MAKING
DESEGREGATION
WORK

A Rand Educational Policy Study

MAKING DESEGREGATION WORK
How Schools Create Social Climates

Robert L. Crain,
Rita E. Mahard, and
Ruth E. Narot

BALLINGER PUBLISHING COMPANY
Cambridge, Massachusetts
A Subsidiary of Harper & Row, Publishers, Inc.

International Standard Book Number: 0-88410-199-1

Library of Congress Catalog Card Number: 81-10971

Printed in the United States of America

Library of Congress Cataloging in Publication Data
Crain, Robert L.
  Making desegregation work.

  Bibliography: p.
  Includes index.
  1. School integration—United States. 2. School environment—United States.
I. Mahard, Rita E. II. Narot, Ruth E. III. Title.
LC214.2.G73   370.19'342   81-10971
ISBN 0-88410-199-1   AACR2

CONTENTS

List of Figures and Tables   ix
Preface   xv

Chapter 1   1
What Makes a Good School?   1

What Can We Learn from City High?   11
The Purpose of This Book   16
Technical Appendix   31

Chapter 2   51
The Effects of the Desegregation Plan   51

Is There a Best Racial Mix for Schools?   51
Busing   56
Dominance and Turf   61
The Myth of the Class Problem   65
Desegregation and Black Achievement   68
Conclusions   75
Technical Appendix   76

Chapter 3   **95**
Staff   **95**

Measuring Teacher Attitudes and Behavior   96
The Effect of Teachers on White Student
Racial Attitudes   97
Teacher Attitudes and Behavior and Black
Students' Reactions to School   99
Teacher Attitudes and Behavior and Student
Interracial Contact   101
Teacher Attitudes and Behavior and Black
Student Achievement   102
Can Teacher Racial Behavior Be Changed?   105
The Principal   108
Conclusions   109
Appendix   111

Chapter 4   **130**
How Schools Handle Race   **130**

Two Successful Programs Using Outside Resources   131
Student Biracial Committees   134
Minority History   137
The Lessons of the Civil Rights Movement   149
Implications   152
Appendix   155

Chapter 5   **168**
Extracurricular Activities   **168**

The Extent of Extracurricular Activities   170
The Effects of Extracurricular Activities   172
High School Extracurricular Activities
and College Attendance   178
Racial Bias in Opportunities to Participate   181
What Can the School Do?   184

Fine Arts Teachers and Gym Teachers   187
Conclusions   190
Technical Appendix   191

Chapter 6   **208**
Structures to Help Teachers Teach   **208**

Heterogeneity and Competition   208
Using a Team Approach   210
Grades   213
Tracking   214
Individualization and Electronic Hardware   220
Making an Innovation Work: The Need for an
Audio-Visual Specialist   223
Helping Teachers Teach: The Instructional Specialist   226
Heterogeneity and Disruption   226
Conclusions   228
Technical Appendix   229

Chapter 7   **234**
Thinking About Making Desegregation Work   **234**

The School as a Place for Adolescent Development   236
The Two Social Environments of the High School   238
Race Relations   243
Changing a School   244
Technical Appendix   250

Appendix A   **257**
Methodological Appendix   **257**

Variables   260
Aggregation   260
Estimates of Sampling Error in School Means   268

References   **272**
Selected Rand Books   **278**

Index   **281**

LIST OF FIGURES AND TABLES

Figure

1A–1   Graphic Display of Variation in Achievement
(Tenth Grade White Students)   45

Tables

1–1   The Difference between the First and Fifth Quintiles of Schools on Several Student Outcomes   23

1–2   Correlations among Student Outcome Variables
after Schools are Matched on Student, School,
and Community Characteristics   27

1A–1   Factor Analysis of White and Black Dependent
Variables   33

1A–2   School-Level Correlations of Major Dependent
Variables for Each Race with SES of Some
Race   39

1A–3   Estimated School-Level Standard Deviations of
Typical Student Responses to Questionnaire
Items, in Percentage Units   41

1A–4   The Percentage of the Total Variance That Lies
between Schools in the Achievement Test
Scores   42

2–1   The Effect of School Racial Composition   52

2–2   The Effect of Busing on Student Attitudes and
Student Racial Contact   59

2–3   Busing and Racial Tension   60
2–4   Peer Pressure against Racial Contact, by
       Race of Student and Racial Composition of
       School   64
2–5   School Racial Tension and Black Student Racial
       Contact, Attitudes toward School, and Delin-
       quency, by Social Status of Black Student
       Body   65
2–6   The Effect of Student Body and Community So-
       cial Status on School Racial Tension   68
2–7   Black Achievement Test Scores, by Sex, and Ra-
       cial Composition of High School and of Earlier
       School   71
2–8   Achievement of Black Students, by Sex, School
       Racial Composition, and Social Class of White
       Students   72
2A–1   Regression Equations with Standardized
       Regression Coefficients (Betas) Used to Construct
       Tables 2–1, 2–4, and 2–5 and Text Discussion
       of Black Happiness   85
2A–2   Regression Equations with Standardized
       Regression Coefficients (Betas) Used to Construct
       Tables 2–1, 2–4, 2–5, and 2–6 and Text
       Discussion of Happiness   86
2A–3   Regression Equations with Standardized
       Regression Coefficients (Betas) Used to Construct
       Tables 2–2 and 2–3   88
2A–4   Regression Equations with Standardized
       Regression Coefficients (Betas) Used to Construct
       Table 2–2   89
2A–5   Regression Equations with Standardized Regres-
       sion Coefficients (Betas) Used to Construct Table
       2–7   91
2A–6   Regression Equations with Standardized Regres-
       sion Coefficients (Betas) Used to Construct Table
       2–8   92
3–1   Influence of Teacher Racial Behavior on White
       Students' Feelings about Blacks   98
3–2   The Influence of Teacher Racial Attitudes and
       Behavior on Black Students' Feelings
       about School   100
3–3   Impact of School Staff Racial Attitudes and
       Behavior on Level of Student Interracial Con-
       tact in School   101
3–4   The Effects of Teacher Racial Attitudes and
       Behavior on School-Level Black Achieve-
       ment   104

3–5   The Effect of Staff and School Characteristics on
        Teacher Racial Attitudes and Behavior   107
3–6   The Relationship between Liking the Principal
        and Other Attitudes about School, for White Stu-
        dents   109
3A–1   Zero-Order Correlations of Items in Teacher Ra-
        cial Behavior Scale   114
3A–2   Zero-Order Correlations of Items in
        Teacher School Racial Attitudes Scale   115
3A–3   Zero-Order Correlations of Items in Teacher
        Nonschool Racial Attitude Scale   116
3A–4   Zero-Order Correlations of Teacher Attitude and
        Behavior Scales   117
3A–5   Regression Equations with Standardized Regres-
        sion Coefficients Used to Construct
        Table 3–1   119
3A–6   Regression Equations with Standardized
        Regression Coefficients (Betas) Used to Construct
        Tables 3–2 and 3–3   121
3A–7   Regression Equations with Standardized
        Regression Coefficients (Betas) Used to Predict
        Teacher Perception of Black Ability and Black
        Achievement (Table 3–4)   122
3A–8   Regression Equations with Standardized
        Regression Coefficients (Betas) Used to Construct
        Table 3–5   125
3A–9   Percentage of Variance Explained by Teacher
        Background and Environmental Variables in Re-
        gression Equations Predicting Teacher Racial
        Behavior, School-Related and Nonschool-Related
        Racial Attitudes   127
3A–10   Regression Equations with Standardized Coeffi-
        cients (Betas) Used to Construct Table 3–6   129
4–1   White and Black Student Attitudes in Schools
        Which Did and Did Not Use Human Relations
        Materials in Last Two Years   131
4–2   Black Student Attitudes in Schools Which Had
        In-Service Race Relations Programs for
        Teachers   133
4–3   Student Attitudes and Amount of Tension in
        Schools Where Teachers Say the Student Biracial
        Committee Is Effective   136
4–4   Black Student Attitudes and Achievement in
        Schools with Minority Culture Classes   138
4–5   Black Student Attitudes in Schools Where Black
        Students Score Well on a Test of Knowledge of
        Black Leaders   140

4–6   White Student Attitudes and Behavior in Schools
        Where Classroom Discussions of Race Are Fre-
        quent   142
4–7   Black Student Attitudes and Achievement in
        Schools Where Classroom Discussion of Race
        Are Frequent   143
4–8   White Student Attitudes in Schools Which Ob-
        server Did or Did Not Like   145
4–9   Black Student Attitudes, by Amount of Civil
        Rights Activity in Community   150
4–10   Black Student Attitudes, by Amount of Civil
        Rights Activity in Community   151
4–11   Level of Racial Tension, by Three Measures of
        Community Conflict over Desegregation   152
4A–1   Regression Equations with Standardized Regres-
        sion Coefficients (Betas) Used to Construct Table
        4–8   156
4A–2   Regression Equations with Standardized Coeffi-
        cients (Betas) Used to Compute Tables 4–6 and
        4–7   158
4A–3   Regression Equations with Standardized Regres-
        sion Coefficients (Betas) Used to Construct
        Tables 4–1 and 4–2   160
4A–4   Regression Equations with Standardized Regres-
        sion Coefficients (Betas) Used to Construct
        Table 4–3   161
4A–5   Regression Equations with Standardized Regres-
        sion Coefficients (Betas) Used to Construct
        Tables 4–4 and 4–5   163
4A–6   Regression Equations with Standardized Regres-
        sion Coefficients (Betas) Used to Construct
        Tables 4–9, 4–10, and 4–11   167
5–1   Effects of Low and High Extracurricular Participa-
        tion on Parental School Visits, Student-Teacher
        Talk about Personal Matters, and Teacher En-
        couragement to Attend College   173
5–2   Effects of Low and High Extracurricular Participa-
        tion on Liking School, Time on Homework, and
        Acceptance of School Rules   174
5–3   Effects of Low and High Extracurricular Participa-
        tion on Self-Esteem and Happiness   176
5–4   Effects of Low and High Extracurricular Participa-
        tion on Racial Contact and Racial Attitude Mea-
        sures   177
5–5   Effects of Low and High Extracurricular Participa-
        tion on Achievement   178
5–6   The Effect of High and Low Male and Female

Participation on White and Black Attitudes toward Desegregation and on Black Feelings of Happiness and Self-Esteem   183

5–7   The Effect of One Additional Music, Drama, Art or Gym Teacher on Self-Esteem, and Achievement   188

5A–1   Regression Equations with Standardized Coefficients Used to Predict White Outcomes in Tables 5–1, 5–2, and 5–5   194

5A–2   Regression Equations with Standardized Coefficients Used to Predict White Outcomes in Tables 5–3, 5–4, 5–6   195

5A–3   Regression Equations with Standardized Coefficients Used to Predict Black Outcomes in Tables 5–1, 5–2, and 5–5   196

5A–4   Regression Equations with Standardized Coefficients Used to Predict Black Outcomes in Tables 5–3, 5–4, 5–6   197

5A–5   Standardized Regression Coefficients (βs) from Equations Predicting Individual-Level Extracurricular Participation by Region, Race, and Sex   199

5A–6   Regression Equations Used to Predict College Attendance in NLS Data from Individual and School-Level Extracurricular Participation   202

5A–7   Regression Equations Predicting Black and White Sex-Specific Self-Esteem and Achievement from per Capita Number of Music/Drama/Art Teachers   204

5A–8   Regression Equations Predicting White and Black Sex-Specific Esteem and Achievement from per-Capita Number of Gym Teachers   205

5A–9   Individual-Level Regression of Extracurricular Participation on Student Outcomes   207

6–1   Percentage of Students Reporting High Interracial Contact by Race, Presence of Tracking, and Staff Racial Attitudes   216

6–2   Percentage of Students Who Say They "Belong" in Tracked and Untracked Schools with Liberal and Conservative Staff   217

6–3   Percentage of Students Who Like School, by Race, Presence of Tracking, and Staff Racial Attitudes   218

6–4   Mean Achievement of Students, by Race, Sex, Presence of Tracking, and Staff Racial Attitudes   219

6–5   Achievement Test Scores of Black and White Students, by Presence of an Audio-Visual Specialist in the School   222

6–6   Percentage of Black and White Students Report-
         ing Personal Conversations with School Staff, by
         Presence of an Audio-Visual Specialist   223

6A–1   Regression Equations with Standardized Regres-
         sion Coefficients (Betas) Used to Construct
         Tables 6–1, 6–2, 6–3   230

6A–2   Regression Equations with Standardized Regres-
         sion Coefficients (Betas) Used to Construct Table
         6–4   231

6A–3   Regression Equations with Standardized Regres-
         sion Coefficients (Betas) Used to Construct
         Tables 6–5 and 6–6   232

A–1   Selected Questionnaire Items   262

PREFACE

The task of this book is simple and important: we want to know what makes schools effective. To find out, we systematically looked at 200 high schools, tested the students, and asked the students, teachers, and principals to describe their feelings and evaluate their schools. We selected the schools that are superior in one way or another and identified some of the reasons for their success. From our findings we have made a list of recommendations for improving schools and written this book in the hope that teachers, principals, administrators, and board members will read it and consider some of these ideas for their schools.

There are many books about how to improve schools. This one is a bit different. It does not present a sweeping theory of school reform or a novel philosophy of education. The book is not intended to be imaginative, creative, or utopian. It merely tries to list a dozen tried-and-proven things that good schools are doing now. This book also differs from others in that it focuses on the whole school, not on the classroom. Through looking at the 200 schools, we have convinced ourselves that good schools have an overall feeling tone, ambience, or what we call "social climate." This book describes how some schools create a social climate which is favorable not only to learning but to adolescent development generally—a side of the high school that academic researchers have not paid as much attention to as they should.

Conservative critics often accuse schools of being more concerned with social development than with the three Rs. (They often follow this criticism by demanding that schools do something about drugs and violence.) It is silly to tell schools to avoid influencing students' social development; students will develop socially while they are in high school, and the school will be a major source of socialization, like it or not. The admonition is more than silly; it is also harmful. A school which makes no effort to influence student behavior in a positive manner will almost certainly influence it negatively. Such a school will wind up with more delinquency, more dropouts, worse race relations, lower test scores, and will graduate a generation of ill-equipped and antisocial young adults.

Since the book is a study of 200 schools, it is necessarily statistical. This created a problem, because the readers most important to us are educators, who are a lot more interested in schools than they are in the mechanics of our statistical techniques. But we had to describe what we did. Many of our readers will be faculty and students in schools of education and in social science departments, and they will want the methodological details. We tried to satisfy both our audiences by presenting our results in each chapter in the simplest fashion but adding an appendix to each chapter which contained the full statistics. The reader interested only in what we found can safely skip most of the appendixes.

A book like this owes many debts. Our greatest is to the 10,000 students and 2,000 educators who took the time to answer our questions. Second to them in importance are all the people who traveled about the country asking the questions and all the people who took the answers and converted them into magnetic tape. The data was gathered by the National Opinion Research Center. We cannot name everyone who helped, but we do want to single out

Eve Weinberg, Fansayde Calloway, Ellen Mitchell, and Jean Schwartz, who oversaw the survey, and Scott Harrison, who supervised the computer programming. The project was funded by the U.S. Office of Education; their project monitor Bob York was helpful in many ways and a good friend throughout. Chapter 3 is his idea. Many people contributed to the analysis that appears in this book. The most important are Carol Stocking, Jean Jenkins, Jim Vanecko, and Cindy Farquahar.

Financial support for writing this book was provided by the National Institute of Mental Health, Center for Metropolitan Problems (GRANT MH-18060); The Ford Foundation; The Rand Sponsored Research Program; and the National Institute of Education through its funding of the Center for Social Organization of schools at Johns Hopkins University. The London School of Economics and Political Science provided office space and other assistance; Donald MacRae, chairman of the Sociology Department, was very helpful. We are indebted to Valerie Campling, Dolores Sullivan and Barbara Hucksoll for their fine typing.

This book began as Ruth Narot's doctoral dissertation at Johns Hopkins University, and Chapters 3, 4, and 5 draw heavily from her work. Ruth Narot was killed in a car crash before she could see the final manuscript. She felt strongly that sociology is only worth doing if it can help people; we hope this book will live up to her hopes for it.

Robert Crain
Washington, D.C.

Rita E. Mahard
Ann Arbor, Michigan

1 WHAT MAKES A GOOD SCHOOL?

Reading about American high schools can be depressing. Apparently everything is getting worse: Scholastic Aptitude Test (SAT) scores are falling; drugs and crime are epidemic; businesses and colleges complain that high school graduates cannot read or write. Even more discouraging are all the accounts of failed attempts to improve schools. Title I has not solved the problems of inner city education; the open classroom movement is in retreat; desegregation has not worked. All of this is frequently summed up in the phrase "Schools don't make a difference." The phrase comes from the many popularizations of the Coleman report (Coleman, et al. 1966) and means simply that the ability of a student to learn is almost entirely a matter of family background (or maybe genetics) and not a question of which school the student attends. Parents, free to choose their child's school, really have no choice—no matter which school the child attends, his or her SAT scores will come out about the same. Because of the differences in family background, the schools can do little to create equality in our society and eliminate the gap between rich and poor, or black and white.

However, this pessimistic analysis is wrong. It may be that we cannot erase the racial gap in achievement—at least not in one generation—but some schools do raise the test scores of minority and poor students noticeably. Of course, schools are supposed to do

1

more than just teach reading and math. They are expected to socialize students—teaching them citizenship and the work ethic as well as how to relate to other students and to adults. Schools provide a set of experiences which help students create images of themselves and their world. There are vast differences among high schools in the kinds of experiences they provide.

This book is optimistic. It makes ten specific recommendations for improving desegregated high schools (most of which would be applicable to segregated schools as well). These recommendations are not highly abstract, impractical, or utopian; they are drawn from actual experiences in the best schools among those which we have studied. Of course these ten recommendations are only a few of the things a school can do, but perhaps the book compensates for their small number by being able to show that each one is based on a systematic statistical analysis of 200 schools.

A CASE HISTORY OF A GOOD HIGH SCHOOL

We think our optimism is justified. There are good high schools in the United States. A few years ago the U.S. Office of Education asked the Educational Testing Service (ETS) to look systematically for good desegregated high schools. Here, with the school's name changed, is a memorandum that Garlie Forehand of ETS wrote after visiting one school:

memo: to file
from: Garlie A. Forehand
re: Site Visit Report,
       Springfield City High School

A large addition is being added to City High. The temporary partitions and barriers, decorated with student art work, feature innumerable purple dragons (the school's athletic symbol), various cartoons, and one vaguely revolutionary painting—a map of Africa, black faces, an uplifted fist and a broken chain.

The school is a busy, informal place. There seem to be few rules, but no extreme disorderliness. There is neither the library-like quietness of an authoritarian school nor the bedlam of one out of control. Between classes the noise level is about what one would expect in an informal crowd—conversation and an occasional shout of greeting.

The atmosphere in the central office is one of amiable chaos, largely because all students are made to feel welcome. The vice-principal and his staff deal with problems, issue passes, provide information and sometimes just shoot the breeze with students.

Students who want to see a vice-principal or the dean are not turned away, though they may have to wait. Students need not state their business to the secretary unless they choose to. The administrators greet them warmly, usually by name, and take their problems seriously. If a faculty member wants to talk to the vice-principal and a student is there first, the faculty member waits. As a result, the administrators are always dashing around, catching students on the way to a meeting and being late for appointments while they finish working with students. They treated me the same way they treat their colleagues; they were gracious and sincere, but if students were there first, I waited.

The students mirror the attitude of relaxed courtesy. They are open and friendly in dealing with adults and with each other. For example, when several students had to adjust their schedules for my research, their attitude was one of positive cooperation rather than resistance or apathetic obedience.

City High was black, white, Mexican-American and Asian students and teachers. Though staff and students now speak of the ethnic diversity as something to be proud of and to preserve, the school's present positive social climate grew out of crisis. The late sixties were described by all respondents as stormy, with the school beset by every problem that can afflict an inner-city school. Newspapers and TV newscasts carried frequent stories of race riots. Ethnic groups in the community organized protests about racism. Students and staff were afraid to come to class. Parents routinely kept their children home, and in some cases withdrew them from school. There were problems with drugs, dropouts, motivation and morale—all the problems that a high school can have.

The present principal, Mr. Washington, took over then, and is universally credited with "turning the school around." Among the descriptions applied to him are: "a real leader," "charismatic," "dynamic," "a go-getter" and "a 20-hour-per-day worker." Thirty one years old, Washington has now been principal for 4 years.

Themes

The programs and practices initiated after Washington arrived are so numerous and complex that people have difficulty recalling them all. Many activities were temporary and faded away once they had served their purpose. This is still the case. People continue to see the school as in transition and to view programs as process rather than as permanent.

Several common themes appear in descriptions of what has taken place. These themes take the form of four slogans which we heard from nearly everyone.

The City High Family.   "It was Mr. Washington who got us to think of ourselves as a family," one staff member reported. When school opens, posters welcome teachers and students to "the City High Family." The same phrase appears regularly in student publications, on bulletin boards, and in conversations. Among the ideas explicitly associated with the concept are unity, cohesiveness, mutual respect, and cooperative problem solving. The family includes staff, students, and interested community members.

Communication.   Another slogan was, "Don't hate, communicate." One staff member outlined five rules for communication that characterize the school's philosophy.

1. Try to get everybody (students, staff, community members, policymakers) to understand the philosophy of what you're doing. This requires open communication—listening as well as talking, an ability to change old ways of thinking, and a free exchange of information and opinions.
2. Know that you will encounter hostility and that a positive approach is vital.
3. Reinforce people when they take a positive approach. They need to see the results of their efforts.
4. Back up communication with an ongoing program.
5. There must be a strong foundation that can weather problems—a philosophy, a purpose. The philosophy must be simple, not bogged down by rules and regulations no one understands.

Individual Recognition.   "Mr. Washington was strong on individual recognition for students and teachers." Methods of recognition included mention in the daily bulletin (a mimeographed newsletter written by the principal), numerous awards, recognition in assemblies, and bulletin board notices.

Everything Is Education.   A philosophy of education which goes beyond traditional limits is another characteristic of City High. Activities range freely from academic work for credit to volunteer work, in-service training, formal instruction, counseling, tutoring, and administration. Students and staff treat these as one fabric without boundaries rather than as discrete activities.

Community Relations

Relations with the community were seen as the most urgent and immediate problem. City High serves a cross section of the region's population. Students come from wealthy areas, middle class neighborhoods, poor areas, and various ethnic ghettos. Pressures from these various communities pull in conflicting directions. More or less militant Mexican-American, Asian, and Black groups have made demands. There has been picketing, marching, lobbying, enlistment of students, and criticism by an effective minority press.

When the school building was scheduled for replacement to meet earthquake safety requirements, members of the white community and the establishment pressed to abandon the school altogether in favor of rebuilding on the edge of town. According to one teacher, the city's newspapers "would like to have seen us belly-up." At the same time, there was a great deal of sentiment for the school and its traditions. As the oldest high school in the area, City has acquired symbolic significance as an enduring institution in an atmosphere of change.

Washington stressed this last argument as he fought to save the school. To abandon City High was to abandon the city. Washington argued that City High, with its natural social and ethnic integration, was an opportunity rather than a cross to bear, that the city was fortunate to have such diversity, and that the school was the major cohesive force in the community. The argument found ready acceptance within the school—at least among some energetic and influential students and staff members. "He believed in this school and made us believe in it," said one teacher. Washington and the school family set out to sell the idea to the community. Students played a major role in the attempt to better community relations. They wrote for the minority press, spoke before the school board, and campaigned for school budget approval.

Washington emphasized communications with minority organizations, accepted speaking engagements, went to coffeeklatches, encouraged visits and meetings in the school. He made similar efforts to reach establishment groups and the press. He is said to have won them around, to have enlisted and gained their support. The new building is now going up on the same site as the old.

Press. Special steps were taken to improve relations with the press. The staging of newsworthy events was just one part of an attempt to present the school as a place where many things happened, not just riots and sports. For example, actors from the TV series *Room 222* came to the school and posed with prominent local politicians and celebrities (in Room 222, of course).

Police Department.   During the school's most difficult years the police department offered to provide counselors—armed and in uniform—from the department's Human Relations division. Washington put the question to a student referendum, allowing time for consideration and debate. Though fear ran sufficiently high that many students and parents wanted police protection, the majority did not. The police were not invited, and there are no police on campus now.

Faculty

When Washington became principal, the staff was discouraged and had difficulty working together. A number of teachers, considered bigoted and inflexible, were asked to leave. (A previous principal had made a similar attempt but without the support of the central office. By the time Washington arrived, a desparate administration was willing to cooperate.) Present faculty members say there was little difficulty in identifying the prejudiced teachers. Minority teachers were recruited in greater numbers. But most of the staff were good teachers who needed to learn to work together. Over the next four years, they worked on a variety of school problems.

Human Relations Development.   The staff's most important project was their human relations development program. The teachers set the agenda for this effort in a three-stage process.

First they chose a small committee to build a framework. Committee members elected a spokesperson who took a strong leadership role throughout the work. The committee began by writing a document to serve as a framework. It included a plan for faculty workshops which would "provide a learning environment in which the staff can function professionally with unity, freedom, and personal integrity for the good of the students, the staff and the school." The framework emphasized the need for teamwork "whereby City High reaches optimum performance." The whole faculty then discussed the framework and broke into small teams with committee members serving as team coordinators. The teams aired their concerns in noholdsbarred rap sessions and reported back to the faculty.
The concerns raised at the rap sessions included the enforcement of present rules, the importance of interdepartmental understanding and good working relationships, and the need for both a clearinghouse for idea exchange and a rap center. This process was repeated with the teams reacting to the comments generated during the first meetings. From this beginning, this committee facilitated a variety of in-service programs.

Some used input from the school district, but these were judged less effective than the activities originated by the school staff. As one committee member said, "We found it best to work from the inside out rather than from the outside in."

When asked about the results of the human relations work, the former committee spokesperson said that the faculty learned to work with others, to be considerate, and to understand that people have a right to their feelings and a right to be heard.

Curriculum Changes. Ad hoc faculty committees developed courses in Asian studies and AfroAmerican art. Teachers asked for student reactions and suggestions.

Sponsoring Student Activities. Faculty members sponsored a host of student activities. Washington formally made major assignments, such as newspaper and student government; teachers volunteered for others.

Students

Everyone gives students the major credit for the school's success. When asked how the student work got started, one teacher replied, "The student leaders at the time were sophisticated, aware, sensitive and multiethnic." The major tool for student involvement seems to have been student government led by several very talented and influential students who held changing elective and appointive positions.

The revised student government constitution eliminated a gradepoint criterion for eligibility and established a permanent Human Relations Committee chaired by an elected vice-president. The student government has an executive council, consisting of elected officers (president, two vicepresidents, two secretaries) and a cabinet of nearly fifty students. Student government activities take up one daily class period. Participants receive course credit. One period per week is occasionally set aside for open meetings which all students can attend.

Among the activities sponsored by the Human Relations Committee were the following:[1]

1. *A Minority Council.* The purpose was to get feedback about the concerns of minorities. For example, at the suggestion of the

[1]Like the rest of the school, the Student Human Relations Committee seems to take pride in multi-ethnicity. One of its reports described its membership as, "Four Chicanos, 3 Asians, 2 Blacks, 1 Jew, 1 Native American and 1 WASP."

minority council, the school began having two bands at dances—one appealing to white students and another appealing to blacks.

2. *Grievance Committee.* Students could file a grievance, saying anything they wanted. When a grievance came through, the principal received a copy, and the committee would ask for his help. If the grievance involved a teacher, the principal decided whether to handle it himself or to forward the grievance to the teacher in question. The committee followed up on all grievances.

3. *The Human-of-the-Week Award.* Each week, The Human Relations Committee selected student, teacher, administrator or community member for this award. The criteria for human-of-the-week were first, being human; second, being a member of the City High family; and, third, showing and demonstrating outstanding human qualities, that is, love, joy, sincerity, forgiveness, understanding, kindness, generosity, patience, courage, truthfulness, or integrity. The award, presented on behalf of the student body, consisted of recognition in the daily bulletin, a certificate and "an allexpense paid interschool exchange with free food and transportation." The award was sometimes used to highlight achievements such as winning a debate or managing a student play.

4. *Awareness Forums.* These were programs on such topics as black, Chicano, women's, and Asian awareness.

5. *Cultural Assemblies.* Students planned programs on ethnic heritage.

6. *Retreats.* Camping and lodge weekends for all comers for discussion and problem solving. (The faculty advisor said they did not work as well as was hoped since they sometimes became just a fun thing.)

7. *Hospitality.* A committee member was assigned the following responsibilities: first, writing thank you, congratulations, and sympathy cards; second, sending birthday cards to students and faculty; and third, writing and sending out buttons and other items to people who have done something for the school. A card was sent out at the request of any student government member.

School Newspaper. The student newspaper (and a fifteen-minute weekly radio show run by the newspaper staff) was credited with being a positive and constructive force. The staff made special efforts to promote a favorably community image. For example, they staged an elaborate schoolwide birthday celebration for the principal with coverage by the Springfield daily paper. The administration encouraged the newspaper staff to identify with their heritage, and ethnic columns in the paper served as a forum. Black, Chicano, and Asian columnists discussed school and national problems, reported on the ethnic studies classes, and sometimes just let off steam. Editorials, editorial cartoons, and letters to the editor were open to other statements of opinion. The principal wrote often for the paper. The paper pounded home his themes: the school family, one group, unity.

Students are said to have felt that everything was wide open—that they knew about everything and could express themselves. The paper did not treat as news the incidents that the local newspaper did, and there was never an underground press in the school (although there was occasional pamphleting).

The paper was not without its problems. A student was attacked, and the parents sued the school district, charging incitement to violence by the paper. A period of censorship followed, but now, according to the faculty advisor, "The paper has real freedom."

I looked through several volumes of the paper, expecting militant rhetoric and dirty words. But even the opinion columns endorsing militant and revolutionary ideas were generally wellreasoned, well-written, and restrained.

Students for a Concerned Society, an improvisational theater group organized and advised by a speech teacher, provided another avenue for communication. The group presented skits on intergroup themes such as prejudice and interracial dating. In performance at City High and other schools, blacks, whites, Asians, and Chicanos played the roles of parents, children, politicians, and so forth. The students usually played a character of an ethnicity other than their own.

Students took an active role in working with the community. Students in the ethnic journalism class wrote for community ethnic papers. Student government officers frequently attended school board meetings and became articulate spokesmen for the school. A speech teacher coached them on parliamentary procedure and helped the Mexican-American students improve their speaking style. The success of this effort persuaded the superintendent to organize a Superintendent's Advisory Council, consisting of the studentgovernment presidents from all the high schools. Students also distributed literature and knocked on doors in support of a bond issue. As one teacher said, "Students are the best PR people a school can have. The message they take home determines the results in the ballot box."

Administration

A chronic problem in most large schools is the runaround—students not knowing which administrators to see and being shunted from office to office. At City, the administrative offices are located in two adjacent suites, one for the principal and office staff, the other for the assistant principal and the dean. The counselors' offices are nearby. The four administrators try to act interchangeably; if a student asks for one who is unavailable, another sees him.

The administrators seem intent on solving problems if at all possible. They do this informally as well as formally; administrators passing through the hall stop to ask waiting students if they can help, often taking care of the problem immediately. The administrators selfconsciously model positive human relations among themselves and with students and faculty. An interethnic group themselves, they make a point of demonstrating mutual respect and positive cooperation.

The Future

The years of work on interpersonal relations have left a legacy of tolerance and friendliness which protects the school when potential trouble appears. For example, during a Black History Week assembly program, many nonblack students were offended by the material. A letter to the editor called it "White put-down week," and some students walked out. Yet the incident was generally shrugged off by staff and students. Several years ago, I was told, there would have been fights. The second incident involved racist literature which was apparently distributed by the American Nazi Party. Again, there was much talk and unhappiness, but the reaction was calm.

Students and staff are satisfied with the present but concerned about the future. One teacher, a leader in the earlier faculty human relations program, feels the school may be running into a problem now because it has not had a continuous program of human relations for people new to the staff. The faculty adviser of the newspaper worries that the students now on the paper do not see themselves as reformers. They are more interested in abortion, contraception, and the like than with school social issues. "The big problem now is that we may let all of this slip away."

The student body recently revised the constitution by restoring the gradepoint average criterion for participation in student government, which had been dropped a few years ago. The former adviser said that the old student government represented a great deal of liberal thinking and that the new one seems more conservatively oriented. He feels the school needs to go back and "do some of those things again. You work hard to get them going and then forget how much time they took." One teacher put it simply: "Without strong leadership we could lose what we have."

WHAT CAN WE LEARN FROM CITY HIGH?

Clearly, this is a school where race relations work. That's not all that works in this school. The school has little problem with violence. Students do well in their courses, and many students are involved in school projects. In short, this is a good school—the kind of high school we would like for our own children. We think the students at City enjoy school. We suspect that they are gaining selfconfidence as a result of the respect shown them by the staff and the opportunities they have to experience selfgovernment.

The problem with reading a description of a school like City is that it is hard to know, in the midst of all this detail, which particular programs can be borrowed and applied in another school. What can a principal or a school board learn? Case studies like this are also discouraging because they make it seem that the only hope is to find a great man like Washington. What can people who are not supermen do? This is why we prefer a statistical analysis. Admittedly, it is less exciting, but we can identify particular components that repeatedly work when implemented by different staffs in different kinds of schools. We will not present more case studies of schools. We wanted to begin with the description of City High because it vividly reminds us that there are some very good high schools and because Forehand's portrait of City High School makes two points which are central to our whole book. First, a good school does more than have high test scores, and, second, teachers working alone cannot make a good high school; everyone must work together.

Education Is More Than Test Scores

Interestingly, nowhere in the description of Springfield City High School is there mention of the achievement test performance of the students. Nor does Forehand talk about special educational programs or the academic curriculum. Instead he focuses on social relationships in the school as a whole. In this sense, Forehand's project is atypical of federally funded education research. Federal officials have been slow to discover that high school quality encompasses more than mastery of the material covered on standardized tests. In the 1960s the civil rights movement demanded that measures be taken to alleviate the inequality of educational opportunity. Congress interpreted this as a call to eliminate the achievement gap between black and white students. Title I of the Elementary and Secondary Education Act of 1965 was the vehicle by which Congress poured millions of dollars into schools in poor neighborhoods on the premise that more money would bring higher achievement test scores which in turn would help blacks to get better jobs. Closing the achievement gap, so the argument went, would result in less of an income gap between the races.

Christopher Jencks (1972) pointed out the fallacy in this whole endeavor by demonstrating what should have been obvious all along—merely raising a student's test scores would not guarantee him a good job, nor a happy and useful life, nor even a college diploma. The people who succeed in the world of work are not necessarily the brightest though they may be more ambitious, more able to put up with frustration, better judges of character, and so on. The same can be said for the other areas of adult life—a high score on an achievement test does not insure that someone will be a good spouse, parent, citizen, or neighbor. We think good schools help students develop the qualities they will need to assume all these adult roles successfully (even though we do not have tests to measure all these qualities).

Schools do not just teach youth; they socialize youth into adulthood. In our society the school is the major institution outside the family that prepares children for adult roles. The school may actually be more important than the family since it is there that the individual first encounters the society. The family primarily teaches children how to act in a small, intimate group, which is what a family is. We depend upon the school to teach the more complex behaviors required in an industrialized society where people relate to one another according to formal rules. School is where students first meet bureaucratic organization. It is also where students first meet people who are not their kin. It is where they are first presented with the opportunity to achieve against supposedly objective standards and where they first learn to deal with rules which supposedly apply to everyone. It is where they first deal with friends, acquaintances, strangers, and authority figures—where they learn what is and what is not appropriate behavior with each of these different kinds of people. It is where they learn to win the friendship and respect of strangers. Of course the desegregated school teaches an additional set of lessons. In our segregated society, students have little contact with people of other races outside of school, so we depend on the school to teach our children how to deal with people of other ethnicities.

If American educators understood this better, they would recognize the danger in encouraging students to play a passive and silent role. They would realize that when students play only one role, that of student, and achieve in only one dimension, scholarship, they will be ill-prepared for adulthood and a complex world. Educators would also be more concerned with the lessons in human relations and formal organization that many high schools teach. Although we would like all our high school graduates to be hard working adults and good citizens, many high schools teach by their example that students should not expect fair and equal treatment, that authority is arbitrarily used, that some students get the breaks and others do not. Some high schools also teach that rules can be broken with impunity, that there is no reason to respect people of other races, and that cooperation with others is not really necessary.

Of course one might argue that these concerns do not fall within the purview of formal education. But to claim that our schools exert no influence beyond that of the three Rs is to tilt at windmills. The school will convey attitudes about work, play, relating to others, and citizenship—if not in words, then by example. The school that claims it does not teach these lessons is almost certainly teaching them badly. The prescription "teach the whole child" implies falsely that the school has a choice in the matter. The school will teach the whole child by design or otherwise. The question is what it will teach. Even if we reject the view of the school as a socializing agency—if we insist that schools concentrate exclusively on the three Rs and that preparing children to become adults is someone else's job—the fact remains that we cannot teach students who have been turned off by school. Students will not learn if they do not like or respect the school, if they are unhappy, or if they have come to think of themselves as unable to learn.

City High impresses us because it attempts to meet the psychic and social needs of its students. Adolescence is a time of identity formation. The teenager seeks knowledge about who he is; he questions whether he can achieve and whether others will accept him. He needs to achieve, to belong, to be a successful member of a community. The school provides his only opportunity to meet these needs. Adults have several different and independent chances to succeed. An adult who fails to achieve occupational status can still find popularity with friends, success in love and parenthood, or prestige through his church or other voluntary associations. The teenager plays out all of these different roles at school. This is why when two teenagers meet, the first question is "Where do you go to school?" The adolescent finds his community at school. His occupation is that of student, school is his place of work, and his social relationships are with other students. It is largely at school that the adolescent gains information about his identity.

Much unhappiness stems from the adolescent's difficult search for identity, and more often than not, the school only adds to his burden. Thus our last, and perhaps most important, reason for being concerned with the nonacademic side of school: Students have a right not to be made more unhappy than necessary. Children are more than partially developed adults in need of training, education, and socialization. They are also human beings with a right to happiness. Although the rights of children are not well defined by the constitution, this does not mean that society is free to make their lives unnecessarily unpleasant. We have an obligation to our children to make schools as humane as possible.

A School Is More Than the Sum of Its Classrooms

Forehand's memo and this book differ from most writing about schools in another way. Rather than focus on the individual classroom, we look instead at the school as a whole. The usual view holds, falsely we think, that the classroom is the only important part of school. Indeed the schools themselves generally operate from this perspective. Yet the individual high school teacher works with groups of students for only forty-five or fifty minutes at a time. While he has almost total responsibility for what happens during that time, he has little control over what students experience before and after his class. In some schools, the students come to class ready to learn; in other schools, they arrive apathetic or angry, preoccupied by something that happened earlier in the day. It is this mood which students carry from one class to another throughout the day that we refer to as the social climate of the school.

We thus arrive at a peculiar irony—the school as an organization has an impact much beyond that of the individual teacher, but the teacher has little opportunity to affect the school as an organization. The typical school's failure to realize that it must function as a unit—that it is a unit—that it is a family—is one of its most serious shortcomings and puts each teacher in an impossible situation.

The prevailing ideology of education holds that we teach students one at a time, rather like a philosopher tutoring a protégé. Yet students also come to class in groups. Two or 3 students talking to each other form one kind of group; 2,000 students at a pep rally become another kind. What a student learns in class depends a great deal upon the influence of the group. If the group says, "Don't study," that norm will override the most eloquent teaching. Worse yet, if the student feels rejected by the group, his loneliness and alienation will create a wall between himself and his teacher. One of the best portraits of high school life is Philip Cusick's *Inside High School,* written by a researcher who spent a year going to classes as a pseudo-senior. Cusick quotes a student on being outside the group: "I skipped fifty-eight days last year because I couldn't stand to come to school because I didn't know anyone...I felt like a real outsider" (1973: 65). Obviously, the group process prevented teachers from reaching this student, yet the school claims no responsibility for manipulating the group process.

If the school wishes to teach students how to live in a multiracial society, then the role of groups—whites, blacks, Chicanos, and others—becomes central to the educational process. Yet most high schools view the group process as irrelevant. A speech given by Harold Spears, a former superintendent of the San Francisco schools, captures the essence of this ideology. While his speech was a statement in opposition to desegregation, its point about the irrelevance of the group process to the purpose of the school is what is important to us.

It is quite apparent that as more courts face the technicalities of the [school desegregation] issue, we should expect the injection of the question of the purpose of the American public school, a matter that has been somewhat ignored up to this point.

Without a doubt, state school codes do not speak of social adjustment as a purpose in the establishment of public schools. Instead, they speak specifically of subjects to be taught....

It is true that any school or any classroom provides a social situation, for when two pupils or more are grouped for instruction the element of human relationships enters the picture. But this social situation has never been stated in law as a purpose of a school. Rather it is a condition that arises because efficiency of school operation demands that children be grouped for instructional purpose, rather than to be tutored individually. The teacher naturally takes advantage of the group situation to teach beyond the subjects which constitute the curriculum, but nobody has ever justified through public expenditure the organization of schools primarily for the social purpose (quoted in Crain 1968: 83).

THE PURPOSE OF THIS BOOK

Forehand's memo, and what we have just written, may give the impression that good schools have an aura about them, a mysterious air of good will. They do have an aura, but there is nothing mysterious about it. The aura results from the sum total of hundreds of actions by school staff. Those actions in turn result partly from a set of policy decisions by faculty and administration.

In this book we describe specific school policies which have worked to make some schools more effective. We have tried to steer clear of general maxims and concentrate instead on specific and practical suggestions. While our focus is on desegregated schools, the techniques would be effective in all-white or all-black schools as well. In order to be a good desegregated school, a school must first be a good school.

How We Did the Research

In spring of 1972 the staff of the National Opinion Research Center (NORC) visited 200 southern high schools. They interviewed school district administrators and building principals. Fifty-five tenth grade students and ten tenth grade teachers completed questionnaires which described each school and their feelings about it. Finally, the students were given an hour-long standardized achievement test.

The first thing we learned from all this information was what kind of problems these schools had. We found that some schools had racial problems (although not as many as we had expected), and we found that many schools had students who could only be described as alienated.[2]

Is Racial Tension a Serious Problem?

At the time of the survey, most of these schools had been desegregated in more than token numbers for only two or three years. The South had just completed a decade of massive resistance to desegregation, and the newspapers still carried stories of anti-integration riots. Most of these high school students had attended segregated elementary and junior high schools, and most of their teachers had spent their entire lives in a segregated society. Knowing all of this, we expected the worst and were surprised to find that most schools were not racial battlefields. Our data indicate that one southern high school in five was experiencing servere racial tensions. The remaining four appeared quiet—whatever problems they had lay below the surface.

We also surveyed 400 elementary schools and found that desegregation seemed to be working very well. These schools had some difficulties—half of the students reported that students of the opposite race caused trouble, and some teachers said that fighting had increased since desegregation began. Yet as many students reported being personally in a fight in segregated as in desegregated schools, suggesting that both teachers and students were construing ordinary childen's fights as racially motivated. On the positive side, both black and white students reported many interracial friendships. Forty-three percent of the white students said that one of their three best friends was black; 52 percent of the black students said that one of their three best friends was white.[3] Eighty-six percent of elementary school teachers reported only minor racial problems; 78 percent said that white students were becoming less prejudiced. Only 18 percent described the relationship between the races as very tense.

---

[2]More detailed statistics on student responses and a longer description of the research design appears in the appendix to this chapter.

[3]The typical school had more white students than black and, therefore, blacks had more opportunities for interracial contact. Thus there is the slightly higher percentage of blacks reporting opposite-race friends.

Finally, desegregation appears to have broken down some standard racial stereotypes. Only 8 percent of the white students and 1 percent of the black students said that white people were smarter than blacks.

The responses of tenth graders were much less positive. Only 18 percent of whites and 37 percent of blacks said that one of their three best friends at school was of the opposite race. Only a quarter of the white students had ever telephoned a black student. Most whites said that their friends would think badly of them for associating with a black student after school.

The limited contact between black and white high school students enabled harsh stereotypes to survive. For example, 22 percent of white students thought that whites were generally smarter than blacks. Asked to describe the black students in their school, 37 percent said they were dumb.

Whereas white students expressed discomfort or prejudice concerning black students, black anger seemed to focus more on the school's administration than on white students. Most blacks said that white students "get special advantages around here," that some of the teachers were unfair to blacks, that school rules were unfair. In part, these students may have been overreacting, revealing their own prejudices by seeing white racism everywhere. But they were correct to some extent. White teachers and principals were having trouble adjusting to desegregation, and in many schools blacks were suffering because of this. There has been some racial tension in nearly all these schools. Two-thirds of the black students said that blacks in their school had complained about white racism, and nearly half of all students agreed with the statement, "Tensions have made it hard for everyone." Still, less than one-quarter of either students or teachers said that their school had serious racial problems. In a minority of the schools racial fights have occurred, but even this was not seen as a serious problem by most students. The typical principal reported only four incidents of physical violence during the year of our survey. In a minority of schools there were interracial attacks, and both black and white students said that black fighting gangs were a problem. (Forty-three percent of whites said that groups of black students had attacked whites; 14 percent said that groups of whites had attacked blacks. Thirty-four percent of blacks said that black groups had attacked whites, and 26 percent said that white groups had attacked blacks. Thus, each group tended to blame the other, but both saw groups of blacks initiating more of the assaults.)

We see two important lessons in these data. First, the amount of racial tension varies enormously among schools. Some schools have no problems; others have many. Second, most of the tension was verbal, not physical, and students and teachers are apparently able to tolerate a certain amount of tension. In the typical school, students said that tensions had made things hard but that problems were only minor.

Most of the high school students in our survey attended segregated elementary and junior high schools. The large difference between elementary schools and high schools in the quality of race relations suggests that high school race relations should improve each year as each class of entering high school students has an additional year of desegregated experiences in junior high and elementary school. This may be true, but elementary schools will probably always have better race relations than high schools. Adolescents are more status conscious, need to express their sexuality, and are strongly oriented toward peer groups and cliques. Conflict between rival groups of adolescents is common, and it is natural for this to occur on racial lines. We do not think that the low amount of interracial contact in high school in 1972 was simply because the students were new to desegregation.

How Students Feel about Their Schools

The radical critics of public education have accused the schools of being irrelevant, boring, and oppressive. While their criticism is too well known to require repeating, we think it important to point out the highly personal quality of much of this writing. The reader who wishes to disentangle truth from fiction will have his work cut out for him. Havinghurst has described the radicals as philosophical anarchists, and it does seem likely that many of them would have great difficulty accepting the idea that some rules are necessary or that there are important things to learn which all students would not volunteer to study.

It is more difficult to ignore the students in our survey. Their responses seem to us to reflect a widespread cynicism and alienation.

Three out of five black students say school rules are unfair. The fact that two out of five whites agree suggests that the issue is more than just race. Similarly, one-half of blacks and nearly as many whites said that when they got punished at school it was usually for no good reason at all.

Schools are commonly criticized for being rigid bureaucracies which depersonalize students. We asked our tenth graders, "Have you ever talked to a teacher or other adult here about things you are doing outside of school...?" One-third of the white students and nearly half of the blacks said that they never had. It is easy to forget how little real interaction occurs between students and teachers. In his study, Cusick (1973) estimated that the average student said only one sentence to an adult during a normal school day.

Many critics attack the judgmental nature of schools. Success, they argue, depends unduly on evaluation, and although the testing and grading are constant enough, the success remains elusive, contingent on yet another test. Not surprisingly, many students feel intense pressure. One-third of all students agreed with the statement, "I get so nervous on tests that I can't think straight."

Our data also suggest that school is unnecessarily boring. Asked if any of their school work in the last week was interesting, one-third of blacks and one-half of the whites said no. A majority of students could not recall having ever discussed two of the most talked about news items of the 1971–1972 school year—women's liberation and the India-Pakistan war. Finally, 51 percent of whites and 39 percent of blacks agree that "a lot of what they teach you in school is not worth learning."[4] Given these responses, it comes as no surprise that many students dislike high school. When asked if they are usually glad to go to school in the morning, less than half said yes.[5]

How We Will Evaluate Schools

Using the survey data, we identified the particularly successful schools in our sample. These data point to three different types of success. We found some schools especially effective in helping

[4]In all attitudes blacks express less alienation from school than whites. While often angry about racial issues, blacks seem more willing to accept the school qua school than whites.

[5]Furthermore, one study concludes that most students who do like school say it is because they enjoy seeing their friends (Benham, Giesen, and Oakes 1980).

students succeed academically, others in establishing good race relations, and still others in combatting student alienation. From the student achievement test and questionnaire we developed ten measures of school success in these three areas.

Academic success has two aspects: first, *achievement,* the score on a one-hour test of reading, mathematics, and science skills, and, second, *self-esteem,* measured by four questions about student feelings of academic self-confidence. Most students feel reasonably good about their academic abilities, and blacks are as confident as whites despite their generally lower test scores. Two-thirds of both races said that they had the ability to complete college. Students resist labelling themselves as poor students. We asked, "Forget for a moment how teachers grade your school work. How do you rate yourself in school ability compared with those in your class at school?" Thirty-five percent of whites and 21 percent of blacks said they were above average, and only 5 and 9 percent, respectively, said they were below.

The quality of race relations was measured in three ways. We assessed racial contact by asking students whether any of their three best friends at school were of the opposite race, whether they had ever telephoned someone of the opposite race, and whether they had helped or been helped with classwork by a student of the opposite race. We also questioned students on their racial attitudes—whether they disliked going to an integrated school, whether they were uncomfortable around persons of the opposite race, and whether they wanted more opposite-race friends. These two scales are referred to as *racial contact* and *racial attitudes.*

Interestingly enough, some schools with high racial contact also experienced a great deal of *racial tension.* The data on racial tension come from the reports of principals, teachers, and black and white students. The scale includes measures of racial violence, such as asking students whether there had been incidents of groups of black students attacking white students or groups of white students attacking black students. Students and teachers also reported on public controversy—charges of favoritism, for example.

Student attitudes toward self and school were measured along five dimensions. One of the most important is the degree to which students accept school rules as fair and legitimate. For example, students were asked, "When you get punished at school, does it usually seem it's for no good reason at all?" and "Do you get really angry when teachers try to make you do things you don't want to do?" We call this scale *acceptance of school rules.*

Students also provided information on whether they had been in a fight, whether they had been sent to the office, and how often they had intentionally stayed away from school. While we will call this dimension *delinquency,* we do not use the word in any legal sense— these violations are not that serious.

We asked students whether they *like school:* "In the morning are you usually glad to go to school?" "Do you usually hate school?" "Do you like the principal of the school?"

Finally, we asked students whether they were happy and whether they agreed or disagreed with the statement: "I feel like I don't belong in this school." Black students more often say they don't belong—32 percent compared to 21 percent of whites—and that they are not happy—37 percent compared to only 19 percent of whites. These items, called *sense of belonging,* and *happiness* have strong racial overtones for blacks but not for whites. A black student who says he feels like he doesn't belong or that he is not too happy more often than not attends a school with poor race relations. In addition, he is likely to hold negative attitudes about whites. For white students, happiness has nothing to do with racial feelings.

How Large Are The Differences Among Schools?

In the following chapters we seek to isolate those school characteristics which encourage more favorable student attitudes about school or self, which improve race relations, or which increase achievement. This means finding the schools which have attained unusual success in one of these three ways and seeing which characteristics these schools have in common.

We first attempted to verify what may or may not be obvious— that schools differ significantly from each other in these respects. We ranked the 200 schools on the various student outcome dimensions, divided them into five equal groups, and then asked, "Does the difference between the scores of the highest and the lowest groups indicate that variation in school quality can have an appreciable effect on students?" Table 1–1 shows the scores of the lowest and highest fifths of all schools on the eighteen dimensions we will use.[6]

[6]The ten factors described earlier yield eighteen different dimensions. Eight of the factors are computed separately for blacks and whites. Racial tension is computed for the whole

Table 1–1. The difference between the first and fifth quintiles of schools on several student outcomes.

Outcome Variable	School Mean		
	In Lowest One-fifth of Schools	*In Average Schools*	*In Highest One-fifth of Schools*
Achievement			
White	402	463	524
Black	306	346	386
Academic self-esteem			
White	46%	59%	72%
Black	32%	51%	69%
Racial Contact			
White	17%	34%	52%
Black	29%	50%	72%
Racial Attitudes			
White	17%	37%	57%
Black	40%	62%	83%
Racial Tension	76%	44%	12%
Acceptance of School Rules			
White	41%	58%	74%
Black	28%	47%	67%
Delinquency			
White	47%	63%	78%
Black	46%	66%	85%
Like School			
White	28%	46%	65%
Black	22%	45%	69%
Unhappiness			
Black	56%	37%	18%
Sense of Belonging			
White	36%	21%	7%
Black	56%	32%	8%

school, not for each racial group separately. Happiness is not computed for white students because significant differences among schools do not appear for whites. We hypothesize that black happiness is closely tied to feelings about race and that there are important school differences which affect black racial feelings. For white students, we suspect that a sense of happiness is unrelated to the school experience.

Of course, we cannot interpret Table 1–1 as indicative of what would happen if we took the worst one-fifth of all schools in the South and introduced new programs, curricula, and staff to make them as good as the best one-fifth. If we did, their student responses would not change to the degree shown in the table. Some of the differences between the lowest and highest fifth of the schools are due to student background characteristics, and some are due to statistical error. Even so, the differences among schools are large enough to make it seem likely that differences in school structure, personnel, and curriculum affect students.

We have computed achievement test scores in units similar to those used for the SAT, setting the means for blacks and whites at the national mean for each race in 1974 (Report on Education Research 1979). (Of course, this does not imply that the students in our survey would score this high since SAT scores are computed only for college-bound seniors. We used this scale only to obtain some sense of whether the between-school differences are large or small.)

Table 1–1 shows that in the one-fifth of schools which have the lowest white test scores, the average score is 402; in the one-fifth of all schools where scores are highest, the average is 524, over 100 points higher. In some schools, tenth graders are capable of junior high school work; in others they can do junior college work. Partly this is due to differences in family background. Most of the low schools are in areas which are poor and rural, and most of the high performance schools are in affluent urban and suburban communities. A considerable part of this difference is due to differences in quality of teaching in both the high schools and their elementary and middle school feeders.

It is often said that researchers believe that schools do not make a difference—that student achievement is determined by family background, and it does not matter which school one attends. The famous 1966 study, *Equality of Educational Opportunity* (the Coleman Report), is often accused of making this assertion. Both apologists for and critics of the public schools have had reasons to endorse the "schools don't make a difference" statement. The critics could use it to argue that all schools were failures, and the apologists could argue that schools were innocent victims since achievement was entirely due to family background. Coleman argued against this view and pointed out that school quality factors were as important as family factors. In the appendix to this chapter, we look at this issue in some detail and conclude that the effects of school quality found in both this study and in the Coleman Report can be made to look small if the differences are stated in statistical language. However, if schools are ranked, not simply by their overall test scores but by actual quality of instruction, the best one-fifth of all schools would produce for the average white student a test score 50 to 70 SAT points higher than this same student would make if he or she were in one of the schools in the lowest fifth of school quality. To put it another way, if 40 percent of the students in the bottom fifth of the schools could pass a college admission test, 60 percent of them would pass if they had attended one of the schools in the top one-fifth. Stated this way, the difference is not at all trivial, and no one would claim from these numbers that schools do not make a difference.

The fact remains that blacks score 117 points below whites on this test. If every black student transferred into the best schools in the nation, their scores would still be below whites. This conclusion has dumbfounded intellectuals, implying as it does that even the best education we know how to provide would not erase the white-black achievement gap. Some researchers even argue that there are inborn racial differences in academic talent. Such a conclusion is, to put it mildly, premature. First, a complicated and not infallible set of statistical assumptions underlies any interpretation of these numbers. Second, even the best southern black student bodies suffer from disadvantage. We have no way of knowing what black scores would look like following several generations of genuinely equal treatment in and out of school.

If we assume that our statistics are roughly correct, then systematic improvement of the worst schools would be expected to raise scores for many black students by 50 SAT points or more. Rather than debate the role of genetic factors in determining academic ability, we might instead concentrate on obtaining the improvement in black test scores that we know we can get; after we have done this we can decide whether we have really done all that is possible.

We wish neither to minimize nor to exaggerate the differences in achievement test scores among schools. The 50 to 70 points, which we estimate is the difference in black achievement between two schools of very different quality of education, is equivalent to one and one-half grade levels. It follows that a school which embarks on even a highly successful effort to raise achievement test scores must not expect to obtain gains this large. An educator who does not understand this may be discouraged without reason, feeling that gains of, say, only one-half of a grade level signify failure rather than success. Education, like politics, is the art of the possible.

Arguments about the extent to which a school can influence student performance do not apply to our sixteen nonacademic dimensions. There the differences between the top and bottom fifths of all schools are large and, except for self-esteem, are unrelated to social class. Racial tension and alienation are as common in middle class schools as in lower class schools. No school can blame its troubles on having poor students, nor can a school assume it is safe because of its comfortable suburban location.[7]

Table 1–1 shows striking differences between schools which perform well and those which perform poorly. For example, in the bottom fifth of the schools, 76 percent of the students describe racial tensions as severe compared to only 12 percent in the top fifth of the schools. The other racial variables also show large differences. For example, if we rank schools by level of white contact with black students, we find that in the bottom fifth only 17 percent of the white students report a high amount of interracial contact, compared to 52 percent in the schools of the top fifth. If we rank schools on the black response to "I feel like I don't belong in this school," we find a range from 56 percent to 8 percent.

Tradeoffs among Student Outcomes

The large differences among schools in the various student outcomes imply that there are things schools can do to increase each of these outcomes. Are there tradeoffs so that schools that place an emphasis on one outcome, such as achievement, lose ground in other areas such as race relations? Are some schools in which unhappy students learn a great deal all work and no play and other schools in which students enjoy school but do not learn much just fun and games? Must schools choose between favoring whites and favoring blacks, or

---

[7]Similar results have been obtained in a study of school violence, which found that the costs of vandalism and theft of school property was the same in suburban as in central city schools; there are also seemingly small differences between suburban and inner city schools in attacks and robberies of students. There is, however, a very large difference in attacks on teachers, which are much more frequent in black schools (National Institute of Education 1978).

can they only make desegregation work by deemphasizing academics? Table 1–2 shows the correlations among schools in three kinds of outcomes: achievement, the extent to which students like school, and race relations. Achievement and liking school are computed separately for white and black students.

The figures in the table are partial correlation coefficients. A positive number indicates a tendency for the schools which have high scores on one outcome to have high scores on the other outcomes as well. The figures have a theoretical maximum of 1, but in fact the difficulty of measuring these outcomes and the sheer complexity of high schools makes it very difficult to conceive of any two different outcomes having a correlation higher than 0.5. (For example, the correlation between white student body socioeconomic status and white student body achievement is only 0.42.) A figure of 0 means that the two outcomes are completely unrelated, and a negative value indicates that schools with a high score on one factor tend to have a low score on the other.

Table 1-2. Correlations among student outcome variables after schools are matched on student, school, and community characteristics.

	Achievement Test Scores		Like School		Racial Contact[a]	Racial Tension
	White	Black	White	Black		
Achievement Test Scores						
White	—	.24[a]	.05	.05	.03	−.04
Black	.24[a]	—	.05	.19[a]	.11	.06
Like School						
White	.05	.05	—	.39[a]	.08	.19[a]
Black	.05	.19[a]	.39[a]	—	.25[a]	.18[a]
Racial Contact[b]	.03	.11	.08	.25[a]	—	−.32[a]
Low Racial Tension	−.04	.06	.19[a]	.18[a]	−.32[a]	—

[a]Probability of a correlation this large by chance is less than .05 (p < .05).
[b]Racial contact is reported by black students.
Note: Correlations are partial correlations controlling on white and black student socioeconomic status, school racial composition, community urbanism and educational level, and region within the south.

Do schools tend to favor one race at the expense of the other? Apparently not. The upper left block of the table shows a positive relationship between black and white achievement; schools which have higher than expected white test scores also have high black scores. The block in the center of the table shows that if a greater than average number of white students say they like school, more blacks will say so too.

Is there a hard "guns or butter" choice between having students like school and having students score well on tests? Again, apparently not. The first column of the table (or the first row since the table is symmetrical) shows that there is little relationship between white student morale and the quality of the school's race relations. All the numbers are close to 0, ranging from −0.04 for the relationship between high achievement and the absence of racial tension to +0.05 for the relationship between white achievement and the degree to which either white or black students say they like school. This suggests that one cannot solve a school's morale or race relations problems by improving the quality of formal instruction, and, conversely, one cannot expect white achievement to go up if one improves the school's social climate. To look on the bright side, we see that doing either of these two things will not make matters worse in the other area. The data for blacks, in the second column, are different. For blacks, achievement is noticeably higher in schools where black students say they like school and slightly higher in schools with more interracial student contact. These relationships apply only to the achievement of black males; black female achievement is not related to either the percentage of students who like school or the amount of interracial contact. This indicates that creating a favorable social and racial climate is a definite prerequisite for raising black male achievement.[8] We see a similar pattern in the block of four correlations in the bottom center of the table. Both whites and blacks like schools more if there is less racial tension, or else they get into less racial controversy in schools they like. Only for blacks is liking school related to increased racial contact. In general,

---

[8]It does not imply the opposite, that is, that improving the teaching of blacks would improve student morale. Any policy which improved black achievement could not be sex-specific and would improve both male and female achievement. If better black achievement improved morale, female achievement would also be related to liking school and racial contact. The only hypothesis that fits the facts is that black males are distracted from school work by a bad social climate, while black females are not.

it seems that for blacks, but not whites, the racial climate of the school is central to their feelings about school, and for black males, feeling about the school are critical to their ability to do school work well. This is perhaps the central finding of this book. For whites, school race relations are secondary; for blacks they are not.

Table 1–2 makes one other point. In the lower right, we see that the relationship between high interracial contact and the absence of racial tension is negative. Good interracial relations and racial controversy and violence go together. It is important to recognize this fact. We think the reason is that the easiest way to suppress tension in a newly desegregated school is simply to allow the school to become internally segregated. As students overcome some of their prejudices, they also overcome their fears of interracial conflict. When school race relations get better, the honeymoon ends. We think this explains why racial tension is worse in the upper south and in high-status urban areas. In the rural deep south, whites do not want good race relations, and blacks do not expect them; both groups see little point in fighting about it. This creates a damned-if-you-do, damned-if-you-don't situation for school people, who may have to face the fact that efforts to improve school race relations may raise racial tensions, at least temporarily.

The Plan of This Book

The last and most important questions to ask are: "What fraction of these differences between schools is due to school policies? How much can we change schools?" Our task in this study was to discover some of the policies and practices which can be used to improve schools. We did this by looking at the schools which were especially effective in one way or another to see what programs or policies they had in common. We then asked ourselves whether other school administrators could copy the policies of the successful schools, and if they could, whether their schools would really improve as a result. We came up with ten specific recommendations.

In the course of locating these policies, and deciding why they would help schools, we have also learned a bit more about how schools create social climates. More research is needed, but we think we have illuminated some of the ways schools work, and we hope that this will also be useful to policymakers.

The book contains five analytic chapters and a conclusion. Chapter 2 analyzes the effect of the kind of desegregation plan used—what difference it makes if the desegregated schools are predominantly white or predominantly black, the effect of busing, and the effect of mixing students of different social class backgrounds. Chapter 3 examines the effect of the racial attitudes and behavior of the school's teaching staff on the students and looks at some of the factors that make a school staff more liberal or more conservative. In Chapter 4 we look at programs, such as black studies programs and student biracial committees, which schools institute to improve race relations. Chapter 5 analyzes the effects of an emphasis upon extracurricular activities and considers what the effect would be if a school hired more gym, music, art, and drama teachers. Two factors we think can reduce some of the problems caused by too much academic competitiveness—the use of team projects in the classroom and the use of ability grouping (which our data suggest is more beneficial than harmful)—are discussed in Chapter 6. This chapter also analyzes the effects of intensive use of audio-visual materials and electronic media. Chapter 7 presents our conclusions.

APPENDIX IA
TECHNICAL APPENDIX

The methodological appendix at the end of the book contains basic information about the sample of high schools; the way in which the data was collected; and the contents of the questionnaires administered to students, teachers, principals, community leaders, and central office administrators. The appendix also deals with certain general statistical issues such as the logic of using aggregate data, the error introduced by using samples of students in each school, and weighting. The technical appendixes following each chapter deal with the theoretical and methodological issues raised in each chapter.

Chapter 1 presents the premise which underlies the entire analysis of this book—namely, that schools vary in their educational effectiveness. If they did not, there would be no way that a survey could locate school policies which would work to make schools more effective. In this technical appendix we will examine this premise, separating it into two questions: First, what are the main dimensions of the student outcomes with which we are concerned? Second, how much do schools differ on these outcomes? The first part of the appendix presents the factor analysis of the student outcomes which was used to locate the basic outcome dimensions; the second part discusses the amount of between-school variance in the outcomes.

A Cautionary Prologue

In any survey one is tempted to believe that one has simply asked questions and received objective answers. Of course, this is not what happens. For example, we find that white students in the upper South are much more likely to say that the school staff discriminates against black students than are the whites in deep South schools. This occurs not because the schools in the upper South are more racist but probably because white students in the upper South hold more liberal views on race and hence are more likely to admit that racist behavior has occurred or more willing to agree with black students if blacks claim that racism exists. Similarly, we find more complaints about rules being unfair from black students in middle class urban schools than from black students in low income and rural schools. Again, this is not because the higher income urban schools are less fair but rather because their students are more sophisticated and outspoken.

In this survey, as in any survey, we should think of the instrument as a series of microexperiments. A stimulus, in this case a question, is administered to the subject who responds in some fashion. It is the task of the researcher to decide what it means when a group of students tends to answer yes rather than no to a particular question.

A Factor Analysis of the Dependent Variables

The sixteen attitude variables used as the main dependent variables were selected from an original set of thirty-four attitude variables (seventeen for each race). Variables were dropped because they were uninteresting, because of their small between-school variance (see the next section of the appendix), because they stubbornly refused to correlate with anything, or because they were either so similar to other dependent variables as to be redundant or so different from other dependent variables as to be uninterpretable. Redundancy and uninterpretability were partly determined by factor analysis.

For each item or scale, regression was first used to compute the variable's residual score net of the effect of socioeconomic status (SES), so the factor analysis is an effort to isolate the dimensions of the school for students of one race, independent of the social class of the student body. The results are shown in Table 1A–1. In the table, the factor weights above .40 are shaded. Other factor weights are above .20. Those below .20 are omitted.[9]

The Variables

The ten marked rows show the ten variables which are the main dependent variables in this book. They are all described briefly in Chapter 1 and the full scales are given in the methodological appendix. (One of them, "racial tension," is in fact only the white or black student component of the scale; this is done to make it respond

---

[9]Note that the values shown are factor weights, not factor scores; they indicate the degree to which each variable can be predicted from knowledge of the schools' score on each factor.

Table 1A–1. Factor analysis of white and black dependent variables.

| | Whites | | | | Blacks | | | | | |
| | | | | | *Factor Scores* | | | | | |
	W1	W2	W3	W4	B1	B2	B3	B4	B5	B6
1. Delinquency[a]	**63**[b]				**62**[b]					
2. Accept School Rules[a]	69		23	29	47	33			28	-27
3. School Work Interesting	48				43					
4. School Work Worth Learning	59				44					
5. Happiness[a]	52				29		36	30		
6. Like School[a]	75		26			**42**[b]	24			
7. Sense of Belonging[a]	52	21				62	24			
8. Racial Tension[a]	20	**75**[b]				52				
9. Racial Climate	21	82	24			75	33			
10. Racial Contact[a]			**78**[b]				**56**[b]			
11. Racial Attitudes[a]	20	38	86		22		57			
12. Internal Control		21	26	**43**[b]				**59**[b]		
13. Test Anxiety		21		50				55		
14. Self-Esteem[a]				84				33	**54**[b]	
15. College Plans				59					67	
16. Achievement[a]				54	20			20		**76**[b]
17. Black Knowledge		-23	29	26						60
18. People Can Be Trusted	27	24	24	23						-30

[a] One of the ten variables which are the main dependent variables in this book.
[b] Factor weights above .40 are bold. Other Factor weights are above .20. Factor weights below .20 are omitted.

to the factor analysis similarly to the other outcome variables. The fact that all the other items are from one race of students means that a fairly high correlation is built in to all these items; this would almost guarantee that the full tension scale, from four different types of informants, would have a lower correlation and would be identified as a separate factor.) The remaining eight variables in Table 1A–1 are used less often in our analysis. They are:

- *Schoolwork interesting:* "In the past week, did you do any schoolwork or homework which was interesting?"
- *Schoolwork worth learning:* (agree/disagree) "A lot of what they teach you in this school is not worth learning."
- *Racial climate:* a scale, constructed from "On the whole, how would you say things are working out with both blacks and whites in the school?" (responses from "almost no problems" to "many serious problems") and "The way things are going between blacks and whites this year, do you think things will be better or worse next year?"
- *Internal/external control:* a scale of five agree/disagree items: "When bad things are going to happen, they are just going to happen no matter what you try to do to stop them." "Good luck is just as important for success as hard work is." 'Some kids are just naturally lucky." "When I make plans I am almost sure I can make them work." "Most of the time it doesn't pay to try hard because things never turn out right anyway."
- *Test anxiety:* "When a teacher says that she is going to give the class a test, do you become afraid that you will do poor work?" and (agree/disagree) "When taking a test, I get so nervous I can't think straight."
- *College plans:* "Do you think you will go to college?"
- *Black knowledge:*this scale of knowledge of famous black persons is described in detail in Chapter 4 and in the appendix to that chapter.
- *People can be trusted:* (agree/disagree) "Most people can be trusted."

The Factor Analyses

There are four factors for whites, and six for blacks. Looking at the simpler white factor structure first, we see that the possible effects that schools might have on their white students fall into four dimensions. The first dimension, *W1*, is a general acceptance-rejection of school. *W2* is racial climate. *W3* is racial behavior, and *W4* is achievement. Much of this seems quite reasonable, but there are some surprises. One is that racial factors split into two dimensions—racial tensions versus racial contact and attitudes.[10]

There are two racial factors for blacks as well. One of the main reasons why racial contact and racial tension are not antithetical is because at least a moderate amount of contact must occur before there are sufficient grounds for conflict. If students are rigidly segregated, or voluntarily withdraw from contact with the other race, there is less opportunity for incidents to occur which might lead to friction. This is reflected in the fact that the simple correlation between the racial contact scale and the racial tension scale is .00 for blacks and only .09 for whites. In later analyses we will see that it not unusual for a school to have good racial attitudes among students but also a great deal of racial tension; conversely, a school can have very little racial tension but very poor human relations among its students.

In general the dimensions of attitudes toward school, racial tension, racial interaction, and achievement are related in a weak positive fashion. All else equal, a school which has a favorable score on one dimension will have a slightly more favorable score on the others as well (although most of the positive factor weights are below .20 and thus appear as blanks in the table). The one exception is the negative loading of the scale of white knowledge of black history on the white racial tension dimension—high knowledge is associated with high tension. This suggests that racial tension is to some degree a necessary price to be paid for progress along the road to equality. Not that our data constitute an apology for severe racial tension; factor *B2* shows that black students resent a school where racial tension is high. Feelings about school and racial tension are closely linked for black students.

For blacks, factor *B1* is not the all-inclusive dimension that W1 is for whites. Delinquency, acceptance of school rules, enjoying

[10]Since racial contact depends greatly on opportunity, the racial contact measure used here is a residual which has removed not only the effect of student socioeconomic status, but also the effect of school racial composition. White students have considerably more contact with blacks in predominantly black schools, and, conversely, black students have considerably more contact with whites in predominantly white schools. The measure here removes that relationship.

schoolwork, and not complaining that school material isn't worth learning all lie on B1 but feelings of belonging in the school, liking school, or happiness do not; these are racial responses for blacks. The things which make white students feel good about school have nothing to do with race. For blacks, race relations are an important part of school. Hence, some attitudes toward school form a nonracial factor, *B1*, while others contribute to a racial climate dimension, *B2*, similar to the white *W2* factor.

The dimensions *B3* and *W3* are similar, with racial contact and racial attitudes having the highest scores for both races. Note that for blacks happiness is related to factor 3, a racial factor, not to factor 1, a "like school" factor. Happiness apparently has a foundation in racial experiences for blacks.

An interesting difference between the two factor analyses is the separation of the single white achievement dimension, *W4*, into three dimensions for blacks. Those schools where white students have high test scores also have white students with high self-esteem, college aspirations, low anxiety about tests, and a high sense of internalization of control of environment—all this after SES effects are removed.

Internal Control and Test Anxiety. While the single achievement dimension for white students seems relatively simple, the corresponding three dimensions for blacks seem very difficult to understand. First, we see that sense of control forms a separate dimension with test anxiety, and this dimension modestly predicts academic self-esteem, achievement test performance, and feelings of happiness. Other research on blacks has suggested that control of environment and happiness have distinctly racial overtones for black students (Crain and Weisman 1972). One must bear in mind that the environment in which a black student must learn to operate is largely white dominated. If he believes that by trying hard he will be able to obtain a good job, he is in effect saying that whites are going to be fair in evaluating him since most employers are white. It is only a small step further to hypothesize that the black who perceives the environment as racist and unfair will more generally see life as outside his control, in the hands of circumstance, and will respond by agreeing to such statements as "Good luck is just as important as hard work for success." Believing this, he will tend to not try as hard to succeed. Other research has shown that prisoners who disagree with statements such as these "high-internals" are more likely to learn about parole (Seeman 1964), high-internal tuberculosis patients are more likely to learn about how to treat disease (Seeman and Evans 1962), and high-internal black adults are more likely to own their own homes and have savings accounts (Crain and Weisman 1972). Yet in this factor analysis, control of environment does not form a factor with any racial items.

We do not understand this complex issue, and in fact will not use internal control in the analysis in this book. The between-school variance is relatively small, meaning that schools cannot have much effect on this variable, and we were unable to locate any interesting school characteristics which were correlated with internal control scores. The same is true for test anxiety, which is also not analyzed in our report.

Dropping the internal control-test anxiety dimension still leaves us with two achievement dimensions. Why should a school with unusually high black achievement test scores be different from a school having high black self-esteem, or many blacks planning on college? The separation of these two dimensions seems to raise some serious problems. Although both self-esteem and achievement are analyzed in this book, we were unable to arrive at an answer to the question, How is it that some schools teach black students more without elevating their academic self-esteem? We suspect that this unanswered question is very important, because we think it holds a clue to important questions about the failure of school to motivate black students. For if it takes different processes to obtain high test scores and to obtain students who believe their performance is high, then the rewards are going astray; we think this conforms to our sense of what is wrong, but that doesn't help us understand why or what to do.

Bear in mind the fact that these variables load on different factors does not mean they are uncorrelated. For blacks, a school with high achievement test scores does have high black self-esteem, $r = .38$. The problem is that the same correlation for whites is .64! In general, all the dependent variables are positively correlated; a school where students feel school rules are fair has better racial attitudes ($r = .38$ for blacks, .23 for whites) and higher achievement (.11 for blacks, .18 for whites). And finally, a school that blacks like is a school that whites like, too ($r = .40$)

The correlations among the outcomes vary from strongly positive down to zero, but in only one case is there a significant correlation implying a difficult tradeoff. Racial contact and racial tension are positively correlated, which implies that one strategy for minimizing racial tension is to simply keep white and black students apart. We are not sure what this means. It may be simply that interracial friendships and acquaintanceship creates opportunity for friction to appear. It is more likely a less direct link, that is, that a certain quality of school climate in which white and black students feel free to interact enables students to both recognize their racial grievances and feel free to express them. The correlations shown in table 1–2 are partial correlations, controlling on black and white SES, school percentage white, the percent urban, the median educational level of the county, and the region within the south. Racial tension is discussed in more detail in Chapter 2.

How Large are the Differences between Schools?

Commentators on the Coleman report frequently conclude that little of the variance in individual achievement lies between schools. There is a considerably greater difference between the performance of any two students selected at random than there is between the means of two schools selected at random. If the main explanation for a student's academic performance or his attitudes lay in the quality of the school he attends, then it would follow that good schools would have a high percentage of high-performing students or students with positive attitudes, while a few very bad schools would have a high percentage of low-performing or dissatisfied students. If this were true, then the difference between the best and worst schools would be nearly as great as the difference between the best and worst students, and most of the variance in individual achievement would indeed lie between schools. By this argument, then, the extent to which school mean achievement or attitude scores differ, after the student bodies have been matched statistically on SES, is an upper limit of the size of the school's effect.

How large must the between-school variance be before it is considered meaningful? We converted the between-school variance into a more meaningful statistic in Table 1–1, using a procedure developed by Jencks and his colleagues in *Inequality* (1972). We imagined the schools ranked by the responses to a question and divided into five equal groups. Then a table of the cumulative normal distribution shows that the typical school in the lowest group would have a score 1.25s below the mean, and the typical school in the top fifth would be 1.25s above the mean. Let us see what this means for the percentage of white students saying they liked the principal of their school, which has a mean of 65 percent and a standard deviation of 19.3 percent. The typical school in the top fifth would have (65 ± 19.3 × 1.25) = 89 percent of the white students saying they liked the principal, while in the typical school in the bottom fifth, only (65 − 19.3 × 1.25) = 41 percent of the students would say this. The differences between high schools in the response of students seems quite apparent.

Table 1A-2. School-level correlations of major dependent variables for each race with SES of same race.

Dependent Variables, White:	Correlations: With White SES
Achievement	.59
Academic Self-Esteem	.38
Racial Contact	.10
Racial Attitudes	.25
Racial Tension	.20[a]
Rule Acceptance	.03
Nondelinquency	.15
Like School	−.09
Sense of Belonging	−.07
Dependent Variables, Black:	With Black SES
Achievement	.53
Academic Self-Esteem	.32
Racial Contact	.07
Racial Attitudes	−.01
Racial Tension	.33[a]
Rule Acceptance	−.05
Nondelinquency	−.25
Like School	−.20
Happiness	.23
Sense of Belonging	−.06

[a]indicates that high SES schools have more tension

These between-school differences in Table 1–1 are based on between-school variances which are inflated by sampling error due to small samples of black or white students in each school (see the Methodological Appendix for details of this) and in the case of achievement and self-esteem, by school differences in SES.

Our analysis of the between-school differences is simplified because most of the dependent variables we are using are not correlated with student body social status—which means we are not in danger of saying the differences among schools are due to school characteristics when in fact they are only due to differences in student body social class.

Of the dependent variables, only achievement, self-esteem, internal control, and test anxiety are correlated with SES, and the latter two variables are not used in our analysis. This perhaps surprising result is shown in Table 1A–2. The tables show the correlations of the eighteen main dependent variables with the socioeconomic status of the same-race student body. Since tension is correlated with both white and black SES, there are nineteen correlations in all. Of the nineteen, only the correlations of SES with achievement and self-esteem are positive and above .30. Of the remaining fifteen, three are positive and above .10, three others are small but in the expected direction, and nine run opposite to our expectations.

Estimating the Standard Deviation of the Distribution of School Means

We were not able to arrive at firm estimates of the amount of between-school variance which was really due to sampling error in the computation of each school's mean. (See the Methodological Appendix for a discussion of this.) Our best estimates of the standard deviations of the distribution of school means (that is, the square root of the between-school variance) net of sampling error, are shown in Table 1A–3.

This table indicates that questions asking students to report on school race relations have very large between-school differences for both blacks and whites. Questions asking about attitudes toward school (such as "Do you like your principal?") and questions about personal racial attitudes or behavior (such as having an opposite-race friend or feeling that one doesn't belong) both show large differ-

Table 1A-3. Estimated school-level standard deviations of typical student responses to questionnaire items, in percentage units.

Types of Items	Corrected for Sampling Error	
	Blacks	Whites
Reports on School Race Relations	15–25	15–30
Racial Attitudes, Behavior	8–17	8–19
Questions on Black Knowledge	8–22	10–17
Attitudes toward School	8–15	8–18
Delinquency	8–15	8–12
Self-esteem	8–15	0–12
Rule Acceptance	5–15	0–10
Control of Environment	5–15	0–8
Test Anxiety	5–12	0–6

Note: All standard deviations are for variables with means of 50 percent.

ences. Control of environment and self-esteem show small between-school differences, but these variables are correlated with SES, so much of this is due to the variability in social status among schools.

For whites, personal attitude questions show only small standard deviations, net of sampling error. Apparently differences among schools have little effect in creating differences among white students in their personal attitudes. For blacks, the between-school differences in these variables—control of environment, rule acceptance, and test anxiety—are slightly larger. This is consistent with our hypothesis that these attitudes are based in part on the student's racial environment and hence are somewhat affected by school.

Whether the between-school differences given in Table 1–1 and in Table 1A–2 are large or small is very much a matter of interpretation. The smallest differences are in the personal attitudes items, and even these seem important to us. Our admittedly rough estimate of the true between-school standard deviation, net of sampling error, of the percentage of black students who say that they are happy is 6.6 percent. The mean is 61 percent, so if we use the top fifth-bottom fifth comparison, we find that in the lowest fifth of the schools only 53 percent of the black students say they are "very happy" or "pretty happy" while in the highest fifth 69 percent say they are. This is one of the smallest between-school differences among our dependent variables, but we believe this difference between two schools would be readily apparent to someone who spent a few days observing them.

The Effect of School on Achievement

Estimating the magnitude of school effects from the between-school variance is most complicated for achievement test performance because of its high correlation with school mean socioeconomic status. Of course, it is achievement which has been the subject of the long debates about the magnitude of school effects. As Table 1A–4 indicates, the amount of variance between schools on the achievement test is one-fifth of the total variance. This is greater than the figure obtained by Coleman for southern whites and about the same as his estimate of the between-school variance for southern Blacks.

The intellectual community responded to the Coleman report by concluding that if most of the variance in achievement did not lie between schools, schools must have little power to create equality of educational opportunity. This conclusion is badly overstated. To understand this, we must understand what it means to say that only one-fifth of the total variance in achievement lies between schools. Most writers have taken this to mean that most of the variance is outside the control of the school and have concluded that there is little that the school can do to influence achievement. No doubt it is important that we recognize that the school is not all-powerful. We should know by now that no amount of improvement in the educational system will create impressive gains in tested achievement in large numbers of students. When we recognize this, we can become more realistic about what to expect from the schools and perhaps place our desire to reform the educational system into a healthier perspective. Recent writing by social scientists, however, has taken the extreme position that significant improvements in tested achievement are impossible to accomplish and, therefore, that

Table 1A-4. The percentage of the total variance that lies between schools in the achievement test scores.

Black Students	19.5
White Students	20.5

educational reform is hopeless.[11] For this reason, we must examine very carefully what "20 percent of the variance" means.

For this analysis, we will look at the white high school student data. We have transformed the test scores approximately into the metric used by the SAT, standardizing scores to a white mean of 466 and a standard deviation of 108. The Coleman (1966) report finds that one standard deviation on this type of test will equal approximately three grade level equivalents. Thus we will estimate that a difference of 108/3 = 36 points corresponds to a difference of about one grade level. The total variance on the test, both within and between schools, is $(108)^2$ or 11664 units. To say that 20.5 percent of this total variance lies between schools is to say that the standard deviation of the distribution of school means is

$$\sqrt{.205} \times 11664 = \sqrt{2391} = 49. \qquad (1A.1)$$

What is the difference between an individual standard deviation of 108 and a school mean standard deviation of 49? One answer is to look at graphs of the distributions in the top and center drawings of Figure 1A–1. The top figure shows the distribution of individual test scores, s = 108. The center figure shows the distribution of school means, s = 49. If we assume normality, the best one-fifth of all high schools in the South should be 1.25 standard deviations above the mean on the average, while the worst one-fifth should be an equal distance below. This means that the two groups will be 2.5 standard deviations apart, or 2.5 × 49 = 122 points apart on our test. This is a difference of slightly over 1 individual-level standard deviation, or converted to grade equivalents, slightly over three grade levels. Consequently, the bottom fifth of the high schools in our sample have white students performing, on the average, below ninth grade level, while the top fifth have sophomores performing near the level of high school seniors. This conclusion is shown visually in the center graph in Figure 1A–1, which shows some schools with means at grade thirteen and others with means at grade seven. Stated this way, the differences between schools do not seem so small.

This is not to say that we have shown that differences in quality of schooling are capable of producing differences of this magnitude.

---

[11]At least that is our reading of Jencks and his colleagues (1972), the Editors' Introduction to Mosteller and Moynihan (1972), and a host of popular magazine articles.

The students in the high achieving schools will usually be from better family backgrounds than those in the low achieving schools. Social class and achievement are not perfectly correlated; our correlation, at the individual level, between social status and achievement for tenth grade white students is only .26 (Coleman's, using a better SES scale and a longer achievement test, was .38). Obviously, social status is not the whole story. Furthermore, there is no system of perfect economic segregation that places the very highest SES students together, without error, into certain schools. (Twenty percent of the individual variance in SES lies between schools.) If we work out the computation, we find that using either our data or Coleman's, only a small portion of the between-school variance in achievement is the direct effect of social class.[12]

Since individual social class alone is not the entire explanation for between-school differences in achievement, we must also consider the contexual effect of social class. Social class has a sort of multiplier effect in schools. Thus, the high status student, already a high achiever due to family background, benefits from economic segregation; he is more likely to be placed in a school where other students have high social status and this means that the school pushes his achievement even higher. This phenomenon is reflected in our data in the fact that while the correlation between social class and achievement at the individual level is 0.26 for the white tenth graders, the correlation between white mean social class and white mean achievement at the school level is .59. The school with uniformly high status students will find that the students tend to be overachievers, while the school with uniformly low status students will find that the average student tends to do worse than would be expected on the basis of his family background alone. This is depressing news for educators, for it suggests that while schools are making a difference, one of the most significant ways that they make that difference is through a factor beyond the control of the school faculty, one that can only be combated through economic desegregation.

---

[12]It happens that in these data, about the same percentages of variance in social class and in achievement lie between schools. This means that if there were no measurement error and no contextual effect of school mean social status on individual achievement, social status would have the same correlation with achievement at the school level as it does at the individual level, explaining either 6 percent ($.26^2$ from this study) or 14 percent ($.38^2$ from Coleman) of the between-school variance.

Figure 1A-1. Graphic display of variation in achievement (tenth grade white students).

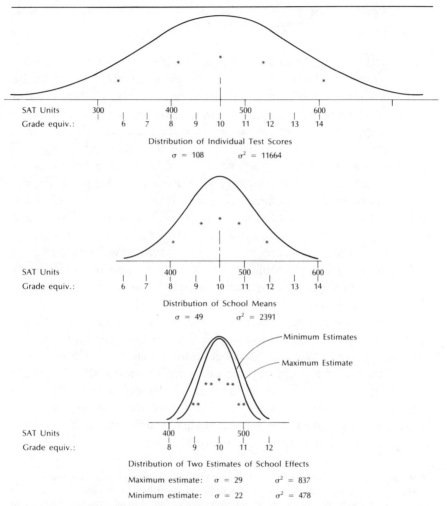

Note: * indicates mean quintile of the distribution.

How much variance is unexplained after we allow for both individual and contextual social class effects on achievement? Since our social status scale has a correlation of .59 with achievement at the school level for whites, $.59^2$ or 35 percent of the school-level variance in achievement is accounted for by the student body social status. We can do a bit better than that if, instead of building a simple scale of the SES items, we use multiple regression to pick the best fitting linear sum of the SES items. When we do this, we are able to generate a multiple correlation coefficient of .67 between school mean white social class and school mean white achievement, explaining .67^2 or 45 percent of the variance.

A Maximum Estimate of School Quality Effects.   Now let us see if we can estimate how much variance between schools might be attributed to differences in quality between schools. We can arrive at a maximum estimate by arguing that whatever we cannot explain with individual and contextual social status and sampling error is explainable by school quality.[13] Let us assume that quality of education can explain 35 percent of the difference in achievement (the amount left after subtracting 45 pecent for school social class and 20 percent for sampling error which occurs because we have used only a sample of fifty students in each school).[14] Thirty-five percent of the between-school variance of 2391 is 837. This means that if a set of schools were given identical students, the distribution of achievement scores would still vary, with a standard deviation of $\sqrt{837} = 29$ points. This distribution, labeled "maximum estimate," is shown in the bottom drawing of Figure 1A–1.

To obtain a minimum estimate, we computed a series of multiple regression equations using the school characteristics measured in our survey. We found that after social class and racial composition effects were removed, we could explain uniquely an additional 12 percent of the variance with seven school characteristics.[15] This is a conservative estimate since it assumes that these seven variables comprehensively measure school quality. Furthermore, these variables do not include some of the teacher characteristics Coleman

[13]This is an obvious overstatement (for example, it assumes no measurement error in school status). On the other hand, this assumption actually underestimates the effect of school quality in one way. By removing not only the direct but also the contextual effects of socioeconomic status, we are, in effect, saying that all the differences between middle class and working class schools are due to the difference between students; we are arguing that the quality of educational effort is the same in middle class and working class schools. If middle class schools are superior in quality (as many people suspect), we are ignoring this difference in quality. Thus, we are overestimating the effect of quality by assigning all residual variance to it, but at the same time, we are underestimating the effect of quality by ignoring all differences in quality which are correlated with school social class (so perhaps the two false assumptions will cancel each other out).

[14]See the Methodological Appendix.

[15]Three teacher attitude variables, three school program variables, and student reports of the amount of homework.

used, with which he was also able to explain 12 percent of the between-school variance.[16]

It seems reasonable to assume that more and better measures of school quality will increase the percent of variance uniquely explained. In addition, we should probably allocate at least a small amount of the variance shared by social status and school quality measures to school quality, rather than arbitrarily attributing it all to social class. It seems reasonable to assume that doing this would raise the total fraction of the between-school variance in achievement attributable to school quality to at least 20 pecent. This would mean that the between-school variance attributable to educational quality would be .20 × 2391 = 478 and that a collection of schools with identical students would have mean achievement scores distributed with a standard deviation of $\sqrt{478}$ = 22 points. This is the minimum estimate shown at the bottom of Figure 1A–1.

The bottom drawing of Figure 1A–1 is thus our answer to the question: "How much difference can a school make?" The answer is that a typical student in an unusually good school (one near the right tail of the distributions in the graph) will be achieving anywhere from three-quarters (the minimum estimate) to one (the maximum estimate) grade level above the norm (that is, the overall individual-level mean for southern schools), and he would score somewhere around 490 or 500 on the SAT. The same student in an unusually bad school would fall three-quarters to one grade level below the norm, and his SAT score would be around 430 to 440. Thus the difference between our best and worst high schools is a difference of one and one-half to two grade levels, or 50 to 70 SAT points. To put it another way, if we brought all our southern high schools up to the level of the best southern schools—pushed them all up to what is now the upper tail of either the minimum or maximum estimate in the bottom of Figure 1A–1—we would raise the regional norm for white tenth graders by 30 points on the SAT.

What percent of the variance in individual achievement is represented by this residual school-level variation, which we argue is the maximum which can be achieved by variations in school quality? The answer is that 837 (the variance of the maximum estimate in Figure

[16]*Equality of Educational Opportunity* (Coleman et al. 1966:317) shows seven teacher variables uniquely explaining 2.49 percent of the individual variance in Southern white ninth grade achievement. This is 12 percent of our estimated between-school variance (.0249/.205 = .12).

1A–1) divided by 11664 (the variance of the individual distribution in the top drawing) is 7 percent of the total variance in achievement. Using the minimum estimate, we get 478/11664 = 4 percent. In other words, only 4 to 7 percent of the variance in individual achievement can be explained by school quality. The amount of differentiation among schools can be made to look large or small, depending upon the kinds of statistics that are used and the way in which common sense is used to interpret those statistics.

Whether school effects appear large or small depends on the units we use to measure them. Indeed, demonstrating this is the main point of this exercise. If we say that school quality can explain no more than 4 to 7 percent of individual achievement, how can we help but conclude that this is a miniscule effect? If we call the same thing a difference of one and one-half to two grade levels or say it indicates that school reform could lead to possible gains for the entire South of 30 SAT points, the same differences look more impressive. Furthermore, if we accept for a moment that 4 to 7 percent of the individual variance is the total effect of school quality, then some of Coleman's results change sharply in interpretation. For example, his finding that 2.5 percent of the variance in achievement can be explained uniquely by teacher quality implies teacher characteristics are a major part of school quality.

An English study in 1978 compared twelve secondary schools serving working class students in South London and found what seemed to be quite large effects of school on achievement test results (Rutter et al. 1979). That study compared the test scores of students before entering the schools (at age eleven) to their performance on the English national tests (the "O-levels") given at age sixteen. The study found, for example, that the brightest one-third of students (based on their scores at age eleven) in one of the schools passed exams in fewer subjects than the dullest one-third in another school. The study uses a complicated scoring system, giving students 1 point for each subject passed with a high score and 0.5 points for each subject passed at a lower level, and finds that a student of average ability would get a total score of 2.38 if he or she were in the best school and a score of only 0.62 in the worst school.[17] This implies

[17]There are two sets of exams used in England. The older "O-level" exams are supplemented by an easier set of exams. Rutter scores 1 point for each O-level pass, 0.5 point for each pass on the easier exam. For example, a student who took an O-level exam in English language and easier exams in woodworking, math, and English literature would get 2.5 points.

that in the best school around 85 percent of the students must have earned a pass in at least one subject, and around 30 percent got one or more high passes; while in the worst school, only 40 percent passed any test, and only 15 pecent got one or more high passes. These differences do seem quite large, and articles in the English press hailed the study as a major refutation of Coleman's results. They differ more in the way the results are stated than in the magnitude of the between-school differences. We used our computations (which agree reasonably well with Coleman's) to estimate the chances of a student of average socioeconomic status passing a test in a single subject (such as mathematics) in a high achievement American school and how much his or her chances would change if he were in a low achievement school. We made the following assumptions: that within any one school the individual-level standard deviation of test scores was 100; the standard deviation of the distribution of school quality effects was 25 (midway between our low estimate of 22 and our high estimate of 29); and that the correlation of general achievement (measured by our test) and achievement in a specific subject was 0.87. We then simulated an American version of Rutter's study, assuming that we selected twelve schools at random. We also assumed that the one of the twelve with the lowest quality and the one with the highest quality had students with the same normal distribution of SES. We found that we would expect 15 percent of the students in the lowest quality school to pass a difficult math test, compared to 35 percent in the best quality school. While this difference does not seem to be as great as that found by the English study, it is certainly not small.[18] Had Coleman stated his results in these terms it seems likely that the school don't make a difference interpretation might never have become popular. Again, what appears to be a substantive difference is mainly a difference in statistical presentation.

Comments.   Finally, we should point out that the maximum effect attributable to school quality is based on the existing distribution of school test scores. In saying that by bringing the average southern

---

[18]We are estimating the probability of a high pass on a single test which is not the same as Rutter et al.'s (1979) estimate of the number of high passes on a battery of tests, but it does seem as if we are finding a smaller difference. If so, this could be mainly explained by the fact that the students in the London schools had been in the same secondary school since age eleven, which allowed more time for the quality of their school to affect them.

school up to the quality of the best southern school, we can raise test scores three-quarters to one grade, we say nothing about what could be accomplished by a school superior to any existing southern school. Any variance analysis can only tell us about the variability that exists in the environment right now, not about what is possible.

2 THE EFFECTS OF THE DESEGREGATION PLAN

One of the problems with school desegregation is that the intense controversy occurring in so many communities has meant that feelings have been expressed and repeated, quoted and reprinted until we forget that they are only feelings and not facts. In every school desegregation controversy, whites have said that desegregation is acceptable, but busing is not—meaning that whites should be left in their own schools, which should be desegregated by bringing in a small number of (preferably middle class) blacks. This message has been relayed so many times that we assumed it had some basis in fact—that the best desegregated schools were indeed predominantly white schools in white neighborhoods where middle class blacks were bused in. We decided to demonstrate the truth of this, if we could, and we could not. At this point we realized that much of what we thought we knew about desegregation was simply mythology and decided to begin this book with a chapter devoted largely to debunking some of these myths.

IS THERE A BEST RACIAL MIX FOR SCHOOLS?

A common claim is that large numbers of black students in a school hold back instruction, thus slowing the academic growth of whites.

When we looked at the data, we found that the whites in predominantly black schools had higher achievement than similar whites in
predominantly white schools. Majority white schools, majority black
schools, and schools with equal numbers of blacks and whites each
have their advantages and disadvantages. There is no such thing as an
ideal racial composition.

We used the same technique for analyzing racial composition as
we did for studying all the other school characteristics reported in
this book. A full description of this procedure are given in the
appendix. Briefly, what we did is this: We used multiple regression
to see if schools which differed in racial composition, size, student
body socioeconomic status, or the urbanism, educational level or
region of the community in which the school is located, also differed
on measures of school success such as achievement test scores,
student or racial tension. We used these results to predict how much
difference there would be between schools if they were alike in all
respects but racial composition. We thus isolated the effect of this
single characteristically by matching schools on the other important
factors.

Table 2-1.   The effect of school racial composition.

Student Attitudes, Behavior	Percent White Students			
	0–40%	40–65%	65–80%	80–100%
Black Students:				
Sense of Belonging	82%[a]	68%[a]	67%	59%
Nondelinquency	69%	67%	65%	64%
Self-Esteem	57%	61%	50%	51%
Achievement Test Score	340	344	348	344
White Students:				
Sense of Belonging	73%[a]	76%	81%	82%
Nondelinquency	59%	59%	64%	65%
Self-Esteem	65%[a]	60%	56%	57%
Achievement Test Score	477	472	463	458
Withdrawal from School	27%[a]	7%	6%	11%
Racial Tension	45%	52%	44%	32%

[a] $p < .05$.

Note: Effects shown are after schools are matched on community educational level and
urbanism, region within the South, school size, black student social status; for white outcomes, schools are matched on both black and white social status.

Table 2–1 summarizes the effect of school racial composition on ten different school outcomes. The equations were constructed to compare four common types of schools: those that are predominantly black (i.e., less than 40% white), those that are approximately half black and half white (40 to 65% white), and those that are predominantly white with a small proportion of blacks (over 80% white). The four types of schools are matched on region within the South (upper vs. deep South), community urbanism and educational level, school size, and student socioeconomic status. (The full regression equations are given in the appendix to the chapter.) Thus, in the first line of Table 2–1 we see that in an otherwise typical school which was less than 40 percent white, we would expect about 82 percent of the black students to say they felt like they belonged in the school. If that school were over 80 percent white, this percentage would drop to 59 percent. The same procedure is used to compute white feelings of belonging in the lower part of the table, except that the schools are then matched on white, rather than black, student socioeconomic status.

We looked at a total of thirty-four different black and white student outcomes. The ten results shown in Table 2–1 are the most interesting. The strongest effect is in the response to the statement "I feel like I don't belong in this school." Apparently black students in predominantly white schools are the most alienated since only 59 percent disagree with this statement. White students in predominantly black schools are also likely to say they do not belong, but not to the same degree. Comparing black and white responses to this question, we would have to conclude that each race is somewhat more comfortable when they are in the majority in their school, but the effects of racial composition are stronger for blacks than for whites. This may seem surprising; blacks are a minority group in the United States and should be accustomed to being outnumbered by whites. We can think of two reason why whites should have an easier time being in the minority. We suspect that when the whites are a minority in the school, the administration goes out of its way to make sure that they are satisfied. In addition, given the realities of academic achievement, the whites in predominantly black schools are likely to collect far more than their share of the academic honors, which should ease much of their discomfort. The differences in sense of belonging between the predominantly black and predominantly white schools are large, especially for blacks, but they should not obscure the fact that even for the most alienated group—blacks in predominantly white schools—most students do not complain.

Other student attitudes show relatively small differences. There is a tendency for students to get into trouble less if they are the predominant race in the school, but the differences are slight. Nondelinquency here refers to not skipping school, not being sent to the principal's office for disciplinary reasons, and not getting into a fight at school. Blacks are about 5 percent more likely to have been involved in trouble in a predominantly white school, and whites about 6 percent more likely to have been involved in trouble in black schools. The differences are too small to be worth much attention. Most of the other student responses show the same pattern—a slight tendency for each race to like school more and to complain less when they are in the majority. (One must bear in mind that this may only apply to the first few years of desegregation; students who are desegregated from kindergarten may react differently.)

One exception is academic self-esteem. The results for blacks look like what we would expect—a slight difference favoring predominantly black schools. Fifty-seven percent of the blacks in predominantly black schools say that they are doing well in their school work, compared to 51 percent in predominantly white schools. For whites, however, the pattern is reversed—white students think less of their school ability in predominantly white schools and have higher self-esteem in predominantly black schools. We think both whites and blacks establish a sense of academic self-esteem by comparing themselves to the other students in the school. In predominantly black schools, white self-esteem is boosted by the presence of large numbers of (usually) poorly performing blacks; black self-esteem is enhanced by the absence of large numbers of (usually) better performing whites.

We think that the higher academic self-esteem of black and white students in predominantly black schools results from their comparing themselves to other students, and not from any differences in absolute test scores. The fourth and eighth lines of the table show very weak relationships between test performance, measured in the same score units used by the SAT, and school racial composition. Each race does slightly better when they are in the minority. The differences for blacks are very small. This does not mean that desegregation does not raise test scores of black students; most of the black students in predominantly white schools in this study attended segregated elementary schools. One might conclude that desegregation of high school students will have little immediate impact on their test performance; other studies have also shown this. The results for white students are more interesting since they show a noticeable difference (19 SAT points) favoring predominantly black schools. At first we thought that this was because the white flight from predominantly black schools had removed the duller students; other researchers studying Florida schools found that it is the high income families who pull their children out of desegregating schools, which makes it unlikely that these are low achievers (Giles, Cataldo, and Gatlin 1976). We suspect that black schools often make a special effort to provide a good school experience for their white minorities, and that this explains the high test scores of whites in predominantly black schools, but the high white withdrawal from these schools makes it hazardous to try to interpret the scores for the students who remain.

Predominantly black schools provide slightly better environments for black student attitudes and white achievement but have other problems. When we study black achievement in more detail, we will see that after several years of desegregation achievement test scores for blacks are generally higher in predominantly white schools. For most school boards, the major difficulty with predominantly black schools is that whites do not want to attend them. The ninth line of the table shows how principals responded when asked, "About how many white students who are assigned here have transferred to another public or private school?" The number of whites leaving the school is small except in schools that are under 40 percent white, where a quarter of the white students have transferred.

If predominantly black schools are unacceptable to white students and have low black achievement, and predominantly white schools alienate black students, then perhaps the best answer is that schools should be well mixed, with white enrollments between 40 and 80 percent, for example. This does seem reasonable, but the last line of Table 2–1 shows that schools in the middle range of racial composition have the highest level of racial tension. One of us taught a class in which a black undergraduate who had attended a quiet, predominantly white junior high and a more combative, racially balanced high school offered a plausible explanation. He said that when either group is badly outnumbered, they have to be docile; racially balanced schools have more tension because the conflict between the races is a fair fight.

Where does this leave us? Obviously, no racial composition is perfect, and which one to choose is partly a matter of taste. Personally, we prefer schools in the 65 to 80 percent white range, despite their greater racial tension.

BUSING

Predominantly white school districts usually desegregate by making the racial composition of every school in the district equal. This has several advantages from the school administration's point of view. First, it makes all schools predominantly white. Second, it ensures that every white neighborhood has desegregated schools, leaving no havens which might cause white flight by attracting whites from desegregated areas. Finally, this kind of plan minimizes the amount of busing of white students. (Busing does not refer to students' riding a school bus, but to their attending school in the opposite-race neighborhood. As far as we can see, white parents have little objection to their children traveling to school by bus; busing is controversial only if the student is traveling to an opposite-race neighborhood.) A racial balance plan, which gives every school the same racial composition, usually works by converting the schools in black neighborhoods into learning centers serving only certain grades. For example, when metropolitan Wilmington, Delaware was desegregated, the school board proposed a plan in which all of the schools in predominantly black Wilmington city would serve only fifth or ninth grade students. This meant that black students would be bused to white suburban schools ten grades out of twelve, while the white suburban students would be bused to formerly black schools two grades out of twelve. Since there are many more white students than black in the metropolitan area, there are approximately as many whites in grades five and nine as there are black students in all ten of the remaining grades. In order to use school buildings most efficiently, as many students must be transported into minority schools as are transferred out. The court did not accept the Wilmington plan since it involved transporting slightly more blacks than whites. The court argued that in order to make the number of transported black and white students as equal as possible, the plan should have placed three grades in the schools in minority neighborhoods, not two.[1]

The courts have only recently begun insisting that white and black transfers be equalized. In the 1960s some southern districts closed all the schools in black neighborhoods on the grounds that the buildings were obsolete. They then took advantage of the excess space in the schools in white neighborhoods and reassigned the black students to white neighborhoods for all twelve grades. No white students were bused.[2]

When blacks are in the minority in the school district, a desegregation plan which converts black schools into learning centers serving two or three grades will make all schools in the district predominantly white, will shift most of the busing onto blacks, and will eliminate any white havens in the school district. When this happens, there will generally be less resistance from whites and less white withdrawal from the desegregated schools.

However, this sort of plan works only if the school district is one-quarter black or less; this strategy will not work in the large central cities of the North, where blacks are often in the majority. Under these conditions, there are only two viable alternatives in the eyes of most school administrators—either to desegregate the entire metropolitan area, using suburban white students to maintain a white majority, or else to leave large areas of the ghetto segregated. Louisville, Detroit, and Wilmington are three districts which pushed for a metropolitan solution, filing suits against their suburban neighbors. When Detroit lost in the Supreme Court, it took the other option and prepared a Detroit-only desegregation plan which left the vast majority of black schools segregated. Dallas and Los

---

[1]The court pointed out that in order to equalize the number of students transported in each direction, the percentage of years that whites are transferred should be equal to the percentage of students who were in minority schools before desegregation. Since minority school attendance constituted about 22 percent of the district, whites should be transported three grades out of twelve, or 25 percent of the time, rather than two grades out of twelve, which is only 17 percent of the time.

[2]This sort of plan would no longer be considered constitutional, but school boards have developed new strategies which avoid busing whites and which are acceptable to the courts. For example, many northern districts are converting some of the schools in minority areas into magnet schools, using new curricula and special facilities to attract white students. If enough whites volunteer for these schools, the school board will not have to assign any whites to schools in minority neighborhoods.

Angeles did not try for metropolitan plans but instead drew desegregation plans which left most of the minority schools segregated.

What is so bad about busing? James A. Davis studied the effects of busing in these 200 high schools and in the elementary schools which we had also surveyed. His lengthy analysis generally found no effect of busing, and his report concluded rather angrily that busing and neighborhood schools were false issues: "We can state emphatically, however, that we will all be better off if we concentrate on the real and terrible problems of desegregation rather than discussing the ridiculous and hypocritical proposition that there is something psychologically or academically edifying in children going to school on foot" (1973: 118).

We will not spend a great deal of time showing the ways in which busing does not affect student attitudes or performance. There are three student variables which do seem to be affected by busing, and these are shown in Table 2–2. In this table, we have assumed the schools to be 65 percent white and have again matched the schools on type of community, school size, and region.

Since busing has little to do with buses per se, we define busing here as meaning not attending the school nearest to one's home. We have divided the high schools into three categories: those in which a large number of black students say they are not attending the school nearest their home (blacks are bused), those in which a large number of white students say they are not attending the school nearest their home (whites are bused), and schools in which neither group says this (neighborhood schools).[3]

The first line of Table 2–2 shows that when blacks are bused they are much more likely to agree with the statement, "I feel like I don't belong in this school." Conversely, whites are more likely to say they do not belong when they were bused, although the differences are not as great for whites, and fewer white students feel alienated. These two lines of the table make a great deal of sense. Students are extremely concerned with territoriality. A school in a white neigh-

---

[3]Blacks are much more likely to be bused than whites; in 43 percent of our high schools, blacks are bused in, while in only 17 percent are whites bused in. Thirty-four percent of the schools are neighborhood schools. Six percent are apparently special schools (probably vocational high schools) where both whites and blacks are attending school away from their home areas. These schools are omitted from our analysis.

Table 2-2. The effects of busing on student attitudes and student racial contact.

(Percentage Units)			
		Type of School	
Student Attitudes, Behavior	Neighborhood Schools	Blacks Are Bused	Whites Are Bused
Black Sense of Belonging	70	44[a]	82
White Sense of Belonging	81	85	68[a]
Black Self-Esteem	54	38	55
White Self-Esteem	59	51	51
Black Racial Contact	49	40	65[a]
White Racial Contact	32	45	45[a]

[a] $p < .05$.

Note: Schools are matched on racial composition, region, school size, community education level and urbanism; and for self-esteem analysis, on student socioeconomic status.

borhood belongs to the white students, and they belong in that school.

The third line of the table shows that black sense of academic self-esteem is lowest when they are bused into a school. We suspect that low self-esteem is part of the feeling of being an outsider. The same pattern occurs for whites—their academic self-esteem is highest in neighborhood schools and lowest when white students are bused.

One should bear in mind that whatever the myths about neighborhood integrated schools, most such schools are not in integrated neighborhoods—they serve either two adjoining segregated neighborhoods or a neighborhood in transition. Under these conditions racial contact may be quite low. White students in these schools often come from segregated junior high schools; they already have a circle of friends and little incentive to make new interracial friendships in high school—particularly if there are long standing neighborhood taboos about the other side of the tracks or neighborhood resentment about "them" taking over. The degree of racial contact in the school is largely determined by the white student social structure. If white students are already organized into a social network of friendships and cliques, blacks will be unable to break in. Viewed this way, the last two lines of Table 2-2 may seem less surprising. They show that both blacks and whites report more interracial contact in schools where whites are bused in. When whites are reassigned, they are often separated from former schoolmates and friends, and hence more likely to establish new interracial friendships.

Another myth about desegregation is that busing increases racial tensions. Our data do not show this. Table 2–3 shows the level of racial tension in schools of different racial compositions which do and do not have students bused in. As usual, the schools are matched on other relevant characteristics such as the region within the South, characteristics of the community, and school size.

The first line of Table 2–3 shows that neighborhood schools which are 10 percent white have considerable difficulty—an average of 51 percent of the students complain about tensions. In contrast, 10 percent white schools where white students are bused in have lower levels of tension with only 24 percent of the students reporting difficulty. These findings seem quite reasonable. First, a neighborhood school which is 90 percent black is almost certainly a school in the last stages of racial transition. There should be considerable conflict between the whites who are being pushed out of the neighborhood and the blacks who have only grudgingly been allowed into the school and are now finally able to take it over. In contrast a school where a small number of whites are bused in is a school which is unequivocally black turf. There will be no conflict over territoriality: The whites have nothing to gain, and the blacks

Table 2-3.   Busing and racial tension.

| | Percentage of High Tension | | |
| | Type of School | | |
School Racial Composition	Neighborhood School	Blacks Are Bused	Whites Are Bused
10 Percent White	51	—[a]	24[b]
40 Percent White	55	77[b]	48
70 Percent White	42	53	—[a]
90 Percent White	26[b]	29[b]	—[a]

[a]Too few schools to analyze.
[b]$p < .05$.
Note: Schools matched on region, community urbanism and educational level, racial composition, school size.

nothing to prove. It is also likely that the school is only 10 percent white because a high level of white flight has taken the more prejudiced students out of the school.

Looking at the other racial compositions, we note little evidence that busing makes much difference. There is an extremely high level of racial tension (77%) in predominantly black schools where blacks are bused in (line two).[4] The 70 percent white schools with blacks bused in also have relatively high levels of tension, but we doubt that busing blacks into previously white schools necessarily increases tension since the last line of the table shows relatively low tension when blacks are bused into 90 percent white schools. The most reasonable conclusion is that there is no evidence that tension is increased by busing.

In summary, our analysis supports Davis's argument—busing is a red herring. There is some tendency for the group which is transported into the school to be more uncomfortable; but overall, the data indicate that busing, like racial composition, is not a major factor in explaining why some desegregated schools are more successful than others.

DOMINANCE AND TURF

These two analyses suggest the importance of territoriality—turf. It seems to us that in thinking about desegregation, both students and parents use a sort of war metaphor. While a school and a battlefield are not necessarily the same thing, each group seems to feel that its members are only safe when they outnumber the enemy and meet them on terrain of their own choosing. One poignant example of this thinking comes from a white student in Boston, on the eve of his first day attending school in all-black Roxbury:

> I don't even know if there's going to be more of them or more of us. My mother says there will be more of them which is weird 'cause I ain't never been with so many of 'em before.... And another thing. They don't live over here. *We* live over here...And if I have to fight in a war then I'll fight over here where *my* friends are, not over there where *their* friends

---

[4]There are only a handful of schools in this category. It seems unlikely that a school system would intentionally reassign so many blacks into a school as to make it predominantly black, which makes us think that a large number of whites must have withdrawn from these schools.

are. That only makes sense. You go where you have the best chance. (Cottle 1976: 113)

There is little justification for this battlefield imagery. In 1978, the National Institute of Education conducted a nationwide study of school violence, the *Safe Schools Study*. That study did find a great deal of trouble in schools—mainly petty theft and fighting. The study did find some support for the safety-in-numbers idea. Students who were in the minority, whether black or white, were more likely to be attacked. This is a minor part of the story; the important point is that rates of theft, robbery, attacks, and vandalism were not much higher in desegregated high schools nor in low income minority schools. It is not so much that we overestimate the trouble in central city schools as that we underestimate the problems suburban schools have. All-white suburban schools have nearly as many assaults and more damage to school property (and frequently have much less administrative preparation for dealing with it).

We can see a number of reasons why white parents will continue to believe that desegregated schools are dangerous, the facts notwithstanding. While attacks on children are no higher in minority schools, the *Safe Schools Study* does show teachers in minority schools are five times more likely to be assaulted. Teachers' experiences are likely to be widely known. (Sometimes it is to the political advantage of teachers' unions or school administrations to publicize attacks on teachers. In the 1960s the Chicago superintendent of schools accused the civil rights movement of fomenting a crime wave in the schools. Under pressure from the central administration, the number of teachers reporting being attacked increased sharply in white as well as minority schools.) A second reason why white parents are quick to believe that their children are in danger in desegregated schools is that black adults commit more crimes of violence than white adults. Rates for specific types of violence may be five or more times higher for black adults, but these differences apparently do not hold for violence among school age children. White students are nearly as likely to hurt other students as blacks are. In the midst of the Los Angeles school desegregation suit in 1978, one white politician charged that his daughter's safety was being jeopardized by a desegregation plan requiring her to attend school in the barrio. Chicano leaders pressured the school system to release data showing that the number of students suspended from school for discipline problems was actually higher in the high income Anglo neighborhood where the politician lived. Of course, a final explanation of white fear is simple racial prejudice. People have always been afraid of other ethnic groups.

Fear of violence only partly explains the popularity of the battlefield motif. Black and white students do compete with each other, but the conflict is usually nonviolent and the stakes are prestige. Bitter racial conflict can occur—over whether the white school mascot will be retained, over whether a black will be elected cheerleader or class officer, over who makes the best grades and who gets the academic honors. This competition leads to an interesting irony.

We noted earlier that students are more likely to have interracial friendships if there are large numbers of opposite-race students in their school. Yet it is precisely when a group is in the minority that it exerts the strongest social pressure on its members to avoid the other race. Table 2–4 gives the percentage of students replying yes to the question, "Do you think that your friends would think badly of you if you went someplace after school with a student of a different race?" The first line of the table shows that whites are most likely to say yes when they are in schools which are 40 to 65 percent white. In these schools whites are not obviously dominant, and we think they are attempting to maintain dominance by practicing segregation and treating blacks as social inferiors with whom they are not to associate.[5] The second line of the table shows exactly the same process occurring for blacks—peer pressure to avoid associating with whites is very low in predominantly black schools and noticeably higher in schools which are over 80 percent white. When whites are the overwhelming majority in the school, blacks apparently engage in self-segregation in order to maintain their group identity.

It is interesting that busing and school racial mix have stronger effects on black students than on whites. Although it is usually white parents that we hear complaining about the need to maintain predominantly white schools or to minimize busing, it is the black students who seem to suffer the most when they are placed in alien territory or are outnumbered in their new schools. It does make

[5]The fact that many prejudiced whites have left the less than 40 percent white schools would explain why peer pressure is not as strong there.

Table 2–4. Peer pressure against racial contact, by race of student and racial composition of school.

| | (Percentage of Students Saying Peers Would Disapprove of Interracial Activity) | | | |
| | Percent White at School | | | |
	0–40	40–65	65–80	80–100
Peer Disapproval Reported by Whites	57	63[a]	58	54
Peer Disapproval Reported by Blacks	33	39	40	51[a]

[a] $p < .05$.

Note: Schools matched on region, community urbanism and educational level, white and black student SES.

sense that the status of blacks is more easily threatened. As the "inferior" group, their prestige is more precarious.

Predominantly white schools are most threatening to blacks when the white students are working class, since working class whites are more prejudiced and more openly aggressive. Black discomfort shows up in the percentage of students who say that they are happy. In schools which are less than 80 percent white, 64 percent of the black students say they are happy.[6] In schools which are over 80 percent white where the whites are working class, this percentage drops to 54 percent. The same pattern appears on several other black student questionnaire responses: In schools with large numbers of working class whites, blacks have less racial contact, like school less, and are more delinquent.

Whites also need a comfortable racial situation in order to be happy, but the definition of comfort for whites is different than for blacks. Blacks, as the inferior social group, feel a need to be accepted by whites. Whites, as the superior group, feel a need to hold onto their position of dominance. This leads to a curious and rather unpleasant finding. White students are happiest when they are in the majority—82 percent of whites in schools over 65 percent white are happy, compared to 74 percent in schools which are less than 40

[6] A table of these figures is not included. As usual, we have controlled the effects of community characteristics, region, and student SES.

percent white. More importantly, there is a 5 percent decline in white students' happiness if the black students in the school are middle rather than working class. Blacks prefer being with middle class whites because middle class whites are more accepting of them. We think whites prefer associating with working class blacks because their own sense of superiority is not threatened.

We realize that this portrait of white and black students is an unflattering one. Of course many students, both black and white, are committed to ideas of racial equality and brotherhood. Nonetheless, if we are looking for practical ways to help desegregated schools, we only make our task harder if we exaggerate the nobility of teenagers.

THE MYTH OF THE CLASS PROBLEM

One puzzling pattern is that high schools seem to have more difficulty if their black students are from middle class families, even though middle class blacks are better students than those from poorer families. Table 2–5 indicates that schools with middle income black students have more racial tension, less interracial contact, and more black students who complain about not liking school. Middle income black student bodies are not even less delinquent.

We thought about this for a long time and finally put together an explanation drawing on the literature on social revolution and some of the ideas in psychoanalytic theory. Research on revolutions shows

Table 2-5. School racial tension and black student racial contact, attitudes toward school, and delinquency, by social status of black student body.

| | Black Student Status | |
	Low	High
Percentage Who Like School	50	42
Percentage Nondelinquent	67	65
Percentage with High Levels of Contact with Whites	49	44
Percentage High Racial Tension	39	48

Note: Schools matched on region, community educational level and urbanism, school size, and racial composition.

that it is never the very poorest who revolt. Revolutions usually occur during periods of prosperity, and are rarely led by the unemployed or the destitute. Apparently, revolutions must be built on hope, and those who are hopeless and cannot imagine a better world do not rebel. A similar theme appears in the literature of psychoanalysis. The most deprived are unable to express their anger because they are too inhibited by their fear of the world around them. Many people were surprised to find that the race riots of the late 1960s tended to involve native northerners who were high school graduates rather than immigrants from the South or persons with less education. Nor did the riots occur in the poorest cities or in the cities with the worst race relations. They began in those cities farthest removed from the South, spread gradually downward toward the border states, but faded out before becoming a significant phenomenon in the South. The more permissive, civil libertarian environment of the North allowed riots to occur. Migrants from the South were less likely to be involved simply because their memories of brutal white police were too vivid and too recent.

Does this argument extend to high school students? It appears that the lower class black students have little reason to be optimistic about the way the school will treat them if they allow their anger to surface. It is easier to say that they like school than to face the consequences of admitting their dislike. If the school has a number of middle class students, these more articulate students who have less to fear from the administration can state their grievances and express their anger publicly. In an environment where protest is more open, it is easier for other black students, who are perhaps less skilled verbally, to express their feelings in physical violence.

There is another plausible explanation for this pattern. It may be that middle class black students are simply opinion leaders, more up to date in their attitudes. In 1972 in the South, the idea that black students should complain about their school was a rather new idea. It was to some degree imported from northern schools. If so, it makes sense that middle class schools would be the first to hear of it. Just as the revolt against the Vietnam war spread first through the most prestigious university campuses, so black student protest in southern desegregated schools should have spread first from those schools where the black students were more successful and from schools located in sophisticated communities. Table 2–6 gives the level of racial tension in different type of schools. Each line of the table shows the effect of one variable when the other four variables listed in the table are controlled. Thus the higher the mean social status of the black students the greater the amount of racial tension, for schools of a certain size, with a certain level of white student social status, in communities of a particular educational level and degree of urbanism. Although middle class white students are more racially tolerant than lower class whites, the presence of high status white students in the school does not reduce racial tension. Similarly, although race relations are presumably more amicable in communities with higher educational levels, the level of tension is in fact much higher in these communities. (This implies that the schools with the worst racial tension will be those located in university towns.) If these protests are part of a diffusion process of a new idea, we should be cautious in making generalizations about social class and tension. The elite universities are now quite apathetic in their politics; it may be that a study done today would find little tension in middle class schools.

The next-to-last line of the table shows that, all else equal, urban communities have somewhat less difficulty than rural schools. The only line which is not a surprise is the last one—there is greater racial tension in larger schools.

All this raises questions regarding our value judgment about tensions. We instinctively assume that tension is a bad thing. In these data, the good schools—those with near-equal racial mixes or in high status communities—seem to have more tension. There is also a high level of interracial contact in tense schools. Furthermore, if the absence of tensions means simply that one or the other group is cowed, perhaps we should reconsider our view of tension as completely bad. Lewis Coser, discussing the work of the German Sociologist, George Simmel, comments:

> Contrary to what common sense might seen to indicate, Simmel asserts that in close relationships where, as we have seen, hostile feelings are likely to be present, the very absence of conflict might be taken as an index of the existance of underlying elements of strain (1964: 4).

The school is like a marriage—no open conflict can be a bad sign.

These tables seem to have done a fairly good job of demolishing one more myth—that the difficulties in desegregated schools are really a matter of class rather than race. Whites often argue that their objections to desegration have nothing to do with color but only

68   MAKING DESEGREGATION WORK

Table 2-6. The effect of student body and community social status on school racial tension.

Independent Variables	Percentage of Racial Tension When Independent Variable Is:	
	Low[a]	High[a]
Student Body		
Black Social Status	39	48
White Social Status	43	44
Community		
Educational Level	29	58[a]
Urbanism	52	33[a]
School Size	33	54[a]

[a] $p < .05$.

Note: For black and white student social status and community educational level, the low and high conditions are assumed to be the bottom and top quintiles of all schools. For urbanism, the low counties are 25 percent urban, the high counties 100 percent urban. For school size, low size is 500 students, high is 1500.

Schools matched on region, community urbanism and educational level, school size, white and black student SES.

with having their children attend school with lower class children. School administrators often complain that the big problem with desegration is the great range in social class in their schools. There are fragments of truth in these arguments, but they are more wrong than right. If the only problem with school desegregation were the unequal ability level of black and white students, then the one condition where ability levels were most equal—when whites were working class and blacks middle class—would be the ideal situation. In fact, this is the worst case of all.

The data make an argument for metropolitan desegregation. In large central cities, most middle income whites have moved to the suburbs and left behind only the poorer whites. These are the wrong whites for desegregation, and a metropolitan plan which brought central city blacks together with suburban, middle class whites would be better.

DESEGREGATION AND BLACK ACHIEVEMENT

The argument as to whether desegregation is educationally beneficial for blacks has raged for most of the twenty-five years since the *Brown* decision. When Chief Justice Earl Warren wrote the 1954 decision, he included a paragraph which implied that black children would benefit academically:

> Segregation of white and colored children in public schools has a detrimental effect upon the colored children. The impact is greater when it has the sanction of the law; for the policy of separating the races is usually interpreted as denoting the inferiority of the Negro group. A sense of inferiority affects the motivation of the child to learn. Segregation with the sanction of law, therefore, has a tendency to [retard]the educational and mental development of Negro childen and to deprive them of some of the benefits they would receive in a racial[ly]integrated school system (*Brown* v. *Board of Education*, 347 U.S. 494).

For a decade very little serious research was done on the question. In the middle 1960s, the federal government commissioned two major studies. One was the Coleman report (Coleman et al. 1966) which tested students in thousands of different schools across the United States. The report showed that black student achievement test scores were higher in predominantly white schools, mainly because there are more middle class students in these schools. Desegregation benefits blacks not because of the presence of white students per se but because going to school with white students is almost the only chance blacks have to attend middle class schools. (Coleman has since changed his opinion about desegregation; he now thinks that it does not help blacks, or at least that"forced busing"does not.)

Two years later the United States Commission on Civil Rights surveyed black adults and showed that those who had attended integrated schools were more likely to have gone to college, have better jobs, and be living generally more successful lives. Perhaps most important, it was the blacks from integrated schools who were most likely to have broken racial barriers by working in jobs traditionally reserved for whites and living in integrated neighborhoods.[7] These results received little attention despite their obvious importance. Most concern was still with test scores.

The debate began in earnest in the early 1970s when David Armor of Harvard University published a paper arguing that the Coleman Report was wrong and that the achievement test gap between blacks and whites did not close as a result of desegregation (Armor 1972).

[7]A more detailed analysis of the commission's data is Crain and Weisman (1972).

Had the paper been written anywhere but Harvard, it might not have been important; but Harvard (where Pat Moynahan was teaching) and the White House had close ties, and President Nixon publicized the paper widely in order to bolster his own antibusing position. Armor's mentor at Harvard, a well known supporter of desegregation, attacked the Armor paper (Pettigrew et al. 1973) and that controversy also made nationwide headlines. The argument about the effect of desegregation on black test scores has sputtered off and on ever since.

One reason why the argument has not been resolved is that the studies which have been done on black achievement conflict. Two of the authors of this book undertook a careful review of the studies that had been done and found that slightly more than half of the studies of desegregation found black achievement test scores going up. Most of the remainder showed no evidence of gain or loss, and a few showed test scores declining. Most researchers have argued that the reason why the studies did not agree was that many of them were done erroneously. We decided that it was more likely that desegregation did not always have the same effect and began looking for explanations of why desegregation might raise achievement in some cases but not in others. We immediately found one answer: Nearly every study of black students who began desegregation in kindergarten or first grade showed achievement test scores going up, but studies of black students who did not begin desegregation until late elementary or junior high school often found no increase in achievement and sometimes found losses (Crain and Mahard 1978b). This was good news from the viewpoint of supporters of desegregation since most of the students involved in court-ordered desegregation plans begin desegregation in the first grade.

In 1972, very few Southern black high school students had come from desegregated elementary schools, so we did not expect to find a desegregation effect of their test scores. There are some interesting differences in test scores of students who attended desegregated junior high schools, however. In Table 2–7 we have divided our schools into those where most black students came from predominantly white junior high schools versus those whose black students came from black junior highs, and then divided the high school by their own racial mix.

The results are shown separately for males and females. For both sexes, the highest black test scores are for those schools over 65

Table 2-7. Black achievement test scores, by sex, and racial composition of high school and of earlier school.

	(Mean Achievement Test Score)			
	Percentage White at High School			
Sex, Desegregation Experience	0–40	40–65	65–80	80–100
For Males in Schools Where:				
Most Blacks Attended Segregated Junior High Schools	334	340	334	317[b]
Most Black Attended Integrated Junior High Schools	—[a]	340	355	347
For Females in Schools Where:				
Most Black Attended Segregated Junior High Schools	347	348	346	342
Most Blacks Attended Integrated Junior High Schools	—[a]	346	355	358

[a]Not enough schools to compute a mean.
[b]Significantly different from overall mean for males.

percent white in which most black students came from predominantly white junior high schools, with scores seven to twenty-one points higher than those in predominantly black schools, or in schools where most blacks came from segregated junior high schools. At the time this study was done, desegregation had been in existence only three to four years in most of the South. It would be worthwhile to do this study again today in order to see if scores are higher now that many southern black high school students have experienced desegregation since kindergarten.

One very important fact appears in this table. It is black male students who seem least able to cope with the sudden shift from a segregated junior high school to a predominantly white high school. Black males in this situation make very poor scores on the achievement test. Their average, 317, is 25 points below the scores of females in the same situation. It makes sense to us that males would have the most difficulty with adolescent desegregation. Black males will have experienced more mistreatment than black females. Males are also more competitive and more aggressive; hence black males are more likely to be paralyzed by their anger when they have to relate to (and compete with) whites.[8]

Part of our reason for thinking that black male students are unable to cope with the stress of competing with whites is that unlike black females they do not benefit from being in school with large numbers of middle class white students. Table 2–8 shows the results of our analysis of the combined effects on black achievement of the school's racial composition and the social status of the school's white students. The lower panel of the table shows for females exactly what Coleman would have predicted—scores are not higher in predominantly white schools unless the white students are of high social status. The lowest scores are in schools where the white students are low status; the highest scores are in schools which are predominantly white with high status whites. This is not the case for male students. The presence of middle class whites raises male achievement only one time out of four.

Table 2-8.   Achievement of black students, by sex, school racial composition, and social class of white students.

| | | (Mean Achievement Test Scores) | | | |
| | | School Racial Composition (Percentage of White Students) | | | |
Sex	White Student Social Class	0–40	40–65	65–80	80–100
Males	Low	330	328	346	335
	High	334	350	343	334
Females	Low	343	343	340	344
	High	349	353	361	361

Note: Controls on black SES, region, community educational level, urbanism, and school size.

[8]The evaluation expert, Donald Campbell, suggested another explanation for the poor performance of black male students in schools where they are a small minority. He hypothesized that when there are few blacks, they will form a tightly knit group, and the group will attempt to maintain an identity by being as homogeneous as possible. One way to do this is to exert social pressure on its members to reject academic achievement, so there will be little competition among blacks for grades.

We studied this problem further and were not able to come up with any simple statement of what conditions were best for black student achievement. We seem to be on the horns of a dilemma. We already know that black students are uncomfortable with working class white students. Yet attending school with middle class whites does nothing to boost achievement for black males. About the best we can say is that apparently schools should not be more than 80 percent white, and it is probably better if the white students are from higher income families. We really do not know what can be done to reduce the pressure which seems to be harming the achievement test scores of male students in newly desegregated schools. We can only hope that now, when most black males have experienced desegregation since first grade, the pressure is easier to take.

THE EFFECT OF DURATION OF DESEGREGATION

Achievement test scores are higher for students who begin desegregation earlier. This shows up not only in our data but in a large number of other studies. A number of studies, including this one, have also shown that white students are more tolerant of blacks if they experience desegregation early.[9] Knowing this, we expected to · find desegregation working more smoothly in other ways if students got an earlier start. We assumed that the first few years of high school desegregation would be the most painful ones, after which things would settle down and race relations would improve since each new class of students entering the school would have experienced desegregation at an earlier age. Having observed a number of ironies and contradictions in our other analyses of desegregation, we were not too surprised to find that our hunch was wrong here as well.

While test scores may improve with time, nothing else seems to improve. For example, 52 percent of the students in predominantly black schools say they like school. At the beginning of desegregation, things get worse for blacks, as we might expect; only 41 percent of the blacks in newly desegregated predominantly white high schools say they like school. The problem is that in those schools where desegregation is not new, and most of the black students came

---

[9]This finding is shown in the appendix to Chapter 3.

from desegregated elementary schools and junior high schools, the percentage who say they like school increases only to 43 percent. Similarly, the percentage of students who say that the rules are fair and who do not complain about school discipline increases only from 44 percent in newly desegregated mostly white schools to 48 percent in schools which have been integrated for several years. Black students in predominantly white schools are generally less sympathetic to desegregation—only 59 percent expressed positive attitudes toward desegregation compared to 65 percent of the students in predominantly black schools. Those who have had several years experience with desegregation have attitudes which are only slightly more favorable—61 percent instead of 59 percent. Finally, the percentage of black students in predominantly white schools who say they "feel like they don't belong in this school" declines only slightly from 40 percent in newly integrated schools to 36 percent in schools which have been integrated for some time. The only place where there seems to be even a noticeable gain resulting from duration of desegregation is in the amount of racial contact reported by blacks. Racial contact increases from 51 percent in newly desegregated schools to 56 percent after several years—a small gain, but better than nothing. Perhaps now, when students in these schools have experienced desegregation since first grade, the news might be better. These data suggest that the third and fourth years of desegregation are every bit as difficult for a school as the first and second years.

Instead of thinking that schools begin with tension and improve with age, it may be more accurate to think that they begin with a honeymoon which then wears off. Certainly we know of schools where race relations seemed to get off to a good start, only to have severe racial tension or even riots in the third or fourth year. In the light of our earlier discussion of the role of black social class, it seems that both black and white students in newly desegregated schools are afraid. Not knowing what to expect, they are on their best behavior, reluctant to complain or start something. After a few years' experience with desegregation, students gain confidence. They may have decided that the school administration will not deal out severe punishments and the students of the opposite race will not start a dangerous race riot. Just as middle class students have the self confidence to speak out and defend their interests (or, depending on one's point of view, cause trouble), so students who have experienced more desegregation will have confidence in their ability to fight for what they feel they should have. When this happens, trouble begins in earnest, not because desegregation has failed but because the honeymoon is over.

CONCLUSIONS

By the time we finished the analysis of this chapter we developed a great deal of sympathy for the faculty of desegregated high schools. The seeming illogic of what happens in the school must be very frustrating. Desegregation does not get easier as white and black students have more time to get used to each other; it may get worse. A school is not lucky if the desegregation plan presents it with middle class black students; it will probably have more trouble. Nor is the staff lucky if the desegregation plan presents them with a group of high income white students; they may find their black male students becoming hopelessly alienated. The faculty of a predominantly white rural school may feel they are better off than they would be in an inner city school with large numbers of black students, but they are wrong. The chances are that the white rural school will have considerably more racial tension.

A second way in which these data are frustrating is that they suggest some highly impractical and even inhuman solutions to school racial problems. For example, racial tension decreases when one group is badly outnumbered and cowed by the other. No one in good conscience would argue from this that the ideal desegregated school should be either 90 percent black or 90 percent white.

There is also an optimistic way of viewing these results. If there is no optimal racial composition, if busing has as many advantages as disadvantages, if there are drawbacks to having middle class students just as there are drawbacks to having working class students, then it follows that just as no school will get a free ride during desegregation, no school is doomed by circumstance to failure. If a school principal feels that the desegregation plan has created an untenable situation in his school, these data say no. Every desegregated school has a chance to be a good one, regardless of its social class, its racial mix, or the number of buses that pull up to its doors. When a high school succeeds, it is not because it was lucky enough to get the perfect mix of students. We shall see in the rest of this book that in a successful high school, the principal and the faculty deserve the credit for its success.

APPENDIX 2A
TECHNICAL APPENDIX

In this appendix we show the statistics which produced the tables in Chapter 2; we also cite some of the research literature which is relevant. We will describe the general techniques used to create the appreviated tables which appear in the text of Chapters 2 through 6 and discuss a problem which appears in all research: How large must effects be for us to take them as important?

This chapter only touches the surface of a number of sociological issues. The reader who is interested in desegregation plans will find papers by Christine Rossell (1978) and Michael Giles (1978) very interesting; both show the extent to which white flight is affected by school racial composition, busing, and other features of the desegregation plan. Gary Orfield (1978) gives an excellent introduction to the policy issues of desegregation, including recent court decisions. The title *Must We Bus?* refers to his very good discussion of whether busing is necessary.

The reader interested in reviewing the literature on the effects of desegregation should begin with the 1978 special issue of *Law and Contemporary Problems* edited by Willis Hawley and Betsy Levin. This issue contains the Rossell piece cited above and reviews of the effects of desegregation on self-esteem and other personal attitudes, achievement, adult educational attainment, occupational mobility, and adult interracial contact.

For the reader who wants to put school desegregation into a historical perspective, we strongly recommend Richard Kluger's *Simple Justice* (1975)—a lovingly detailed history of the events that led up to the Supreme Court decision. The book also contains the full text of the court's opinion. The reader interested in getting the flavor of the more recent debates over desegregation's effect on achievement test scores and on white flight will enjoy Mill's collection of papers called *The Great School Bus Controversy* (1973). It contains the paper by David Armor (1972b) and the rebuttal by Pettigrew and his colleagues (1973).

So little research has been done on desegregation that a serious study of some of the topics touched on in this chapter would quickly exhaust the literature. It is particularly unfortunate that so little desegregation literature deals with the long-term effects of desegregation. Most studies of the effects of desegregation only look at the results during the first one or two years; indeed, the major problem with this book is that most of the students in the high schools we studied have been desegregated no more than three or four years. There have been a few studies of the long-term effects of desegregation, but McPartland (1978) and Crain and Mahard (1978a) have written helpful papers.

It is also disappointing that so little of the research literature on desegregation deals with adolescence, especially adolescent sex differences. Douvan and Adelson (1966) conclude their study of adolescent development by noting that they found strong sex differences in patterns of development. They expected male and female adolescent development to be similar. They conclude: "... In fact we find that the adolescent crisis for boys and girls differs in almost every regard—in the statement of developmental tasks, not just how they are phrased, but whether they arise during the era at all..." (p. 305).

There is also very little written on how desegregation plans should be drawn; the two most helpful papers are by Foster (1973) and Finger (1976), both of whom write from their own experience as designers of major desegregation plans. In thinking about desegregation plans, the issue of turf or territoriality is an important factor. Suttles (1968) discusses the way anthropologists and sociologists have thought about territorial claims.

Crain (1977) analyzes the effects of a number of variables on racial tension. The argument that there should be greater tension in better educated communities or in schools with higher SES students is well supported in the literature (see, for example, Caplan's analysis of ghetto rioters [1970]). Two pieces which take a more psychodynamic view are Kardiner and Ovisey (1951) and Crain and Weisman (1972); both argue that racism inhibits black expression of anger and that higher status persons are psychologically free to express aggression.

The notion that working class and southern-born blacks are more inhibited than middle class or northern-born blacks is also developed by Crain and Weisman (1972). They argue that inhibition of aggression is both advantageous and harmful to working class and southern-born blacks.

This book does not attempt to cover everything that is in the earlier *Southern Schools* (NORC 1973) report, so the reader may find it helpful to read that report as well as this book. In particular, we refer the reader to the chapters by Ruth Narot on the effect of racial composition on black and white achievement and by James Davis, on the effects of busing, both in Volume 2. The Narot analysis is itself taken from a much more detailed unpublished study by Janet Griffith, now of the Research Triangle Institute.

METHODS

Throughout this analysis, we will use a policy model in which we assume that the type of community, the social status of the students, the type of desegregation plan, and the school physical plant are fixed. The policy question becomes, "Given this type of community, students of this SES, this type of desegregation plan and this size school, what would be the effect of a change in school characteristic x?" In each case, x is chosen for study because it is a variable which policymakers can alter to some degree; and the community and student characteristics, type of desegregation plan, and school size are control variables because they cannot be altered. The control variables change slightly in each chapter. In Chapter 2 we were interested in the effects of the desegregation plan; in later chapters desegregation plan factors (such as duration of desegregation) will be added as control variables.

In Chapter 1 we noted that the ecological fallacy (interpreting group-level correlations as if they were correlations among individuals) is only rarely a problem in this analysis. There is a possible ecological fallacy in the social class analysis in which we use black mean SES as an independent variable. For example, we find that high status schools have more complaints from black students and assume, in our argument, that it is the high status students who are complaining. Of course, it may be the few low status students in middle class schools who are doing the complaining.

In this book we are experimenting with a new way of presenting the results of our analysis. We are convinced that multiple regression (or some similar methodology) is necessary in order to adequately understand our data. Replacing old-fashioned cross-tabulation tables with more sophisticated statistics has made social science data more accurate but more difficult to grasp intuitively. The problem is that results of multiple regression equations are normally stated either as slopes, standardized or unstandardized, or else in terms of percentage of variance explained. We have used multiple regression to create simulated cross-tabulation tables. In the technical appendix of Chapter 1, we said that percentage of variance explained has no commonsensical interpretation. While it is possible to interpret a slope, and other disciplines such as economics are quite used to doing so, most other social scientists and educators are accustomed to understanding the effect of one variable or another from a cross tabulation. One can look at a 2 × 2 table and immediately answer a fairly simple question: If A causes B, then if I change from a low value of A to a high value of A, how much difference does it make in B? One can of course derive the answer to this question from the regression slope, and this is exactly what we have done.

Our procedure is intended to create sentences of the following form: "If an independent variable A is changed from a relatively low value A_1 to a relatively high value A_2 without changing other important school characteristics, the effect is to change the dependent variable B from the value B_1 to the value B_2." Making this statement involves three steps: first, values of the independent variable V_1 and A_2 must be chosen which are reasonable examples of low and high values in the real world. We want to see the effect of the kind of change that one could reasonable expect to happen. Second, B must be transformed into an interpretable metric so that the values B_1 and B_2 will have some plausible meaning. Finally, the unstandardized regression coefficients must be used to compute the values of B_1 and B_2 corresponding to A_1 and A_2. The first two steps are arbitrary ones. In choosing values of the independent variable, we have in some cases selected values which are easy to express. For example, in looking at school size we compare the effects of a school which has 500 students to those of a school which has 1500. We select the numbers partly because they are round figures and partly because they represent almost exactly values which are one standard deviation above and below the mean for our sample of high schools. We know (or think we know) how many students 500 is and how large a high school of 500 is, and since 500 is one standard deviation below the mean, we also know that such high schools are not rare. However, we do not know what a SES score of ten, twenty, or fifty means. Since no value of SES has any intrinsic meaning, we have used the value corresponding to the mean of the bottom fifth and the top fifth of the distribution of all schools. Thus, we can study the apparent effect of SES by comparing a typical school in the bottom fifth of all southern high schools in black socioeconomic status to another school which is typical of the top fifth.[10] The means of the top and bottom fifths are assumed to be 1.25 standard deviations above and below the overall mean.

The statistic we see most often in everyday life is the percentage. The Gallup Poll regularly tells us that a certain percentage of the population think this way or that way about a particular issue. For this reason we have transformed all our dependent variables into metrics which correspond to the percentage distribution of responses on a particular question. Thus, when we say that black student self-esteem is around 51 percent in predominantly white schools and 57 percent in predominantly black schools, we mean that on any single self esteem question of those used to make the scale we would expect 51 percent of the students in a predominantly white school to give the answer indicating high self esteem, but 57 percent to do so in the predominantly black school. The reader who has had experience with polls and other surveys will then have some idea of how large a difference this is. Doing this also means that we can compare the effect of school racial composition on two different dependent variables in order to see which one is most affected.

We can demonstrate the computations with an example. We used the following multiple regression equation to compute the effects of school racial composition on racial tension, shown in the bottom line of Table 2–1 in the chapter, and also to compute the effect of black student average socioeconomic status on racial tension, shown in the bottom line of Table 2–5:

$$
\begin{aligned}
\text{Tension} = \ & (0.0186)\ (\text{total enrollment}) + & (2\text{A}.1) \\
& (8.8)\ (\text{median years of adult schooling in county}) + \\
& (-0.250)\ (\text{urbanism of county}) + \\
& (1.69)\ (1 \text{ if upper south, } 0 \text{ if deep south}) + \\
& (0.194)\ (\text{black student SES}) + \\
& 13.2\ \text{PW}_1 + 19.7\ \text{PW}_2 + 11.8\ \text{PW}_3 + \\
& (-55.6)
\end{aligned}
$$

Racial tension has been transformed into a scale representing the approximate percentage of students of either race who complain about racial violence in the school. Thus if a school has a racial

---

[10]We are indebted to Jencks and his colleagues (1972) for a simpler version of this.

tension score of 36, we would expect 36 percent of the students to say that racial violence was occurring in the school[11]

We assessed the effect of racial composition by constructing three dummy variables representing racial compositions of less than 40 percent white (PW_1), 40 to 65 percent white (PW_2), and 65 to 80 percent white (PW_3). If a school is under 40 percent white, the dummy variable PW_1 is equal to *one;* otherwise it is zero, and so forth. If we now select a school which is typical of all the schools in our sample except that its racial composition is less than 40 percent white, we can find its expected level of racial tension by summing [0.0186 times the mean value of school size] + [the other five coefficients times the mean values of the other five control variables] + [13.2 × 1 (the dummy variables PW_2 and PW_3 are zero when the school is less than 40 percent white)] + [the regression constant, which is −55.6]. The sum of the first six terms in the equation plus the regression constant is 32.1 percent, which means that the level of racial tension expected in a school less than 40 percent white is 32.1 + 13.2 = 45.3, in a school 40 to 65 percent white it is 32.1 + 19.7 percent = 51.8 percent, and in a 65 to 80 percent white school it is 32.1 + 11.8 percent = 43.9 percent. These are the three numbers in the next to last line of Table 2–1. For mathematical reasons only three dummy variables are included although there are four categories of racial composition. This means that if the school is over 80 percent white, all three of the dummy variables PW_1, PW_2, PW_3 will be zero, and the fourth number on the next-to-last line of Table 2–1 is simply 32.1 percent. This also means that the three regression coefficients represent the effects of particular racial compositions in comparison to a composition of over 80 percent white, so the equation shows that the level of racial tension should be 13 percent higher in schools less than 40 percent white than in schools over 80 percent white, 20 percent higher in schools which are 40 to 65 percent white than in schools over 80 percent white, and 12 percent higher in schools 65 to 80 percent white than in schools over 80 percent white. Since we are not interested in the effect of the control variables, these effects are not shown in Table 2–1.

11But not necessarily exactly 36 percent of the students would give this response. Tension is a scale built on a number of items, and we are inferring what the response would be on this single item from the overall level of tension. If school x has a tension score of 36, we are precisely saying that its level of tension is about as high as one would expect in a school where 36 percent of the students complained.

Let us consider a slightly different example. In Table 2–5, we are interested in the effect of the socioeconomic status of the black student body of the school. Since socioeconomic status has no meaningful metric, we have set high and low values at the means of the first and fifth quintile. In a normal distribution these quintile means are 1.25 standard deviations above and below the overall mean, respectively. SES has a mean of 30.7 and a standard deviation of 18.0, so low and high values of SES are [30.7] ± [(1.25) (18.0)], or 8 and 53. We can use the same equation for this analysis that we used to analyze the effects of racial composition in Table 2–1, but socioeconomic status is now the independent variable and racial composition a control variable. In order to control on racial composition, the dummy variables must be set to represent the typical condition for all schools. Since 15 percent of all schools are less than 40 percent white, 30 percent are between 40 and 65 percent white, 31 percent are between 65 and 80 percent white, and 24 percent are between 80 and 100 percent white, the typical condition is estimated by setting $PW_1 = 0.15$, $PW_1 = 0.30$ and $PW_3 = 0.31$. We now have a regression equation which has one independent variable, eight control variables, and a constant. The unstandardized coefficient of tension on black SES is 0.194, and the product of the means of the eight control variables times their regression coefficients plus the overall constant of the equation is 37. This means that the level of racial tension corresponding to a low level of black SES is [37] + [(.194) (8)] = 38.6, and the level of tension corresponding to a high value is [37] + [(.194) (53)] = 47.3. These are the two numbers that appear in the last line of Table 2–5, rounded to maintain a difference of 9 between them. If one magically transformed a school from being one that had black students representing the poorest quintile of all southern high schools to one whose students were like those in schools of the highest quintile, without changing anything else, this equation indicates that the effect would be to raise the level of racial tension by 9 percentage points.

This is, of course, an estimate affected by different kinds of error. If there is a systematic bias (e.g., we forgot to control on some critical variable or have misinterpreted what the survey questions meant to the people who answered them), then the 9 percent could be either too high or too low, depending on the kind of bias introduced. In addition, every variable has miscellaneous errors of measurement due to the question's meaning different things to different respondents to respondents' accidentally checking the wrong response, and so forth. To the degree that these errors in either the self-esteem scale or the tension scale are random—some respondents who meant yes said no, others meant no and said yes, with no system to the error—then the effect is to attenuate the relationship, and the 9 percent is an under-estimate of the true effect.[12]

Complete Equations for Text Tables

The regression equations in Table 2A–1 through 2A–6 were used to compute the eight tables given in the text. These tables give the regression coefficients in standardized form. In order to save space, we have collapsed the tables somewhat. For example, the same equation is used to compute the effects of racial composition on black nondelinquency in Table 2–1 and the effects of black student SES on black nondelinquency SES in Table 2–5, so we have shown the equations only once in the second column of Table 2A–1. Table 2A–1 shows the effects of racial composition and black SES on the black dependent variables in Tables 2–1, 2–4, and 2–5, and Table 2A–2 shows the effect of these independent variables on the white dependent variables in Tables 2–1 and 2–4 and on racial tension in Tables 2–1, 2–5, and 2–6. Table 2A–1 also shows three coefficients associated with a dummy variable indicating whether most of the black students in the school attended segregated elementary and junior high schools. If they did, it is likely that the schools were only recently desegregated. These three coefficients are discussed, but without showing a table, in the "Duration of Desegregation" section in the last part of the chapter. In Table 2A–1, we show the coefficients of racial composition, SES, school size, and so forth, before the "students from segregated schools" variable is added because this variable was not included in the equations when Tables 2–1, 2–4, and 2–5 were computed. The parentheses around a coefficient is our way of indicating that a

---

[12]If there is much error in the control variables, their effects are underestimated; if the control variables work to reduce the relationship between the independent and dependent variables (that is, beta is smaller than the correlation coefficient) then the amount of reduction is underestimated, and the effect of the independent variable overestimated. For a discussion of reliability and attenuation, see Nunnally (1967: 203 4, 217 20).

variable was not included in the equation shown. If the "most black students from segregated schools" variable had been included in the equation, it would have the beta shown, and the coefficients for racial composition and for the control variables would change only slightly; we do not show these three equations in order to save space.

All of the data in tables 2–1, 2–4, 2–5, and 2–6 are constructed from Tables 2A–1 and 2A–2 except the data on black and white achievement. The equation for black achievement appears in Table 2A–5 later in this appendix; the equation for white achievement is taken directly from Narot (1973) and is not shown in this appendix. White achievement does not seem to be related to aspects of the desegregation plan, except for being slightly higher in predominantly black schools.

Since our chapter focused only on desegregation issues, we did not consider the relationships between the dependent variables and some of the control variables which are shown in Tables 2A–1 and 2A–2. Some of these are quite interesting. For example, self-reported delinquency—cutting school, fighting, or being sent to the office—is much lower in the deep South for blacks (i.e., a negative coefficient means nondelinquency is less in the upper South). For whites there is no difference. There is less white and black peer disapproval of interracial association in large schools (although only the black relationship is significant). There is more racial contact in the upper South, and for whites, much less peer disapproval of association with blacks (not so for blacks; the coefficient for region in the peer disapproval equation is so small that the computer routine we used did not permit the variable to enter the equation). There is not more white delinquency in urban areas, but there is more in highly educated communities. There is also less delinquency among higher status white student bodies and in smaller schools.

The effects of busing were analyzed by dividing the schools into six categories based on the number of white and black students who were not attending the schools nearest their homes. For example, if 80 percent or more of the white students in the school said that there was no school closer to their homes than this one, but less than 50 percent black students in the school said that they were attending the school nearest their homes, the school was coded as one in which many black students were bused. Similarly, if over 80 percent of the white students and between 50 and 80 percent of the black students were attending the school nearest their homes, the school was coded

Table 2A-1. Regression equations with standardized regression coefficients (betas) used to construct Tables 2-1, 2-4, and 2-5 and text discussion of black happiness.

	Dependent Variables (Black Students)						
	Sense of Belonging	Non-delinquency	Self-Esteem	Lack of Peer Disapproval	Happiness	Like School	Racial Contact
Mean	30.56	66.08	51.75	59.01	63.15	46.33	46.98
Standard Deviation	19.14	15.98	14.80	17.88	15.05	18.91	20.24
Independent Variables:							
Mean Black SES	.126	.066	.353[a]	.015	.226[a]	-.162	-.109
School Size	-.104	.128	-.092	.229[a]	-.121	-.031	.102
Region	-.020	-.268[a]	.022	—[b]	.102	-.039	.169[a]
Community Educational Level	-.109	-.232	.058	-.026	.061	.034	-.062
Urbanism of County	-.045	-.083	.020	.126	.022	-.002	.039
Percentage White:							
(0-40%)	-.526[a]	.149	.171	.432[a]	.076	.127	-.561[a]
(41-65%)	-.213[a]	.092	.004	.320[a]	.072	-.003	-.196[a]
(66-80%)	-.200	.036	-.037	.273[b]	.078	-.058	-.099
Most Students from Segregated Elementary and Junior High Schools	—	(-.079)	—	—	—	(.062)	(-.061)
r^2	.174	.228	.141	.163	.072	.070	.299

[a] $p < .05$.
[b] Unique variance added too small to enter equation.
Note: Parentheses represent beta if variable were to be entered into equation following third percentage white term. This variable was not used to compute the r^2 for the equation.

Table 2A-2. Regression equations with standardized regression coefficients (betas) used to construct Tables 2-1, 2-4, 2-5, and 2-6 and text discussion of happiness.

	Dependent Variables (White Students)						
	Sense of Belonging	Non-delinquency	Self-Esteem	Lack of Peer Disapproval	Happiness	Out Transfer Rate	Racial Contact
Mean	21.03	62.69	58.81	41.84	79.44	8.03	
Standard Deviation	11.40	12.60	13.92	22.76	10.50	19.56	
Independent Variables:							
Community Educational Level	.076	-.429[a]	.094	.135	-.146	-.091	.458[a]
Urbanism of County	-.093	.244	.088	.284[a]	.189	.352[a]	.343
Region	—[b]	.067	.150	.246[a]	.106	-.083	.033
School Size	.116	-.247[a]	-.143	.140	-.260[a]	.044	.404[a]
Mean White SES	.090	.271[a]	.412[a]	-.018	.258[a]	-.450[a]	.010
Mean Black SES	.080	-.077	.016	.031	-.228[a]	-.101	.138
Percentage White:							
(0–40%)	.273[a]	-.151	.194[a]	-.041	-.279[a]	.363[a]	.189[a]
(41–65%)	.258[a]	-.201[a]	.110	-.180[b]	-.211[a]	-.116	.356[a]
(66–80%)	.025	-.039	-.047	-.073	-.005	-.144	.216[a]
r^2	.100	.184	.227	.471	.193	.497	.333

[a] $p < .05$.
[b] Variable possessed insufficient tolerance to enter equation.

as one in which few blacks were bused. If over 80 percent of both whites and blacks said that this was the school nearest their homes, the school was coded as a neighborhood school. Because so many more black students are reassigned than whites, we did not attempt to construct a symmetrical definition of whites being bused. A school is coded many whites bused if as many as 30 percent of the black students and less than 50 percent of the white students say that they are attending the school nearest their homes. If over 50 percent of the black students and between 50 and 80 percent of the white students are attending the school nearest their homes, the school is one in which a few whites are bused. Finally, schools which are not covered by any of these definitions (where fewer than 80 percent of the white students are attending the school nearest their home and fewer than either 50 percent or 30 percent of the black students are attending the school nearest their home) are coded as ones in which both black and white students are bused in. We assume that these are mainly vocational schools and other special interest schools which draw students from a large area.

The combination of six categories of busing and four levels of racial composition would produce twenty-four types of schools. Our sample is not large enough to estimate all such possibilities, particularly since a number of these combinations are quite unlikely (for example, a school which is overwhelmingly black, but which is not a neighborhood school for blacks). We therefore simplified the equations slightly by replacing the twenty-four possible combinations of busing status and racial composition with twelve variables: two representing the percentage white and the square of the percentage white, so as to allow a parabolic form for the effects of racial composition, plus five dummy variables to indicate the school's busing status, plus five variables which are the products of the busing dummy variables and the school percentage white, which gives us the interaction effect between busing status and racial composition. The results are shown in Tables 2A–3 and 2A–4.

Even in this simplified form, the results are quite complex. The most important coefficients are those attached to "many blacks bused." The standardized coefficients are very large, indicating that schools where most blacks are bused in have black students with a stronger sense of not belonging, lower self-esteem, and less racial contact, and that these schools have more racial tension. In all cases, the coefficient for the interaction terms "percent white × many

Table 2A–3. Regression equations with standardized regression coefficients (betas) used to construct Tables 2-2 and 2-3.

	Dependent Variables (Black Students)			
	Sense of Not Belonging	Self-Esteem	Racial Contact	Racial Tension
Mean	30.56	51.75	46.98	29.23
Standard Deviation	19.14	14.80	20.24	14.05
Independent Variables:				
Area Effects				
Region	-.033	.010	.071	-.026
School Size	-.125	-.034	.149	.436[a]
Community Educational Level	-.120	.024	-.102	.498[a]
Urbanism of County	.022	.018	-.047	-.318[a]
Busing Effects				
Many Blacks Bused	.991	-1.154	-.444	.458
Few Blacks Bused	-.022	-.089	.104	-.247
Few Whites Bused	.097	.027	.144	.000
Many Whites Bused	-.127	-.143	.276	-.329
Both Races Bused	-.186	.191	.459	-.162
Racial Composition Effects				
School Percentage White	.455	-.330	.874[a]	.433
School Percentage White^2 ÷ 100	-.129	.206	-.214	-.819[a]
Interaction Effects				
School Percentage White X:				
Many Blacks Bused	-.720	1.051	.397	-.345
Few Blacks Bused	.071	.000	-.115	.224
Few Whites Bused	-.100	-.211	-.175	(-.002)
Many Whites Bused	-.021	.129	-.069	.311
Both Races Bused	.302	-.407	-.333	.161
Mean Black SES	—	.371[a]	—	—
r^2	.277	.235	.489	.360

[a] $p < .05$.

Note: Parentheses indicate the beta if this variable were to be entered into the equation following Few Blacks Bused. This variable was not used in computing the r^2 for the equation.

Table 2A-4. Regression equations with standardized regression coefficients (betas) used to construct Table 2-2.

	Dependent Variables (White Students)		
	Sense of Belonging	Self-Esteem	Racial Contact
Mean	21.03	58.81	34.02
Standard Deviation	11.40	13.92	16.02
Independent Variables:			
Area Effects			
Region	−.047	.171[a]	.223[a]
School Size	.205	−.162	.211[a]
Community Educational Level	.060	.118	.098
Urbanism of County	−.140	.057	.180
Busing Effects			
Many Blacks Bused	−.621	1.222	.963
Few Blacks Bused	.181	−.135	−.044
Few Whites Bused	.392	−.306	.227
Many Whites Bused	.360	−.063	.274
Both Races Bused	.853	1.059[a]	.195
Racial Composition Effects			
School Percentage White	.059	−.971[a]	−1.077[a]
School Percentage White$^2 \div 100$	−.261	.781[a]	.730[a]
Interaction Effects			
School Percentage White ×:			
Many Blacks Bused	.692	−1.352[a]	−.910
Few Blacks Bused	−.119	.111	.042
Few Whites Bused	−.289	.267	−.158
Many Whites Bused	−.073	−.055	−.087
Both Races Bused	−.637	−1.066[a]	−.095
Mean White SES	—	.435[a]	—
r^2	.211	.325	.520

[a] $p < .05$.

blacks bused" has the opposite sign, meaning that these effects are strongest in schools where very large numbers of blacks are present. This is surprising; one would think that a safety in numbers sort of effect would make schools where more blacks were bused in more tolerable. We also see that these effects do not occur when few blacks are bused or when whites are bused. This implies that formerly all-white schools should not be desegregated by busing in very large numbers of blacks, although we earlier saw that too few blacks was also a problem. We do not think anyone can draw any useful recommendations about alternative desegregation plans from this analysis, except to conclude, as we did, that there is no obviously right or wrong way to desegregate a school.

Table 2–2 in the text was computed by collapsing the "many bused" and "few bused" categories together and discarding the few schools where both blacks and whites are bused. This leaves only three categories—neighborhood schools, schools where blacks are bused, and schools where whites are bused. We then selected 65 percent white as a typical racial composition and computed the values of the dependent variable for the six busing categories, and then the average value for the many and few categories of blacks bused and whites bused is computed by averaging. Table 2–3 is computed in the same manner except that four different racial compositions are used in turn in order to produce the four lines in the table.

Tables 2A–5 and 2A–6 show the regression equations used to compute the effects of school racial composition, duration of integration, and white socioeconomic status on black achievement test scores. Since there are eight achievement test scores reported in each table, the regression equations each include seven dummy variables, representing different combinations of school racial composition and high and low duration of desegregation or high and low levels of white student SES.

The effects of the control variables are not surprising except that black achievement seems to be lower in well-educated communities. We do not understand this unexpected finding. The other finding of interest is that black male achievement is not higher in the upper South although black female achievement is. Urbanism shows a similar pattern although neither coefficient is significant: male achievement is lower in urban areas, female achievement higher. Looking at all three lines together we see that the gap between female and male performance is greatest in well-educated urban communities in the upper South. This is consistent with our argument that black male students are crippled by competition and aggression. These communities have more able white students and tolerate more black anger, which results in an increasing sense of failure for black males and leads to more tension and less achievement—or so we suspect, but more research is needed.

Table 2A-5. Regression equations with standardized regression co-efficients (betas) used to construct Table 2-7.

	Dependent Variables (Black Students)	
	Male Achievement	Female Achievement
Mean	406	414
Standard Deviation	56.19	38.83
Independent Variables:		
Region	-.014	.186[a]
Urbanism	-.049	.075
Community Educational Level	-.287[a]	-.183
School Size	.138	.092
Mean Black SES	.538[a]	.421[a]
Percentage White:		
W_1 (0-40%)	-.238	-.247
W_2 (41-65%)	-.082	-.133
W_3 (66-80%)	.087	-.040
A: More Black Students from Predominantly Black Elementary and Junior High School	-.246	-.101
Interaction Terms:		
$A \times W_1$	.316	.224
$A \times W_2$	.215	.115
$A \times W_3$	-.056	-.039
r^2	.319	.292

[a]$p < .05.$

How Big A Difference Matters?

The question of when an effect should be considered large and when small is a continual and serious problem in social policy research. We have already discussed one aspect of this problem—the need for a metric and a method of presentation which common sense can cope with. We still have the problem of deciding whether a change of x percent is large or small.

This problem is usually discussed in terms of personal bias, as the so-called "fully-only" problem (referring to the fact that if the dependent variable has values of 40% and 55%, one can say that it has changed fully 15% or only 15%). The problem is that 15 percent

Table 2A-6. Regression equations with standardized regression co-efficients (betas) used to construct Table 2-8.

	Dependent Variables (Black Students)	
	Male Achievement	Female Achievement
Mean	406	414
Standard Deviation	36.19	38.83
Independent Variables:		
Region	.006	.192[a]
Urbanism	-.099	.021
Community Education Level	-.239[a]	-.176
School Size	.103	.060
Mean Black SES	.525[a]	.391[a]
Percentage White:		
W_1 (0-40%)	-.058	-.025
W_2 (41-65%)	-.107	-.045
W_3 (66-80%)	.094	-.095
White SES Interaction Terms:		
SW_1	.012	.035
SW_2	.192	.072
SW_3	-.016	.184
SW_4	-.001	.128
r^2	.300	.312

[a] $p < .05$.

Note: Interaction term SW_4 is the product of S, mean white SES, and W_4, which is one if percentage white is greater than 80 percent.

must be viewed relative to something. Fifteen percent is small relative to the maximum possible, which in this case is a change from 40 percent to 100 percent, four times as large. Of course, no one has ever seen a correlation this powerful. (For that matter, what really does "four times as large" mean?)

We believe that a difference of 15 percent should be treated as important in some cases, and trivial in others, depending on several things. First, are we interested in proving the existence of an effect or in assessing its size? If we only wish to show that A causes B, then the size of the effect is less important, and its statistical significance is what matters—which is why many laboratory experiments are content to report the results as a simple analysis of variance, without even reporting the magnitude of the effect. However, for policy analysis we need to know more than A causes B—we need to know how important A is. In this book, we are sometimes interested in showing that a relationship exists; more often we are concerned with how large it is.

Second, what is the theoretical model, and what are our assumptions about the relationship being studied? For example, it is well known that the major predictor of academic achievement is SES. In these data, the individual level correlation of SES with achievement is 0.26. Assuming linearity, this implies that only 16 percent of the students in the lowest one-fifth of the SES distribution would achieve a score of 500 on our test, compared to 46 percent of the students in the top fifth. This difference of 30 percent seems important. If the difference had been only 20 percent, we might be surprised, concluding that SES is less important than we thought. For most other relationships, a 20 percent gain in achievement would be considered very large.

Third, what is the maximum the dependent variable can change? For many survey research variables, measurement error considerably restricts the explainable variation. For other variables, such as achievement, we know that history and other fixed factors such as SES explain a good part of the variance. For this reason, we often compare the size of an effect due to one variable to the effect of other variables. For example, in Chapter 6 we will see that one school resource appears to raise white student achievement an average of 39 points—which implies that providing this resource for low SES whites would increase the percentage passing the 500 mark on our test from 16 percent to 29 percent. A 13 percent change might seem of only moderate size for another variable, but since it is close to half of the effect of SES, it seems very large. In the same way, a change of 10 percent in racial attitudes seems less impressive than a 5 percent change in perceived happiness, which has a larger error variance and less between-school variation.

Fourth, for policy the important question is not how large are the effects but how high is the cost-benefit ratio? For example, the finding in this chapter that desegregation seems to raise black achievement by an average of 12 points can be used as an argument against desegregation by critics who implicitly argue that this benefit is too small to justify the political or social costs of desegregation. Indeed, if we thought this achievement gain were truly the only benefit of desegregation, we might agree. At the same time, another policy might cause a less impressive effect—a gain of 5 percent in the amount of interracial contact, for example—but be very attractive because of the low political or financial cost involved.

All of this does not give us any simple answers. Most of the effects of desegregation plan variables on student attitudes seem small to us partly because we expected them to be larger. In the next few chapters, we will take effects of this size much more seriously because the variables that cause them are school features which high schools can incorporate at not unreasonable cost.

School administrators and research analysts should look at effect size differently. If 45 percent of black students say that they think school rules are fair, and we show that in schools with more extensive extracurricular activities this percentage increases to 51 percent, an administrator should be impressed since this represents a drop of a tenth in the number of black students who might complain—which is hardly a trivial accomplishment. A researcher looking for an understanding of race relations might be less interested. In short, whether an effect is small or large depends on which dependent variable is involved, which independent variable we are analyzing, and what one plans to do with the information.

Note that the question of interpreting the size of the effect has little to do with the question of statistical significance. With only 194 schools and a conservative weighting rule to allow for the small number of students surveyed in some schools, effects strong enough to be interesting to policymakers may not be statistically significant. In our analysis, we had to decide for each school characteristic whether its effect was real or merely a statistical fluke. We did so by looking at both statistical significance and its pattern of relationships with a number of different dependent variables. Every characteristic analyzed in this book has statistically significant effects on some student outcomes, but in each case we have also pointed out additional outcomes in which the effect is not statistically significant but is logically related to the significant effects and large enough to be of interest to policymakers.

3 STAFF

It looks as if desegregation works at City High, at least in part, because the staff wants it to work. Forehand was told that the principal forced out some of the most conservative staff and that in-service training changed the attitudes of other faculty members. Both statements are interesting, but they raise three important questions, which this chapter will try to answer. First, every staff reflects both conservative and liberal views. Does it really make sense to talk, as the City High teachers do, about the attitudes of the entire staff as a group? Second, teenagers are notoriously independent. Do staff attitudes really have such a great impact on them? Third, how can a school establish positive staff attitudes?

The data lead to optimistic answers on all three questions. There does seem to be a school-wide faculty attitude; it does have an important impact on students; and it can be changed—the right sort of principal and the right sort of community pressure and in service education can have considerable impact.[1] The analysis points to the principal as the key, and the last part of the chapter shows that how

[1]These conclusions apply to the predominantly white schools in our study. Since we would expect very large differences between the attitudes of black and white teachers, all the analysis on teachers in this chapter is restricted to schools whose student bodies are at least 60 percent white. All these schools have predominantly white teaching staffs so that we can be sure that we are talking about differences between schools in the attitudes of white teachers.

students feel about the principal tells us a great deal about how they feel about the school.

MEASURING TEACHER ATTITUDES AND BEHAVIOR

The cornerstone of this chapter is our measurement of the racial behavior of the teaching staff in each school. We could not observe the racial behavior of the thousands of teachers in our 200 schools. Instead the pupils, teachers, and the principals served as our informants. We asked white and black students whether they thought that most of their teachers liked integration. We asked the principal the same question, and, finally, we asked the teachers themselves what other teachers thought. Note that we are asking people to report on the attitudes of others, but it is behavior that we are measuring. Since our informants are not mindreaders, they can only infer another's attitudes by observing what that person does and says.

Many students, principals, and teachers were reluctant to come down on either side of this question. Many said either that they did not know how most of the teachers in the school felt or else that the staff was divided or neutral about desegregation. We suspect that teachers in most schools keep their feelings about school desegregation well hidden since only a small number of white students said that their teachers were in favor of it. Nonetheless, the students give a fairly good indication of the teacher racial behavior in each school, and it does look as if we can speak of a school staff as having a characteristic racial attitude.

First, the white and black pupils, the teachers, and the principal all tend to agree in assessing the attitudes of the teachers in the school. If one of these four informants sees the teachers in their particular school as especially liberal or especially unsympathetic to desegregation, the others tend to agree.

Second, we find a great deal of difference in the perception of teacher behavior from one school to another. Ranking the predominantly white schools in terms of teacher attitudes, we find that in a school in the lowest quintile, none of the ten teachers we surveyed would say that most white teachers like desegregation, while in a school in the highest quintile, five of the ten would say this. There are similarly large differences between schools in the reports of white and black students about teachers' attitudes toward desegregation.

We also asked teachers about their own attitudes. Teachers seem rather supportive of school desegregation. For example, 71 percent of the teachers say that most black students are better off in integrated schools, and 58 percent say that most white students benefit from desegregation. The between-school differences are quite large on these two questions. For example, 82 percent of the teachers in the highest fifth of all schools say that white students benefit from desegregation, compared to only 40 percent in the lowest fifth of all schools.

Teacher racial attitudes are less liberal on matters not directly related to school desegregation. Only 53 percent disapprove of miscegenation laws, and only 38 percent disagree with the statement that "the amount of prejudice against minority groups in this country is high exaggerated." These teachers do not talk like liberals. We can only sympathize with them when we realize that they were drafted into the front lines in the nation's effort to solve its race problems. It was these teachers, not northern liberals, who had to make desegregation work in southern high schools in 1972. Attitudes about school desegregation and attitudes about other racial issues are related, of course; in schools where teachers have conservative attitudes, teacher behavior is also more conservative. The teachers' behavior is more closely related to their attitudes toward school desegregation than to their general racial attitudes.

THE EFFECT OF TEACHERS ON WHITE STUDENT RACIAL ATTITUDES

Having seen that schools differ in the attitudes of teachers about desegregation and that these attitudes are reflected in teacher behavior, the next question is, Do these differences in staff attitudes and behavior affect the students? We will divide this question into four parts by looking at effects on white student attitudes, black student attitudes, student race relations, and finally black achievement test scores. We will consider effects on white student attitudes first. If teachers serve as models for their students, we would expect more liberal teachers to have more liberal students. After schools were statistically matched on a number of criteria,[2] we looked at the relationship between teacher behavior and student attitudes. We found a consistent tendency for schools with liberal teachers to have students with more positive racial attitudes. Table 3–1 is constructed by computing the percentage of students giving liberal responses in the bottom fifth of all schools in terms of teacher racial behavior as contrasted to the percentage of students with liberal responses in the schools where teacher behavior is in the top fifth. In order to make sure that the analysis is not circular, the behavior of the teachers in the school is an average of the reports of black students, teachers, and principals but not the reports of white students. In this way, we are not merely showing that when white students say nice things about their teachers, they also say nice things about black students.

The first line of Table 3–1 shows that when the school staff behaves in a more liberal manner, the percentage of whites who say that blacks are not dumb is 68 percent, that is, 7 percent higher than

Table 3-1.   The influence of teacher racial behavior on white students' feelings about blacks.

	Percentage of Teachers with Favorable Racial Behavior as Perceived by Blacks, Principal, and Other Teachers	
	Low	High
Percentage of Whites Saying Other Group Is Not Dumb	61[a]	68[a]
Percentage of Whites Saying Other Group Is Ambitious	42[a]	49[a]
Percentage of Whites Saying Color Is Not Related to Smartness	76[a]	81[a]

[a] $p < .05$.

Note: Schools are matched on school and neighborhood racial composition, duration of desegregation, school size, region, urbanism and educational level of the community, and black socioeconomic status.

[2] Black and white student socioeconomic status, school size, the integration experience of the white and black students, the racial composition of the school and the surrounding neighborhood, region within the South, and the urbanism and educational level of the community.

in schools in which teachers behave more conservatively; there is the same gain in the percentage who say blacks are ambitious. Finally, the percentage of whites who say that color has nothing to do with intelligence is 5 percent higher in the schools in which teachers are liberal. (Recall that schools are matched on black student socioeconomic status, so this difference is not due to whites' dealing with brighter black students.) The table indicates that teachers do have an impact on white student attitudes although the effect is not as large as one might hope. High school students arrive in high school with fairly strong racial prejudices, and they cannot be expected to change quickly. We also think teachers avoid talking about desegregation, so they do not present clear models for students.

TEACHER ATTITUDES AND BEHAVIOR AND BLACK STUDENTS' REACTIONS TO SCHOOL

Black students should be less alienated when teachers have more liberal attitudes—not only because black students are more comfortable when teachers are more accepting of them but also because liberal teachers help form liberal white student attitudes. In this analysis, we looked at the impact of staff attitudes and behavior on black students' feelings of belonging in and liking the school. As in all our analyses, the schools are statistically matched on family backgrounds of black and white students, school size, racial mix and duration of desegregation, region, and community urbanism and educational level. The racial behavior scale is here based on the reports of white students, teachers, and principals and not on the reports of black students. We expected a teacher's public behavior to have more of an effect on students than a teacher's privately held attitudes. We also thought that if attitudes did matter, teacher attitudes about school integration would be more influential than their attitudes about other aspects of race relations.

The data in Table 3–2 support our predictions: A liberal staff does make black students more comfortable in a desegregated school, and teacher behavior matters most, school-related racial attitudes less, and nonschool racial attitudes least of all. The strongest difference—11 percentage points—is in the relationship of staff racial behavior to the percentage of black students who like school. Only 38 percent of blacks say that they like school when staff

Table 3-2.   The influence of teacher racial attitudes and behavior on black students' feelings about school.

	Teacher Racial Behavior		Teacher Racial Attitudes— School Related		Teacher Racial Attitudes— Nonschool Related	
	Low	High	Low	High	Low	High
Percentage of Black Students Saying They Like School	38[a]	49[a]	40	47	43	44
Percentage of Black Students Saying They Do Not Belong	41	31	41	32	39	33

[a] $p < .05$.

Note: Schools are matched on school and neighborhood racial composition, duration of desegregation, school size, region, urbanism and educational level of the community, and white and black socioeconomic status.

racial behavior is unsympathetic to desegregation; the percentage increases to 49 when teachers appear more accepting of desegregation. The impact of teacher attitudes toward school desegregation is slightly weaker, and the impact of teacher nonschool racial attitudes is the weakest. The percentage of black students who say, "I feel like I don't belong to this school" shows the same pattern—the weakest effect (a 6% difference) is for the nonschool-related attitudes, and the strongest effect (10%) is for teacher racial behavior, with school-related attitudes in between. Again, these differences are large—a change in teacher racial behavior reduces the number of alienated black students by a quarter.

That teacher behavior is more crucial than general teacher attitudes is welcome news. If a teacher's personal feelings about miscegenation or the civil rights movement were the critical issue, one would almost want to give up. Instead, the critical issues are, first, how the teacher feels about desegregated schools, a feeling which can be influenced by the way in which he or she is helped to prepare for desegregation and, second, how the teacher behaves in the desegregated classroom. The teacher who has difficulty accepting the principle of desegregation can learn to convey a sense of acceptance even if it is not completely heartfelt. Sociological theory leads us to believe that it is easier to change behavior than it is to reshape attitudes. Indeed, one of the easiest ways to change attitudes is to change people's behavior so that they must deal with the contradiction between what they feel and what they do. Often, attitudes will then tend to change in order to be consistent with the new behavior.[3]

TEACHER ATTITUDES AND BEHAVIOR AND STUDENT INTERRACIAL CONTACT

The relationship between teacher attitudes and behavior and student interracial contact is in the expected direction, but this time not as neat as we would wish. The data do show that when teachers set examples by their attitudes and behavior, there is more contact between blacks and whites. Table 3–3 shows that both blacks and

Table 3–3.   Impact of school staff racial attitudes and behavior on level of student interracial contact in school.

	Teacher Racial Behavior		Teacher Racial Attitudes— School Related		Teacher Racial Attitudes— Nonschool Related	
	Low	High	Low	High	Low	High
Percentage of Black Students Reporting Friendly Interracial Contact	48[a]	61[a]	53	57	55	54
Percentage of White Students Reporting Friendly Interracial Contact	30[a]	37[a]	29[a]	37[a]	29[a]	37[a]

[a] $p < .05$.

Note: Schools are matched on school and neighborhood racial composition, duration of desegregation, school size, region, urbanism and educational level of the community, and white and black socioeconomic status.

[3]This may explain why these teachers seem so sympathetic to desegregation; their attitude has changed to be consistent with the fact that they are willing to teach in a desegregated school.

whites report more friendly relationships with the opposite race in schools where teachers are perceived as more sympathetic to desegregation. (Again we delete perceptions by either black or white students from the teacher behavior scale to eliminate circularity.) For blacks, the difference is reasonably large (13%); and again we see it is the public behavior of teachers, not their personal attitudes, that matters. For whites, the data are less clear. The effect of teacher behavior is less, and the two teacher attitude variables work equally well in predicting white student racial contact.[4]

TEACHER ATTITUDES AND BEHAVIOR AND BLACK STUDENT ACHIEVEMENT

A school with liberal teacher attitudes and behavior should see better academic performance from its black students. Certainly if black students are less alienated, like school more, and have better relationships with white students, it should be easier for them to study, and they should be more motivated to learn. There is another reason, however, why the attitudes of teachers are important. Over a decade ago in a California school a social psychologist conducted an experiment that is now so famous that we need hardly describe it. Briefly, Rosenthal (1966) went through a bit of shenanigans with a pencil and paper test of students and persuaded the teachers that the test indicated which students would blossom over the next few months. Returning a year later, he found, at least in certain classrooms, that those students who were supposed to blossom had blossomed—despite the fact that he had selected their names using a table of random numbers and that the test was a complete fraud. There have been dozens of replications of Rosenthal's study, many successful and others not. We are convinced that the general point is well taken—students do well when teachers expect them to do well, and they do poorly when teachers expect little.

We suspect that if teachers are unsympathetic to black students and to desegregation, they will have low expectations for their black

---

[4]The fact that teacher attitudes are as highly related to white student racial contact as is teacher behavior suggests that there may be technical problems with this analysis. It may also be that white students, having been around other whites all their life, are more sensitive to subtle expressions of prejudice than are black students. We discuss this issue in the appendix, Table 3A–4.

students. The teachers in our sample were asked, "What proportion of your minority group students would you say are performing adequately by your standards for this grade level?" and "What proportion of your minority group students would you say have potential to attend the largest university in your state?" The response to both items are combined into a single scale and pooled for the ten teachers in each high school in the usual fashion. We then compared the average teacher's racial attitudes in each school to the staff's average perception of minority ability.

We found a close association between prodesegregation attitudes and behavior and high teacher expectations for minority students. In the one-fifth of all schools where teacher racial behavior is most favorable to desegregation, 45 percent of the teachers judge their minority students to be performing adequately or to have the ability to attend the state university. In the one-fifth of all schools where teachers have the least sympathetic attitudes, only 36 percent evaluate minority students this favorably. (See Table 3A–7).

Teachers' perception of minority ability is also related to teacher attitudes about school desegregation, but it is not very strongly related to general (nonschool) racial attitudes. This is again encouraging because it suggests that there is no need to alter the deep-seated racial attitudes of school staff as long as their attitudes about school and their behavior in school are as they should be.

One might argue that our cause-and-effect interpretation is wrong. It is not the teachers' behavior that influences their perception of minority ability but their perception of minority ability which influences their behavior. If, after all, the black students in the school were performing badly, then it would make sense that the teachers would be less likely to believe that desegregation is working, and they would appear less sympathetic to desegregation. However, we have tested for this possibility. We used the actual test performance of the black students to predict teacher evaluations of the students (as usual, controlling on school and community variables). Teacher evaluations of the students are influenced by the overall ability of the black student body, but not very strongly; in fact, one can predict staff evaluation of the students as accurately by knowing the staff's attitudes about desegregation as one can by knowing the actual performance of the students in the school. This means that there is little chance that student achievement is affecting the faculty's racial behavior. The faculty's perception of student achievement is not very accurate, and they can hardly be influenced by a reality they cannot perceive. Thus it must be, that the teachers' perceptions of minority ability are based partly on objective reality and partly on their general attitudes about blacks.[5] The school's social climate is as crucial for teachers as it is for students. We believe that when the majority of teachers serve as models of good racial behavior—models for each other as well as for the students—then teachers will expect more from their black students.

We now see two reasons why teacher racial attitudes should affect black student performance. First, liberal racial behavior should increase black student motivation. Second, if teachers' perceptions of black academic ability have as much to do with personal prejudice as with actual ability and teacher expectations influence student performance, then liberal teachers should expect, and hence get, better performance from their black students.

Table 3–4 shows that liberal staff racial behavior is related to higher black achievement. In predominantly white schools in which teachers behave liberally, black students score around 360 on our SAT-like scale; when teacher behavior is not so liberal, the expected school mean is 346 points.

Table 3–4. The effects of teacher racial attitudes and behavior on school-level black achievement.

	Teacher Racial Behavior		Teacher Racial Attitudes— School Related		Teacher Racial Attitudes— Nonschool Related	
	Low	High	Low	High	Low	High
Mean Black Achievement	346	360	341	358	342[a]	362[a]

[a] $p < .05$.
Note: Schools are matched on school and neighborhood racial composition, duration of desegregation, school size, region, urbanism and educational level of the community, and white and black socioeconomic status.

[5]This casual analysis is developed in more detail in the appendix. Note that we are not saying that teachers cannot accurately judge the ability of individual students but that they cannot accurately judge the average ability of their school's entire student body relative to other schools.

Teachers' school-related racial attitudes are also important predictors of black student achievement. A liberal attitude toward school desegregation adds to the school's mean black achievement performance. Finally, teachers' private racial views are associated with the school's mean black achievement level. Staffs falling in the upper fifth of our distribution tend to be in schools in which mean black achievement is around 362, that is, 20 points higher than in schools where teachers are less liberal on racial issues.

The results of Table 3–4 are encouraging but not exactly what we want. We expected the strongest effects on school achievement to come either from teacher racial behavior or from the school staff's school-related racial attitudes, not from the staff's nonschool prejudice. The most reasonable conclusion seems to be that teacher racial attitudes and behavior do influence black achievement but not by 20 points as the last two columns of Table 3–4 would suggest. The 17 and 14 point differences which appear in the first four columns of the table seem more likely. Consider the smallest difference in the table, which is 14 points. Is 14 points in the average SAT performance of black students in high school a worthwhile gain? On the one hand, a gain of 14 points on the SAT for any one student is not very large. However, for some students in the school that gain of 14 points is exactly what is needed for them to be admitted into college. Imagine, for example, that a score of 400 were required for admission to a particular college. If the scores for all black students in a particular school were distributed in the normal bell-shaped curve with an overall school average of 346 (which is the average for all blacks in this study), then a gain of 14 points due to a change in staff attitude would have the effect of increasing the percentage of black students who passed the college admission requirement from 26 percent to 31 percent—an increase of one-fifth in the number passing.

CAN TEACHER RACIAL BEHAVIOR BE CHANGED?

Some civil rights leaders have argued that racist white teachers cannot be saved and should be fired. Undoubtedly some teachers should be dismissed because of their racial prejudice, but are there other prejudiced teachers who will become more tolerant as they adapt to desegregation? How much can the average teacher be expected to change? The teachers in our sample represent the full cross-section of southern high school teachers. Nearly all were themselves educated in segregated schools and have taught in segregated schools most of their careers.

Can these teachers adapt to desegregation? Our analysis indicates very clearly that they can. First, we have already seen that the percentage of teachers who believe that desegregation is beneficial is quite high—higher than we would expect given their general racial attitudes. In addition, we analyzed the relationship between the characteristics of the predominantly white schools and the racial attitudes and behavior of school staff. We found several school characteristics that seem to influence teacher behavior (see Table 3–5). Those racial attitudes that had the least to do with school desegregation, such as attitudes towards intermarriage or feelings about the civil rights movement, were not related to school characteristics. On the other hand, school-related attitudes and in-school racial behavior were related to school characteristics. At the same time, nonschool racial attitudes were strongly related to the personal characteristics (race and age) of the teachers while attitudes about school segregation and racial behavior were not. In other words, characteristics of the teaching staff seem to determine general staff attitudes while characteristics of the school seem to determine the attitudes that the staff has about school desegregation itself.

Let us look at some specific examples from Table 3–5. In the first two rows, we see that nonschool attitudes are strongly related to staff racial composition—the more black teachers, the more liberal the staff attitudes on nonschool racial issues. These two percentages are footnoted to indicate that this effect is stronger than the effect of staff racial composition on school-related racial attitudes.

Similarly, rows three and four show that young teachers have more liberal racial attitudes. The more young teachers there are on the staff, the more liberal their nonschool racial attitudes. A young staff also has more liberal attitudes about school desegregation, but the results here are not as strong, and a young staff is not perceived as behaving in a more liberal way.

The next two lines show exactly the opposite pattern. The longer desegregation has been in effect (reflected in the amount of desegregation experience white students have had) the more accepting of desegregation the school staff is and the more favorably their

Table 3-5. The effect of staff and school characteristics on teacher racial attitudes and behavior.

| | | Percentage of Teachers on: | | |
		Racial Attitudes— Nonschool Related	Racial Attitudes— School Related	Racial Behavior
Percentage of Black Teachers	Low (5%)	$15^{a,b}$	60^a	$-^c$
	High (44%)	$39^{a,b}$	70^a	
Percentage of Teachers 35 or Under	Low (35%)	19^b	59^a	86
	High (78%)	31^b	70^a	80
Percentage of White Students Previously Integrated	Low (13%)	22	61	$70^{a,b}$
	High (67%)	28	69	$97^{a,b}$
Use of Human Relations Literature	No	24	65	79^b
	Yes	26	65	89^b
Principal's Racial Attitudes	Conservative	18^a	55^a	$73^{a,b}$
	Liberal	33^a	75^a	$94^{a,b}$

[a] $p < .05$.
[b] Indicates the strongest effect in each row of the table.
[c] Cannot be analyzed because racial behavior scale refers only to behavior of white teachers.

Note: schools are matched on the four other independent variables shown above, staff sex ratio and educational level, school racial composition, urbanism and region of community, amount of civil rights activity in community, presence of a community biracial committee, presence of minority history in curriculum, staff in-service program, principal's desegregation attitudes, and amount of principal-staff discussion of race.

behavior is evaluated by others. Similarly, the more human relations' literature has been used in the school, the more favorable the staff is to desegregation both in attitudes and behavior. Neither of these two factors seems to influence the nonschool racial attitudes of staff. Apparently school staff can learn to accept desegregation and to work effectively in a desegregated school without their attitudes about other aspects of race relations being affected. Table 3-5 shows that some standard tactics of attitude change—giving desegregation time to work and bolstering it with the use of human relations' material in the school—are effective.

THE PRINCIPAL

The last line of Table 3–5 shows an especially interesting and significant point. The more liberal the racial attitudes of the principal, the more liberal the attitudes of the staff will be. We think that teachers, like most people, take cues from others, particularly from persons in authority. The principal who chooses to do so can demand a certain level of staff behavior regarding race. The problem is that many principals either do not approve of desegregation and hence are unwilling to press their staff to make it work or else are so hesitant about exercising leadership that they effectively conceal their own racial attitudes and try not to influence their staff. This table (and a longer analysis in the appendix) indicates that the principal, as head of the school, can influence the school staff to accept desegregation.

The principal thus has an indirect effect on the students through his staff. The principal can also have quite a strong direct effect on each student even though he may have no regular day-to-day contact with most of them. As the person of highest authority in the school, the principal serves as a symbol of the school. He may be the butt of a thousand sophomoric jokes told behind his back, or he may be a father symbol for a thousand students. Our data suggest that how students feel about their principal says a great deal about their whole school experience.

We asked white and black students if they liked their principal. We related the percentage of students who said they did to other student responses.[6] In Table 3–6 we compare schools where the principal is very well-liked to schools where he is not. Line one indicates that students are more apt to feel that they belong in the school when students of the same race like the principal. The difference between the high and low categories for white students is around 8 percent. For black students, the difference is 13 percent. The second line shows that in schools where the principal is not especially well liked by whites, about half of the white students say

[6]In this analysis, we are not concerned with the racial behavior of a principal in a predominantly white school but rather with the overall behavior of the principal. Hence this analysis deals with all schools, not just those over 60% white. We have matched the schools on school and neighborhood racial composition and duration of desegregation as well as school size, the socioeconomic status of black and white students, and the region, urbanism, and educational level of the community.

Table 3-6. The relationship between liking the principal and other attitudes about school, for white students.

		Percentage of (Same Race) Students Who Like the School Principal	
		Low Percentage	High Percentage
Percentage of Students Who Feel They Do Not Belong	White	25[a]	17[a]
	Black	39[a]	26[a]
Percentage of Students Who Feel That School Rules Are Fair	White	50[a]	65[a]
	Black	43[a]	52[a]
Percentage of Students with Favorable Racial Attitudes	White	35	39
	Black	56[a]	68[a]

[a]$p < .05$.

Note: Schools are matched on school and neighborhood racial composition, duration of desegregation, school size, region, urbanism and educational level of the community, and white and black socioeconomic status.

school rules are fair. Where he is liked, roughly two-thirds of the white students feel the rules are fair. We also see the same pattern for black students. Finally, students who like their principal also have more favorable racial attitudes.

We think there are a number of reasons why principals are so important. As the schools' top administrator the principal influences school policy and staff behavior. Most importantly, the principal is also the symbolic leader of the school. His public relations give the school much of its reputation in the eyes of its students.[7]

CONCLUSIONS

The racial attitudes of the school staff and more importantly staff behavior in a desegregated school need not be taken as an uncontrollable given. Much can be done short of the politically outrageous solution of inventing a pencil and paper test to measure

[7]None of the 194 principals in our sample were women.

racist attitudes and firing the teachers who flunk it. A combination of progressive leadership in the school, a serious effort to help teachers learn to deal with desegregation, and simply giving desegregation enough time to work will make a difference in teachers. A difference in teachers will make a difference in school race relations and in minority student attitudes and performance.

Researchers and educators are coming more and more to regard the principal as the critical factor in the school. It is our contention that the principal's leadership, or lack of it, can be the deciding factor in effective desegregation. When all is said and done, when the desegregation plan has been drawn, students reassigned, teachers hired, and materials purchased, it is the principal who will be responsible for the way the school works. The idea of the principal as the single most important determinant of school climate is not a new one. Our own initial chapter provided a pointed demonstration of how the strong leadership of one principal changed the direction of City High.

APPENDIX 3A

The analysis of this chapter implicitly uses literature from several traditions in sociology. The idea that the racial attitudes and behavior of teachers will influence pupil racial attitudes comes from reference group theory. For the student, teachers are what Ehrlich defines as a relevant "reference other," that is, "any person, group, or category of others whom the individual feels is important to him or her and whose expectations for behavior would be given serious consideration" (1973:151). In the same manner the principle is an important reference other for teachers. The opinions of reference others are important in predicting ethnic behavior (De Fleur and Westie 1958; Fendrich 1967; De Friese and Ford 1969). A reference group will be more important if there is a stronger identification with the group. (For example, Ewens and Ehrlich distinguish for college students between reference others who are peers from college versus those who are from the respondent's home town and show that the home town others are more important [1969:157].) The only question about the relevance of this literature is the possibility that the normal superordinate-subordinate conflict between teachers and students or between principals and teachers may prevent the necessary identification between them. Apparently the conflict among principals, teachers, and students is not excessive since our analysis shows principals and teachers influencing teachers and students.

Our decision to distinguish between teacher racial attitudes and racial behavior is derived from a good deal of literature which has contrasted attitudes and behavior. The notion that behavior is simply the public manifestation of attitude has gradually been refuted until the present view is that expressed by Pettigrew (1973): The simplest way to change attitudes is to change the respondent's behavior; attitudes will change to conform to the behavior change. Experiments in attitude change and the work of Festinger (1957) on cognitive dissonance indicate that when behavior and attitudes conflict, the attitude will often change to conform to the behavior. Previous research points out how teacher racial behavior might affect the educational performance of minority students. Katz (1964) identifies four factors which can be characteristic of black performance in a biracial setting: (1) lowered probability of success—the existence of an educational standards gap between black and white schools or strong feelings of inferiority on the part of blacks can lead to decreased expectations which, in turn, can lead to lower achievement; (2) social threat—rejection by representatives of the dominant culture can trigger emotional responses which impede intellectual performance; (3) failure threat—doing poorly academically involves risking the disapproval of significant others such as peers and teachers. The possibility of such disapproval can negatively influence academic performance. Katz suggests that acceptance of blacks by their white peers and teachers can lead to (4) a "social facilitation effect" on learning. The social threat and social facilitation factors referred to by Katz have important implications for our discussion of teacher racial attitudes and behavior.

The teacher expectation literature initiated by Rosenthal (1966) also suggests that teachers' attitudes will affect student peformance. There has been considerable controversy over the "Rosenthal effect," as it is often called. While some social scientists argue that the evidence is inadequate to conclude that teacher expectations affect student peformance, we remain convinced that teacher expectations play a part in student performance.

CONSTRUCTION OF SCALES

The difficult methodological problems in this analysis are the measurement of teacher racial attitudes and racial behavior and the determination of whether teacher behavior is indeed a cause of student behavior. We chose to measure teacher racial behavior by asking other persons in the school to report on the attitudes of teachers. For example, both black and white students were asked, "How about most of your teachers—how do you think they feel about blacks and whites going to the same school together?" (The following responses were offered: They like it; they don't like it; it doesn't matter to them; don't know.) Teachers and principals were asked similar questions. Thus, not only the principal and the students gave their perceptions of the teachers' attitudes, but each teacher served as an informant on the other teachers in the school. The overall scale was constructed by standardizing the four different variables so that each type of informant carried equal weight in the final construction of the scale. (This same balancing of the importance of each informant was done in constructing the racial tension scale.) We called this measure "teacher racial behavior" simply because it is not possible to directly observe another's attitudes. One can only infer from observing what another person says or does what that person's attitudes are. Whether the teachers are unprejudiced, or simply careful to conceal their prejudices, is irrelevant—in either case their behavior is that of an unprejudiced person.

One problem is that the perception of another person's prejudice depends upon the attitudes of the observor. For example, white students in the upper South are more likely to report that their teachers do not like desegregation. This is probably because the whites in the upper South are themselves more liberal than white students in the deep South and hence more sensitive to racial slurs or more willing to agree with criticisms of the teaching staff made by black students. This means not only that our measure of prejudice is relative rather than absolute but also that we need to consider how respondent bias might be affecting our results.

It is understandable that people are reluctant to answer these sorts of questions—they are very general, referring to all teachers in the school, and people should be reluctant to guess about another person's attitudes. The result is a large number of "don't know" and other neutral responses.

When we correlate the responses of our different types of informants, we find that white students, teachers, and principals tend to agree with each other quite well while black students agree less well (see Table 3A–1). There is an old southern saying that "black people can see through the behavior of whites," but we suspect that this does not mean that blacks are better judges of white prejudice than whites are. After all whites are going to be more careful in what they say around blacks, and whites, having spent more time with whites, will be more sensitive to subtle cues in their conversation. We suspect that the saying refers to the fact that the behavior which seems acceptable to prejudiced whites may not be acceptable to blacks.[8]

The correlations in Table 3A–1 are probably too high. In this study, correlations between two different respondents greater than .3 should be read with caution. In this case we think the high

[8]This interpretation is supported by the finding that teacher racial attitudes are only weakly related to black student perception of staff. The correlation between staff nonschool racial attitudes and black perceptions of teacher attitudes is only .127; for white students it is .43. The black correlation is depressed partly by the smaller number of respondents per school.

Table 3A-1.   Zero-order correlations of items in teacher racial behavior scale.

	1	2	3	4
1. Percentage of Black Students Saying Most Teachers Do Not Like Desegregation	—	.196	.041	-.124
2. Percentage of White Students Saying Most Teachers Do Not Like Desegregation		—	.291	-.340
3. Principal Says Most White Teachers Dislike Desegregation			—	-.397
4. Teachers Say Most White Teachers Like Desegregation (reversed)				—

correlations simply reflect the fact that when a school has a generally good racial environment everyone in it tends to give everyone else the benefit of the doubt. We suspect in this case that the schools which have no history of black complaints about white teachers will be schools where the principal, teachers, and white students will all tend to say that their teachers are unprejudiced; the agreement among these measures on teacher behavior is biased upward by the school's history of race relations.

Differences in question wording cause some difficulty. For example, students were asked about teacher attitudes about integration without being given an opportunity to distinguish between black and white teachers. Teachers answered two separate questions, one about white and one about black teachers. In order to keep our analysis clear, we have limited this chapter to the schools whose student bodies are 60 percent or more white so that we can be confident that we are talking mainly about white teachers.

There is considerable agreement among teachers and among students as indicated by the relatively high between-school standard deviations on these items. For example, the percentage of teachers saying that most white teachers like desegregation is 27 percent with a standard deviation of 20 percentage points. If one assumes that there are ten teachers in each school, the variance between schools which can be attributed solely to sampling error in selecting the ten teachers is:

$$\sigma^2 = \frac{(.27)(.73)}{10} = .0197$$

Our actual variance is $.20^2$ or $.0400$, twice as much, and the true between-school variance is $.0400 - .0197 = .0203$, yielding a true between-school standard deviation of $.1425$. If we follow our usual convention of distinguishing between the top and bottom fifths of all schools, we find a difference of 36 percentage points between them (assuming, as we always do, a difference of 2.5 standard deviations). The other items used on the teacher behavior scale also have high between-school variances. Thus it seemed safe to conclude that there is considerable difference between schools in teacher behavior, and enough agreement among students and teachers about this to enable us to measure it.

As usual, we have attempted to minimize any false correlation occurring because of using independent and dependent variables from the same respondent. Thus, we have constructed several versions of the teacher behavior scale. One version eliminates all responses from black students when black dependent variables are to be analyzed. A similar variant is constructed for analysis of white dependent variables. A third variation eliminates all responses from the principal when principal questions are correlated with teacher behavior.

Tables 3A–2 and 3A–3 show the correlation of items in two different measures of teacher racial attitudes as reported by the teachers themselves. Both teacher racial attitude scales are aggregated for the ten teachers surveyed in each school. School-related racial attitudes (Table 3A–2) are measured by the responses to two

Table 3A–2.   Zero-order correlations of items in teacher school racial attitudes scale.

	1	2
1. Percentage of Teachers Saying Most Black Students Are Better Off in Mixed Schools	—	.722
2. Percentage of Teachers Saying Most White Students Are Better Off in Mixed Schools		—

questions: "Do you think that black students benefit from attending desegregated schools?" and "Do you think that white students benefit from attending desegregated schools?" The question referring to black students is not a particularly good measure of racial prejudice since a highly prejudiced teacher might feel that blacks benefit from attending desegregated schools by increased contact with superior white students. However, the same cannot be said of the item about white students—the teacher who believes that whites benefit from desegregation is clearly expressing a racially liberal idea.

The following nonschool race relations (Table 3A–3) items used in this study have appeared in several national surveys:

Listed below are some statements other people have made. For each, please mark whether you strongly agree, agree somewhat, disagree

Table 3A-3. Zero-order correlations of items in teacher nonschool racial attitude scale.

	1	2	3	4	5
1. Percentage of Teachers Disagreeing That the Amount of Prejudice against Minority Groups in This Country Is Highly Exaggerated	—	.356	.258	.376	.504
2. Percentage of Teachers Agreeing That They Would Like to Live in an Integrated Neighborhood		—	.311	.556	.563
3. Percentage of Teachers Agreeing That the Civil Rights Movement Has Done More Good Than Harm			—	.281	.418
4. Percentage of Teachers Disagreeing That Blacks and Whites Should Be Allowed to Intermarry				—	.602
5. Percentage of Teachers Who Feel That Restrictions Imposed by a White Society Account More for the Failure of the Negro to Achieve Equality Than a Lack of Initiative or Drive					—

somewhat, or strongly disagree:

1. The amount of prejudice against minority groups in this country is highly exaggerated.
2. I would like to live in an integrated neighborhood.
3. The civil rights movement has done more good than harm.
4. Blacks and whites should not be allowed to intermarry.

If you had to choose one factor which accounts most for the failure of the Negro to achieve equality, which would you choose—a lack of initiative and drive, or the restrictions imposed by a white society?

Table 3A–4 shows that the two attitude scales are highly related to each other with a correlation of over .7. This is one of the very highest correlations we will see in the study, and it reflects both the close relationship between the school-related and nonschool attitudes and also the high reliability of both scales since this means there is less error variance than usual to attenuate the correlation. (The high correlation between the two scales does not imply that they should have the same means; the school-related attitudes appear to be more liberal than the nonschool attitudes.) The correlations between these two attitude scales and the teacher behavior scale are the highest for data based on different informants that we will see in this study. The magnitude of these correlations supports our

Table 3A–4. Zero-order correlations of teacher attitudes and behavior scales.

	Teacher Racial Attitudes— Nonschool	Teacher Racial Attitudes— School	Teacher Racial Behavior— Others' Perceptions
Teacher Racial Attitudes— Nonschool Related	—	.725	.427
Teacher Racial Attitudes— School Related		—	.461
Teacher Racial Behavior as Perceived by Others			—

argument that the teacher behavior scale is not badly contaminated by bias and does indeed measure teacher behavior.[9]

ANALYSIS OF TEACHER EFFECTS ON WHITE RACIAL ATTITUDES

Table 3A–5 gives the full regression equations for the relationship of the mean teacher racial attitudes and behavior to mean white student racial attitudes in schools which are over 60 percent white. White student racial attitudes are measured with three different items. One item asks whether the students think that white people generally are smarter than blacks. The other items concern their perceptions of blacks in their school. White students are asked to simply check whether they think the blacks in their school are ambitious or whether they are dumb. (These items have an obvious problem: It is impossible to say when an opinion of another group is stereotypic and when it is simply realistic.)

In Table 3A–5 the control variables are generally weakly related to white student prejudice. Prejudice is generally lower in white schools. We suspect that whites in white schools feel under less pressure and are more likely to respond with socially acceptable attitudes. It could also be that the few blacks in predominantly white schools appear in fact to be more ambitious and bright. It is also interesting that the higher the socioeconomic status of white students, the lower the number of tolerant answers. This is complicated because white student status is correlated with other variables such as urbanism, region, and community educational level. If the values of the regression coefficients are taken at face value (we are not at all sure that they should be), then the implication is that the large low status cities of the upper South have the most liberal white students. One reason why whites in high status schools may

---

[9]One might expect the school-related attitudes to be much more strongly related to teacher behavior than the nonschool attitudes. We think they are. The attitudes toward desegregation scale has only two items compared to five for the general prejudice scale; this means that the correlation between behavior and school attitudes is depressed by the lower reliability of the shorter scale.

show more prejudice is because these particular items refer to academic matters, and middle class white students may perceive working class black students as being duller or less ambitious.

Table 3A–5 shows that teacher racial attitudes and behavior are consistently linked to white student prejudices. All nine coefficients are positive, and teacher racial behavior is significantly related to student prejudice in all three equations.

Table 3A-5. Regression equations with standardized regression coefficients used to construct Table 3-1.

	Other Group Is Not Dumb	Other Group Is Ambitious	Color Is Not Related to Smartness
Independent Variables:			
Mean White SES	-.074	-.210[a]	-.332
Black Students from Black Elementary/Junior High	-.141	-.122	.000
White Students from Integrated Elementary/Junior High	.039	.238[a]	.212[a]
High School in Black Neighborhood	.108	.078	.097
School Size	.080	.203	-.012
Region	.266[a]	.104	.241[a]
Mean Black SES	.009	-.057	-.032
Community Educational Level	-.136	-.081	.215
Urbanism of County	.253	.166	.219
Teacher Racial Attitudes— Nonschool	(.167)	(.065)	(.101)
Teacher Racial Attitudes— School	(.150)	(.173)	(.072)
Teacher Racial Behavior	(.186)[a]	(.216)[a]	(.177)[a]
r^2	.260	.226	.294

[a] $p < .05$.

Note: Parentheses indicate the beta if this variable were to be entered into the equation following the control variables. This variable was not used in computing the r^2 for the equation.

TEACHER EFFECTS ON INTERRACIAL CONTACT AND BLACK ATTITUDES

Table 3A–6 shows the relationship between teacher racial attitudes and behavior and measures of student interracial contact and black responses to the "like school" scale and the "I feel I don't belong in this school" statement. Regression equations for all four of these dependent variables were presented in the preceding chapter, and limiting the sample to schools over 60 percent does not change them much, so it is not necessary to review the impact of control variables again. The general findings that attitude and behavior seem to influence both racial contact and black students' responses to the school seem well supported by the data. In the case of the black like and belong items, the strength of the three teacher variables is as it should be—the nonschool racial attitudes are weakest, the school-related racial attitudes next, and the racial behavior scale the strongest. This is also the case for black interracial contact when the teacher nonschool attitude variables seem unrelated to contact. For white racial contact, all three variables are strong predictors.

TEACHER EFFECTS ON ACHIEVEMENT, TEACHER ACHIEVEMENT PERCEPTIONS

Teacher perceptions of the ability of black students are measured by two questions: "What proportion of your minority-group students would you say are performing adequately by your standards for this grade level?" and "What proportion of your minority-group students would you say have the potential to attend the largest state university in your state?" The scale has been standardized so that it represents approximately the percentage of teachers who say that more than half or almost all of the black students are performing adequately, or the percentage of teachers who give the same responses for the second question. Thus about 30 percent of the teachers in the average school would rate the black students favorably on either one of these questions.

The first column of Table 3A–7 shows the factors which are related to teacher perceptions of black student ability. As we noted in the text, the actual level of black achievement is no better a predictor than teacher school-related attitudes. We also see that

Table 3A-6. Regression equations with standardized regression coefficients (betas) used to construct Tables 3–2 and 3–3.

Independent Variables:	Blacks Say They Like School	Blacks Feel They Do Not Belong in Their School[b]	Blacks Report Favorable Interracial Contact	Whites Report Favorable Interracial Contact
Mean Black SES	-.217	-.217	-.079	.068
Black Students from Black Elementary/Junior High	-.008	-.032	-.020	-.085
White Students from Integrated Elementary/Junior High	-.094	.113	.107	.235[a]
High School in Black Neighborhood	.329[a]	.280[a]	.075	-.091
School Size	.021	.089	.104	.049
Region	.011	.056	.040	.240[a]
Mean White SES	-.027	.020	-.080	-.061
Community Educational Level	.164	.115	-.044	.061
Urbanism of County	.002	.130	.073	.360[a]
School Percentage White	.065	-.033	.353[a]	-.242[a]
Teacher Racial Attitudes—Nonschool	(.031)	(.108)	(-.023)	(.241)[a]
Teacher Racial Attitudes—School	(.143)	(.178)	(.097)	(.245)[a]
Teacher Racial Behavior	(.221)	(.192)	(.286)[a]	(.217)[a]
r^2	.122	.142	.156	.483

[a] $p < .05$.

[b] Item reversed.

Note: Parentheses indicate the beta if this variable were to be entered into the equation following the control variables. This variable was not used in computing the r^2 for the equation.

121

Table 3A-7.   Regression equations with standardized regression co-efficients (betas) used to predict teacher perception of black ability and black achievement (Table 3-4).

	Black Student Ability	Mean Black Achievement
Independent Variables:		
Mean Black SES	.064	.452[a]
Black Students from Black Elementary/Junior High	-.010	.176
White Students from Integrated Elementary/Junior High	.056	.086
High School in Black Neighborhood	.129	.170
School Size	.312[a]	.008
Region	-.019	.150
Mean White SES	.065	.305[a]
Community Educational Level	-.154	-.182
Urbanism of County	.251	-.071
School Percentage White	.049	-.007
Teacher Racial Attitudes— Nonschool	(.126)	(.198)[a]
Teacher Racial Attitudes—School	(.315)[a]	(.116)
Teacher Racial Behavior	(.286)[a]	(.136)
Mean Black Achievement	(.310)[a]	—
r^2	.236	.413

[a] $p < .05$.

Note: Parentheses indicate the beta if this variable were to be entered into the equation following the control variables. This variable was not used to compute the r^2 for the equation.

student socioeconomic status is a weak predictor—apparently schools with middle class black populations do not have teachers who evaluate students more positively. The strongest single relationship is with school size. Size is correlated with a high black SES, high community educational level, and upper South region. All of these factors are related to achievement, so it could be that multicollinearity is causing the size variable's effect to be overstated. This cannot explain all of the relationship, however, and we have no explanation of why large schools should have more positive teacher perceptions of black ability. (It may be because large schools have more ability grouping; see Chapter 6.)

The second column of Table 3A–7 shows the regression equation for black achievement. We have already seen this equation in Chapter 2, but this time it is restricted to schools which are 60 percent white or more. This equation, unlike the others we have seen, shows the strongest apparent effect on achievement to be from teacher nonschool racial attitudes—clearly the wrong variable according to our theory. The fact that all three independent variables are positive supports the argument that teacher racial attitudes do affect achievement. At the same time, the relationship may well be spurious. Teacher racial attitudes may be serving as a surrogate for the sort of upper South, sophisticated urban community where teacher racial attitudes are likely to be generally favorable and achievement generally high. If this is the case, then the effects of teacher racial attitudes and behavior may be exaggerated in the table. We do not regard this as sufficient reason to dismiss the results entirely, however, since the equation does control on a number of community and student variables. The findings having to do with black noncognitive effects and with staff expectations build a consistent theoretical model which predicts that staff attitudes affect achievement.

The general problem of whether to take teacher racial attitudes and behavior as cause or effect is a difficult one with no general solution (unless one argues that never drawing conclusions from this sort of data is a general solution; this is indeed what some writers recommend, but we believe social scientists often interpret relationships as causal on less evidence than we have here). We think we have constructed such a model. We have shown that the data fit the argument that liberal teacher behavior sets an example for white students, creates a comfortable school environment for black students, and leads to higher staff expectations for black students— all of which lead to increased achievement. The alternatives are, first, to argue that the relationship is spurious and that other factors are influencing both student attitude and achievement variables as well as teacher racial attitudes and behavior. But our regression equations control on a host of variables, and these control variables generally have little impact upon the relationship between teacher attitudes and student responses. A second alternative is to argue that causality runs in the opposite direction—that when students express good racial attitudes, appreciate school, and have high achievement, teachers will develop more favorable attitudes toward integration.

This alternative seems plausible, but it does not explain why staff attitudes toward racial intermarriage, the civil rights movement, and black poverty should be affected by their school experience. Given that one of these three explanations (*a* causes *b*, the relationship is spurious, or *b* causes *a*) must be true, we think the best argument can be made for our interpretation.

In analyzing the achievement test, we noted that a gain of 14 percentage points for a total school could be translated into a gain of 5 percent in the number of students who score above a particular threshold. We arrived at this conversion by simply assuming that the scores in that particular school were normally distributed with a mean and standard deviation equal to that of the total population in the study. Let us assume that the threshold (presumably the admission requirement for some college) is an SAT score of 400. Let us further assume that the black students in a particular high school had a mean score of 346 with a standard deviation of 84. A score of 400 is 54 points, or $54/84 = 0.64$ standard deviations above the school mean, so we can expect (reading a table for the cumulative normal distribution) 26 percent of the students in the school to score over 400. If the scores of the students in the school were raised by 14 SAT points, then the school's mean would shift to 360 while the standard deviation would remain 84. If this happened, a score of 400 would be only $40/84 = 0.48$ standard deviations above the school mean, and we could expect 31 percent of the black students in the school to score above that point. Thus the effect of a 14 point gain in the mean is a $31 - 26 = 5$ percent gain in the number of students who pass this test threshold. The percentage gain would of course differ depending on which threshold is chosen.

CAUSES OF TEACHER ATTITUDES

The other major question raised in the analysis is whether teacher attitudes should be viewed as fixed or changeable. Using regression, we analyzed the relative impact of different kinds of variables on the three teacher scales now treated as dependent variables. (Since we are using principal characteristics as independent variables, we delete principal perceptions of white teachers from the teacher behavior scale.) The basic equations are shown in Table 3A–8. This table supports the general argument that those teacher attitudes least

Table 3A-8. Regression equations with standardized regression coefficients (betas) used to construct Table 3-5.

	Teacher Racial Attitudes— Nonschool	Teacher Racial Attitudes— School	Teacher Racial Behavior
Independent Variables:			
Teacher Race	$-.402^a$	$-.236^a$	$-.137$
Teacher Sex	$-.079$	$-.042$	$.029$
Teacher Age	$.178$	$.242^a$	$-.072$
Teacher Education Level	$-.103$	$-.031$	$-.019$
Urbanism of County	$.204^a$	$-.005$	$.038$
Region	$.286^a$	$.103$	$.219^a$
School Percentage White	$.056$	$.048$	$.242^a$
White Students from Integrated Elementary/Junior High	$.092$	$.171^a$	$.343^a$
Black Students from Black Elementary/Junior High	$-.005$	$.066$	$.102$
Civil Rights Activity in Community	$-.014$	$.125$	$-.017$
Effective Community Biracial Committee—Leader Report	$-.071$	$-.043$	$-.072$
Effective Community Biracial Committee—Principal Report	$.088$	$.033$	$.112$
Years of Human Relations Literature	$.030$	$-.012$	$.139$
Learned Minority-Group History—Teacher Report	$.149^a$	$.148^a$	$-.055$
Teacher Trained in Intergroup Relations	$.044$	$.007$	$.067$
Principal's Racial Attitudes	$.138$	$.349^a$	$.224^a$
Principal's Desegregation Attitudes	$-.171^a$	$-.083$	$.103$
Principal Has Talked to Teachers about Desegregation	$.021$	$.089$	$-.060$
r^2	$.589$	$.458$	$.398$

$^a p < .05.$

related to school are the ones least affected by what is happening in the school while teacher in-school racial behavior is most strongly correlated with what is happening in the school.

Table 3A–8 shows the combined effect of eighteen independent variables. The first six independent variables are essentially staff background characteristics related to the kinds of teachers who are likely to be hired in a particular school. The sex, age, educational level, and race of the teachers and the region and urbanism of the community are all factors which cannot be altered by the way the school functions. The next nine variables describe the school's racial composition, desegregation history, the amount of in service education, and level of civil rights activity in the community. The last three variables are all characteristics of the principal.

In general we find that the background variables are most strongly related to the teacher nonschool racial attitudes. For example, region within the South and the racial composition of the teaching staff are the two best predictors of teacher nonschool racial attitudes. Black staffs and staffs in the upper South are more liberal. Two school variables, desegregation history and present racial composition, are most strongly related to teacher racial behavior. Teachers are more liberal in white schools and schools where the students have had a long history of desegregation. The principal's racial attitudes strongly influence teachers' school-related racial attitudes but are only weakly related to nonschool racial attitudes. These data are consistent with our general argument that teacher nonschool attitudes are least affected by the school situation and teacher racial behavior is most affected.

The large number of variables in the equations makes it difficult to interpret the size of each individual coefficient. For this reason Table 3A–9 summarizes the variables in terms of the pecentage of variance uniquely added by each group of variables. For this purpose we have divided the variables into four grous: the first six variables which are teacher background characteristics; the second group of six variables which are characteristics of the community and the integration experience of the school; the next three variables which deal with in service human relations programs for teachers and students; and the last three variables which reflect the attitudes and behavior of the principal.

Table 3A–9 shows that teacher background variables explain more variance in teacher nonschool racial attitudes than they do in

Table 3A-9. Percentage of variance explained by teacher background and environmental variables in regression equations predicting teacher racial behavior, school-related and nonschool-related racial attitudes.

	Teacher Racial Behavior	Teacher Racial Attitudes— School	Teacher Racial Attitudes— Nonschool
Percentage of Variance Explained by:			
Teacher Background Variables[a]	.206	.268	.484
School and Community Variables[b]	.105	.030	.032
Race Relations Programs Variables[c]	.023	.014	.017
Principal Variables[d]	.064	.146	.056
Total r^2	.398	.458	.589

[a]Teacher race, sex, age, educational level, urbanism of county and region.

[b]School percentage white, previous integration experience of black and white students, level of civil rights activity in community, and existence of effective biracial committee in community.

[c]Years of human relations literature and teacher training in minority-group history and intergroup relations.

[d]Principal racial attitudes, principal desegregation attitudes, and principal communication with teachers about desegregation.

school racial attitudes. However, the second line shows that the school and community variables add uniquely more variance in explaining teacher racial behavior than they do in explaining teacher attitudes. The same is true of race relations programs variables. Finally, principal variables seem most strongly related to teacher school-related racial attitudes. Thus, of the variance explained in teacher nonschool racial attitudes, over four-fifths is explained by teacher background characteristics. However, only slightly more than half of the variance in school-related racial attitudes is explained by teacher background characteristics; most of the remainder is explained by principal characteristics. Finally, for teacher racial behavior, almost exactly half of the variance is explained by teacher background variables; most of the rest is contributed by principal and school/community characteristics.[10] This seems to us to be

[10]The teacher behavior scale uses only student and teacher data, not principal reports.

reasonable evidence supporting our view that school-related attitudes and behavior within school need not be taken as fixed—they respond to school and community influence.

EFFECTS OF STUDENT PERCEPTIONS ON THE PRINCIPAL

Table 3A–10 shows the relationship between white and black feelings about their principal and their feelings about other aspects of school. These equations violate one of our analysis rules; data from the same respondents was used for both the dependent and independent variables. This means that the correlations will be much higher than usual, and this must be taken into consideration. For example, this table shows that if white students say they like the principal, they will also be much more likely to say that the school rules are fair, which does not mean, however, that a principal who makes a new effort to be liked will quickly see a huge increase in student support for school discipline. It is likely that a variety of different things are going on here. Well-liked principals do inspire confidence in the school's disciplinary policy, but a good set of disciplinary rules makes it easier to like the principal, and a school with a good-natured student body and few problems will have more students giving favorable ratings to both the rules and the principal. In our view the only clear interpretation one can make of the data is that feelings about the principal are a key element in the constellation of feelings students have about school—which probably means that the principal's behavior is of great importance in affecting that constellation of feelings.

Table 3A-10. Regression equations with standardized coefficients (betas) used to construct Table 3-6.

Independent Variables:	White Student Attitudes			Black Student Attitudes		
	Feel They Do Not Belong	School Rules Are Fair	Positive Racial Attitudes	Feel They Do Not Belong	School Rules Are Fair	Positive Racial Attitudes
Mean White SES	.022	.136	.124	-.013	.077	.037
Mean Black SES	.058	-.020	.001	.148	-.032	-.037
Blacks from Black Elementary/Junior High	.016	-.119	-.017	-.002	-.133	.017
Whites from Integrated Elementary/Junior High	-.168	-.033	.016	-.133	-.031	.153
High School in Black Neighborhood	.159	.039	.087	-.220[a]	.186	.010
School Size	.175	-.227[a]	.063	-.098	.027	.167
Region	.058	.189[a]	.214[a]	-.013	-.039	-.071
Community Educational Level	.161	.092	-.015	-.121	.016	-.173
Urbanism of County	-.058	-.005	.337[a]	-.018	-.051	.049
School Percentage White	-.278[a]	-.075	.062	.265[a]	-.059	-.059
White Students Rate Principal Favorably	-.280[a]	.449[a]	.104	-.266[a]	.243[a]	.286[a]
r^2	.236	.275	.349	.273	.115	.139

[a] $p < .05$.

4 HOW SCHOOLS HANDLE RACE

Perhaps the most important message in this book is that for black students, feelings about race relations are central to their feelings about everything else. For most of these students, their only interaction with whites is at school, so race relations at school are of enormous importance. This is not true for whites. Their feelings about the school's race relations have less to do with whether they like school. There is no evidence that white achievement declines in a school with bad race relations. For blacks, however, and especially for black males, achievement is strongly affected by the racial climate of the school.

If the school is going to reach its black students, it must establish a good racial climate. We asked the teachers and the principal a number of questions about school activities dealing with racial issues. The results are mixed and confusing. Some strategies seem to work consistently. Others seem not to work. Frankly, we are not sure what the difference is between the effective and ineffective strategies, but after looking at these school programs, we will speculate on one possible explanation, and we invite the reader to think along with us about this vexing question. At the end of the chapter, we will present our most surprising result—that peaceful desegregation, in the long run, is not good for school race relations. Let us begin by examining three programs which seem to have consistently positive effects.

TWO SUCCESSFUL PROGRAMS USING OUTSIDE RESOURCES

We found two programs in schools which had friendly contact between blacks and whites and where students of both races supported integration. Both involved the use of outside resources: the use of human relations literature in the school and the establishment of intergroup relations programs for teachers. The first involves obtaining materials to be used with students. The second normally involves bringing in outside specialists to conduct workshops or classes with the school staff.

We asked the principal whether the school had obtained literature in the last two years and whether staff workshops in intergroup relations had been held. Table 4–1 shows positive effects of human relations literature on both white and black students. The largest difference is in the percentage of black students who say that their teacher likes desegregation; there is an increase from 14 to 23

Table 4-1.   White and black student attitudes in schools which did and did not use human relations materials in last two years.

	Use of Human or Community Relations Literature	
	No	Yes
Percentage of Black Students Saying Their Teacher Likes Desegregation	14[a]	23[a]
Percentage of Black Students Saying They Like School	41	49
Percentage of Black Students Saying School Rules Are Fair	44	50
Percentage of White Students Saying Their Teacher Likes Desegregation	12	16
Percentage of White Students Saying They Like School	44	48
Percentage of White Students Saying School Rules Are Fair	56	59

[a]$p < .05$.

Note: Schools matched on racial composition of school and neighborhood, duration of desegregation, school size, region, community urbanism and educational level, and black and white student socioeconomic status.

percent if human relations literature has been used during the last two years. The percentages of black students who say that they like school and consider school rules to be fair also increase. A similar pattern appears for white students although the differences are not as large.

How Big an Effect Should We Pay Attention to?

Let us interrupt our argument for a moment to answer an obvious question: Are these results large enough to pay attention to? We will see a number of tables similar to Table 4–1. In this and the next two chapters our technique is always the same—to first show that when a group of schools are matched on the kind of community they are in and the kind of students they have, the schools that have a particular characteristic also have better race relations or higher achievement or higher morale. Second, we try to decide whether there is a very good chance that this trait caused the improvement in these schools. This decision will be derived partly from what we know about schools but mostly from the data. In analyzing the data, we will try to answer three questions: First, is the relationship between a certain school characteristic and a certain outcome really there, or is it only an accident, something we would not find again if we had a different group of 200 schools? (In other words, is it statistically significant?) Second, is the relationship between this school characteristic related to other student outcomes in a theoretically consistent manner? These supporting relationships need not be statistically significant. Third, is the relationship large enough to make adoption of this school practice worthwhile? The answer to the last question is almost always yes since the practices we are looking at are not expensive. For example, in Table 4–1 we see that schools which have purchased human relations materials in the last two years have slightly more white students saying that most teachers in the school like desegregation: 16 percent say this compared to 12 percent in schools which reportedly did not buy human relations material. The difference in a typical large high school is a change in perception of the staff by perhaps only thirty white students—hardly a revolution. But the schools which purchased human relations materials probably spent very little, and it is easy to make the case that what they did spend was a worthwhile investment.

A final point is that one should not construe the school practices in a narrow or literal fashion. Buying human relations materials works, but, obviously, placing the order and then putting the materials on a shelf after they arrive is not enough. They have to be used, which means talking to teachers and students, devising a way of using the materials, making at least some minor changes in the curriculum, and so forth. Of course, if a school does a better than average job of using materials, it will get better than average results.

In-Service Staff Training

Black students also respond well to schools which have held intergroup relations programs for staff. Table 4–2 shows that in such schools black students are more apt to say that their teachers like desegregation and to say that they like school.

Differences in Tables 4–1 and 4–2 are not always large. The only information we have, however, is the principal's statements on whether the school sponsored in-service programs and used literature. We know nothing about the quality of either the materials or the staff programs.

Table 4–2. Black student attitudes in schools which had in-service race relations programs for teachers.

	Teacher Intergroup Relations Programs for Two or More Years	
	No	Yes
Percentage of Black Students Saying Their Teacher Likes Desegregation	15	21
Percentage of Black Students Saying They Like School	42	48

Note: Schools matched on racial composition of school and neighborhood, duration of desegregation, school size, region, community urbanism and educational level, and black and white student socioeconomic status.

STUDENT BIRACIAL COMMITTEES

Throughout the South many communities found that a biracial committee of white and black community leaders was an effective way to deal with civil rights problems. These committees provided a forum for discussion when things were quiet and an avenue for heading off problems during periods of unrest. If racial tensions were severe, the committee was likely to be helpful in resolving the conflict. For example, in Charleston, South Caroline the biracial committee played a key role in negotiating the settlement of a long and bitter strike of black hospital workers. In that situation the biracial committee aided hospital management in locating the real leadership of the strike so that negotiations could begin. A short time later a race riot in a high school provided another opportunity for the committee to help. The committee organized meetings, first of white and black students and parents separately, then of both groups together with school staff, and a compromise solution emerged. The result was to push the school district to make needed reforms (which ultimately led to the dismissal of the white principal).

Although student biracial committees in high schools are not as well known as community biracial committees, they can perform many of the same functions. At the boundary between white and black student groups and between students and administration, the biracial committee can provide a forum for student grievances. By dealing honestly with the grievances, the committee will earn a reputation for fairness, making it difficult for students or the administration to reject its recommendations. In this way a student biracial committee can serve as a watch dog, anticipating problems perhaps before either students or administrators are aware of difficulties. Often the committee can diffuse a tense situation before it becomes serious. Finally, if severe problems do arise, the committee as an accepted body can referee the dispute. Forehand and Ragosta (1976) found that the most effective student committees actively seek to improve race relations within the school rather than simply responding to tension and unrest after the fact. Building harmonious race relations within the school in an ongoing process. This is why it is important that the committee be actively involved during quiet times as well as tense ones.

Forehand and Ragosta recommend that members of a student human relations committee be selected by the students themselves. How the committee is formed is probably less important than that it be representative of all majority and minority groups within the school. The best committees make sure that the normally unrepresented student—the alienated student with poor grades—is also represented on the committee.

An effective student biracial committee has an impact on its own student members (who in many cases learn more from their participation on the committee than they could from any class) and on the school as a whole. Teachers and students were asked to evaluate the student committee in their school. There is, as one would expect, considerable agreement among teachers and white and black students as to how effective the schools' committees are.

Table 4–3 shows that when teachers say that the student biracial committee has been effective, students of both races are more likely to say that the school staff supports desegregation. Of course, a school may have an effective biracial committee because it has a liberal staff, but an effective committee makes the staff appear more supportive of desegregation since the staff will be credited with creating the student committee, and the good atmosphere the committee creates will make the whole school, staff included, look better. The staff may also be pushed into a more liberal position by the committee's presence. Chapter 3 pointed out that teachers behaved more liberally when the committee had experienced extensive civil rights activity and when the school had an aggressive principal. The biracial committee could be an illustration of this same process—external pressure can push teachers to change their behavior.

The third line of the table shows that effective biracial committees are associated with a smaller percentage of black students who feel they do not belong in the school. Similarly, black students in these schools more often say that school rules are fair and that they like school (lines four and five). These results seem reasonable—black students should feel more comfortable when their interests are represented, and they should view the rules as more just when they have an opportunity to appeal decisions or to protest unfairly administered rules. These things together should make it easier for black students to like school.

Table 4-3. Student attitudes and amount of tension in schools where teachers say the student biracial committee is effective.

	Teachers Rate Effectiveness of Student Biracial Committee	
	Low	High
Percentage of White Students Who Say Their Teacher Likes Desegregation	12[a]	17[a]
Percentage of Black Students Who Say Their Teacher Likes Desegregation	15	21
Percentage of Black Students Who Feel They Do Not Belong	36	28
Percentage of Black Students Who Feel School Rules Are Fair	45	50
Percentage of Black Students Who Like School	41	49
Percentage of Multiple Respondents Saying Racial Tension Is High	52[a]	35[a]

[a] $p < .05$.

Note: Schools matched on racial composition of school and neighborhood, duration of desegregation, school size, region, community urbanism and educational level, and black and white student socioeconomic status.

The final line of Table 4–3 shows that there is considerably less racial tension in schools with an effective biracial committee.[1] A biracial committee may reduce tension by training moderate students to fill a political vacuum otherwise available to rabble-rousers. Normally, a racial incident will be greeted with silence until the least inhibited students—the militants of the left and the right—speak up. Militants are likely to make things more tense, not less. The effective student biracial committee, however, will have been quietly training student moderates to deal with racial issues. When the time comes,

---

[1]The difference is substantial, and one should probably not conclude that a biracial committee is as effective as this in reducing racial tension. The reason why the difference is so great may be that in a school with tension the teachers will not credit the biracial committee. Even though the situation might be far worse if the biracial committee were not there, teachers will still be reluctant to give the committee high marks in a situation where things are going badly. Thus, it is not so much that the absence of an effective biracial committee allows increased tension as it is that high tension makes any biracial committee look bad.

they too will speak up, giving liberal students, both black and white, a position to support.

Positive effects are also associated with high black student ratings of the biracial committee (data not shown). Black students like school better and consider the rules fair in schools with well-regarded committees. Racial tension is lower, and black students report more contact with whites and have more favorable racial attitudes.[2] White student results show a similar pattern. Whites like school, are more apt to say the rules are fair, express less racial prejudice, and report slightly more friendly contact with blacks. Finally, racial tension is lower.[3]

Encouraging students to share in the responsibility for successful integration is sound policy. High school students will get involved whether they are asked or not. It makes much more sense to tap their energy and channel it in productive directions; our data indicate that doing so can pay off in better race relations and student satisfaction with school.

Only about a quarter of the black students and less than a fifth of the white students said that their school had an effective biracial committee. Why such low percentages? In addition, most schools treat race relations as a salient issue only during periods of unrest. Unless the biracial committee has had ample opportunity to develop its skills during the quiet times, it is unlikely to be effective in time of crisis.

MINORITY HISTORY/KNOWLEDGE OF THE BLACK EXPERIENCE

Having looked at three strategies which seem effective in improving race relations, let us now look at one which does seem to work as well. The principal was asked whether there was a minority history

[2] A logical problem arises in interpreting these data. It may simply be that prointegration black students who have more contact with whites will praise biracial committees more highly. thus, these findings should not be taken as firm evidence that the biracial committee has created more positive black attitudes.

[3] Again, the results seem slightly suspect—they may merely reflect more generous white attitudes about both blacks and biracial committees rather than a genuine impact of the committee on students. Nevertheless, the solid consistency of all these data, coupled with the variety of different positive effects, is a strong indication that the biracial committee is an important tool.

class and, if so, how long it had been offered. Table 4–4 compares schools which had no course to schools which had offered a course for two or more years. (This was done on the supposition that the classes might be more effective once they had gotten past the first year's start-up problems.) The data of Table 4–4 offer little support for the merits of minority group history courses. Black student attitudes toward integration are more negative in schools that teach minority history, and schools which have had the classes for two years or more have black students who report less contact with whites. Finally, black achievement test scores are no higher in the schools which have minority history. The effects of minority history classes on white students are generally weak and inconsistent.

There are several possible reasons why minority history classes might fail to prove helpful. First, it seems probable that many schools have implemented such classes halfheartedly. Classes set up over-night on a shoestring budget are unlikely to have much of an impact. Another problem with separate minority history classes is their separateness. Catering to black students' racial interests may raise group pride but will probably not further racial integration. Proponents of minority culture classes have argued that black racial pride is a prerequisite for dealing with whites on an equal basis and thus a

Table 4-4. Black student attitudes and achievement in schools with minority culture classes

	Minority Group History or Culture Class	
	No Course	A Course in Its Second or Later Year
Percentage of Black Students With Favorable Racial Attitudes	66%[a]	58%[a]
Percentage of Black Students Reporting Friendly Interracial Contact	55%	48%
Mean Black Achievement	344	347

[a] $p < .05$.

Note: Schools matched on racial composition of school and neighborhood, duration of desegregation, school size, region, community urbanism and educational level, and black and white student socioeconomic status.

prerequisite for successful integration. That argument is not convincing.

Additionally, minority history as an addendum to the regular curriculum is in itself not very supportive of the concept of racial equality. Forehand and Ragosta (1976) make a convincing argument for the multi-ethnic curriculum. They argue, however, that merely having black history materials in the building is insufficient to insure that the curriculum will be truly racially integrated. The history of the black experience in America should be taught as part of American history. This approach also increases the likelihood of staff and students' taking the subject seriously.

Finally, the most important problem with a separate black history course as an elective is that white students will not take it—at least no white students will take it except the handful who have the least to gain from doing so. The implied lesson—that black history is not so important that whites have to learn it—is part of the lesson of separatism which works not only against an integrated curriculum but also against an integrated school community.

Our data also support the other side of this coin; it not only argues against a separate minority history class but also argues in favor of minority history as part of the regular curriculum. In order to examine the impact of teaching the history of the black experience in America to students, we constructed the brief test that follows.

> Here is a list of people. In each case, mark whether the person was white or black. If you don't know, mark "Don't know."
>
> 1. John Wilkes Booth
> 2. Harriet Tubman
> 3. Booker T. Washington
> 4. F. Scott Fitzgerald
> 5. Nat Turner
>
> 6. Which of the following was a scientist?
>   a. Booker T. Washington
>   b. George Washington Carver
>   c. Paul Lawrence Dunbar
>
> 7. Ralph Bunche was—
>   a. A civil rights leader
>   b. A U.S. Congressman
>   c. A United Nations official

The items are not easy for high school sophomores. Fitzgerald is normally not taught this early in the curriculum, and only a third of our black students identified him correctly as white. While only a quarter of the white students knew that Harriet Tubman was black, over half the black students did, which indicates that black history is being taught to some students. Over half (55%) of whites and slightly more blacks (61%) correctly identified Carver as a scientist. The question about Ralph Bunche would normally be considered too difficult for high school students. This questionnaire was administered only a few months after Bunche's death, however, so it seems reasonable to expect an integrated high school to have acknowledged such an important American. In fact this is not the case—only 21 percent of both whites and blacks identified Bunche as a United Nations official; they would have done better by blind guessing.

Table 4–5 shows the relationship between the average score of the black students in the school and black student attitudes. Since we want to be sure that we are talking about the effects of black knowledge and not merely the effects of general intellectual sophistication, we have statistically controlled on the average

Table 4-5. Black student attitudes in schools where black students score well on a test of knowledge of black leaders.

	Black Students' Score on Black Knowledge Scale	
	Low	High
Percentage of Black Students Who Feel They Do Not Belong	38[a]	27[a]
Percentage of Black Students Who Say Their Teacher Favors Desegregation	16	20
Percentage of Black Students Who Say They Like School	44	47
Percentage of Black Students Who Feel School Rules Are Fair	49	45
Percentage of Black Students with High Academic Self-Esteem	48	53

[a] $p < .05$.

Note: Schools matched on racial composition of school and neighborhood, duration of desegregation, school size, region, community urbanism and educational level, black and white student socioeconomic status, and black achievement test scores.

achievement level of the black students of the school in addition to our usual controls for social class, racial composition, and type of community. In this way we can say that a black studies effect is not simply a disguised achievement effect.

Three patterns are evident in Table 4–5. First, a high level of black knowledge sharply increases the chances that the black student will feel a part of the school—hence the drop in the percentage saying they don't belong. However, these students tend to rate the teaching staff as only slightly more favorable to desegregation, like school only slightly more, and are less apt to say the rules are fair. The results are not unreasonable; black history is a history of protest, school rules provide an obvious target, and why not learn to protest about school rules while studying black history?

To our way of thinking, the most important of all these results is the apparent effect of black history on black student academic self-esteem (last line). While not large, the effect is precisely as predicted by the supporters of black history. Students who study their heritage learn to realize its worth and think more highly of blacks in general and of themselves in particular. This favorable self-opinion extends to feelings of academic competence. Proponents of black history have argued that studying black history will build the kind of academic self-confidence that will enable students to set higher educational goals. Schools that have taken that message seriously have apparently motivated more black students to attend college. Our data indicate that a high mean on the black knowledge score is associated with a higher percentage of black sophomores with college aspirations, again controlling on achievement (data not shown).

Two Programs With Inconsistent Effects

One practice which should be helpful, but seemingly is not, is that of assuring the open discussion of racial issues. Many schools wrongly pretend to ignore the question of race. We know principals of newly desegregated schools who have great difficulty using black and white as if it were somehow wrong to admit that the students in the school came in two colors. If everyone in the school in fact did not notice color it would be one thing. It is quite another when everyone notices but no one can talk about it. It came as no surprise to us that only one-fifth of the students said that discussions about race relations occurred in their classes as often as once a month. What did surprise us was how little difference it made whether or not race was discussed.

Table 4–6 shows the apparent effect of classroom racial discussion on white students. First, we see that if the school has more discussion of race, white students are more likely to say that their teachers support desegregation. The difference is fairly strong. In the second line we see that white students have somewhat more favorable racial attitudes in schools where there is more discussion. Similarly, in the third line we find white students in these schools report slightly more contact with black students.

In some ways the last line in Table 4–6 is the most important. In schools that have more discussions of race, white students are more likely to say that they have talked with teachers about personal matters. This makes sense—these schools are probably more informal generally and place more emphasis on good teacher-student relations.

What makes these results for whites intriguing is their contrast

Table 4-6. White student attitudes and behavior in schools where classroom discussions of race are frequent.

	Frequency of Classroom Intergroup Discussions	
	Low	High
Percentage of White Students Saying Their Teacher Likes Desegregation	11[a]	18[a]
Percentage of White Students with Favorable Racial Attitudes	34	40
Percentage of White Students Reporting Friendly Interracial Contact	32	37
Percentage of White Students Saying They Have Talked with Teachers about Nonacademic Matters	60	67

[a] $p < .05$.

Note: Schools matched on racial composition of school and neighborhood, duration of desegregation, school size, region, community urbanism and educational level, and black and white student socioeconomic status.

with the apparent effect of racial discussions on black students in Table 4–7. Increased discussion leads to only a slight tendency for blacks to say that their staff is more sympathetic to desegregation, and black students in schools with high levels of class discussion have less favorable racial attitudes and lower self-esteem. The data are not shown, but there is no tendency for black students to say that they talk more to teachers about personal matters.

The bottom line of Table 4–7 raises a frightening but not illogical possibility—lower black achievement test performance in schools where racial discussions are frequent. If students in these schools do have lower self-esteem and slightly less favorable attitudes about school integration, their motivation may suffer, and they may have more difficulty performing on an achievement test. Frankly, the result seems a bit implausible, but the difference (16 SAT points) is large enough that we are reluctant to ignore it.

Let us consider one last surprising result which is another school characteristic that one would expect to lead to a better school experience for blacks but does not. Surely, a good school should make sure that the student leadership includes minority students. One would expect such an effort to be very important. In fact, it makes relatively little difference. We asked each principal if the

Table 4-7. Black student attitudes and achievement in schools where classroom discussions of race are frequent.

	Frequency of Classroom Intergroup Discussions	
	Low	High
Percentage of Black Students Saying Their Teacher Likes Desegregation	17%	19%
Percentage of Black Students with Favorable Racial Attitudes	64%	59%
Percentage of Black Students with High Academic Self-Esteem	56%[a]	46%[a]
Mean Black Achievement	354[a]	338[a]

[a] $p < .05$.

Note: Schools matched on racial composition of school and neighborhood, duration of desegregation, school size, region, community urbanism and educational level, and black and white student socioeconomic status.

school's student government included both blacks and whites and if the cheerleading team was integrated. Comparing schools where the students leadership was and was not integrated, we found few differences.

Why Good Intentions Fail: A Speculation

We have seen three apparently sensible efforts a school might undertake—a black history class, frequent discussion of race in the classroom, and desegregating the school's student elite—that seem to accomplish little. Why do such well-intentioned efforts not work as expected? We do not know. The best we can do is offer an argument which we cannot prove but may be worth considering.

We think that there are many schools which seem to be good high schools but are not and which we will call "mainstream" schools. They are schools where students are treated decently, where staff-student relationships are reasonably good, where the classes are taught well, and where students have an opportunity to achieve. Students who can perform reasonably well, both academically and socially, will do well and be fairly happy in these schools. Some white students do not perform this well, and they form a sort of "underclass" which causes some trouble but which mainly tolerates (and is tolerated by) the school. The problem is that many black students do not fit into this sort of mainstream school. They arrive considerably behind in achievement test performance, are often frightened (although the fright may be masked by a good deal of bravado), and are usually badly outnumbered. Simply providing the opportunity to succeed will benefit only a small number of very bright, socially skilled black students who will be accepted into the elite positions in the mainstream of the school. While they are occupying positions of leadership and giving the appearance of good race relations, the majority of black students will be left in the cold.

The comments of our own interviews may illustrate this mainstream bias. The person in charge of each site visit was a professional interviewer, usually a college-educated woman, whose own children were of high school age or older. She spent only a few hours in each school, making arrangements with the school secretary, visiting classrooms to administer questionnaires, and interviewing the principal. When she had completed work in a particular school, she filled out a brief form which included the question, "Would you send your own child to this school?" If the responses to this question are any indication, the difference between a good school and a bad school is readily apparent. There was no way for the observer to know what the students had written on their questionnaires. Nevertheless, in schools to which the observers said they would send their children, only 11 percent of the white students said school staff did not support desegregation. In schools the observers did not like, the percentage was 18. This difference is after schools are matched, as always, on student and community characteristics. The schools which the observer liked also had white students who had higher self-esteem and said they liked school. These differences are shown in Table 4–8.

One can walk into a school and immediately sense the ambience or feeling tone of the place. It is the sort of thing that Garlie Forehand referred to in the memorandum which opens this book—a buzz of conversation in the hall which is neither inhibited nor rowdy, the tiny expressions of respect shown by teachers and students, and so forth. Good schools have good vibes.

The schools the observers liked are also distinguished by a second characteristic—they do not have more favorable black student responses. Black students in these schools do say that their teachers

Table 4-8.   White student attitudes in schools which observer did or did not like.

	Observer Would Send Own Child to This School	
	No	Yes
Percentage of White Students Who Say They Like School	50	57
Percentage of White Students with High Academic Self-Esteem	39	44
Percentage of White Students Who Say Their Teacher Likes Desegregation	82[a]	89[a]

[a] $p < .05$.

Note: Schools matched on racial composition of school and neighborhood, duration of desegregation, school size, region, community urbanism and educational level, and black and white student socioeconomic status.

like desegregation and that they often talk personally to them, but they do not particularly like the schools, feel the rules are especially fair, have more contact with whites, or have more positive racial attitudes.

We cannot prove our contention, but we suspect that the schools which appealed to our observers were racially liberal, high quality mainstream schools. Such schools provide equality of opportunity but only for those whom we are calling mainstream students—the students, both black and white, who can perform reasonably well in the school setting. In a newly integrated school, however, both whites and blacks bring a history of racial antagonism. Additionally, large numbers of students, white as well as black, are frustrated daily by their inability to cope with the demands of the school. It is not enough for a newly integrated school to be merely a mainstream school. This would also explain why integrating the school's student council and its cheerleaders accomplishes so little. Cheerleaders and student government officers are part of the school's elite—usually good students, usually middle class and always popular—that wonderful characteristic that some teenagers have and so many others do not. It is important that the school's elite be integrated, but we should not exaggerate the degree to which the mass of students will be impressed by this token integration.

The same reasoning explains why classroom discussion of race seems ineffective. There is a difference between what is said in classroom discussion and what happens in classroom discussion. However liberal the words, the actions may convey something different. Classroom discussions of race, like most classroom discussions, probably are dominated by the more articulate students and by the teachers' favorites. These favorites are students who do well in course work, are well behaved, and represent the school's better students. They will primarily by white students with perhaps a few of the more aggressive blacks joining in the debate. In other words, discussions about race become simply another opportunity for a few students to dominate the classroom. The average students, both white and black, are being put down and would probably be better off if there were no classroom discussion at all.

Another way to phrase our argument is to say that the unsuccessful strategies are unstructured strategies. The few students who can take advantage of a loose structure will do so, but the rest will be left out.

The black male student with below average grades will not regard the election of a bright popular black girl as having any relevance to him. He is not likely to learn the complex message contained in the assigned readings in a black history course, and he will probably not learn very much from a casual classroom discussion of race. The finding that minority students have more negative attitudes in schools where there is more frequent discussion of race may be because of these schools have less structure. Group discussions of race frequently do not proceed past the superficial and consequently cannot penetrate the tough veneer of prejudiced white comments and militant black opinions. The result is a discussion limited to half-truths and to unresolved conflict.

In short, these unstructured, elitist programs ignore the class and ability divisions in the school and assume that students can behave like adults in dealing with race, rather than like adolescents. They also assume a high level of cognitive ability and objectivity on the part of students. Race relations is not an elective class for honors students. Everyone who enters a desegregated school automatically signs up for the course.

In summary, there are three points to be made. First, appearances can be deceiving. The school which appears to be making a conscientious effort to make desegregation work may in fact not be succeeding at all. Second, one must be concerned with the mass of students and not merely with the student elite. Good race relations among the elite do not necessarily mean good relations among the other students in the school. Finally, one cannot achieve successful desegregation with a simplistic approach which says that students, given the opportunity to express their feelings and work things out, will in fact work things out. The white and black students are not entering school on an equal footing—the whites are better students, usually in the majority, and represent the dominant group in the United States; the school itself is likely to have been white before desegregation. In this situation, simply providing unstructured egalitarianism is an invitation to chaos.

Thinking about things this way gives one a new insight into the problems of racial tension. Racial tension often seems to occur in schools which do not deserve trouble—schools where the staff are well-meaning liberals and the white students sympathetic to racial equality. The problem is that these schools only look like good schools when viewed with a mainstream bias. Bright students do well in these schools, but without a formal organized curriculum to help deal with racial issues the average student will suffer.

Does this mean schools should avoid the race issue? We do not know but we do not think so. We think that schools must teach race relations, but that occasional casual discussions, no matter how well-intended, are no substitute for a real curriculum. Desegregation only works when good intentions are implemented as they are in City High by a carefully orchestrated school program which creates situations in which blacks and whites are on truly equal footing and in which the mass of students is directly involved. Every school will have to find its own particular approach. Whatever approach is used, it should involve four elements:

1. Activities must not be couched in the abstract academic style that high schools normally use; race relations are not taught with graded homework assignments and essay competitions.
2. Students must be involved actively, not passively, in intergroup activities. They must be given help in the hands-on experience they receive each day in the school. Students learn best by actively participating in learning.
3. The lessons of good race relations must be learned with real examples. Dealing with race means dealing with contemporary and close to home issues that directly concern students. Unless the rules of good race relations are applied unhypocritically to the school's own problems, students will not believe that intergroup harmony is serious school goal.
4. A desire for good race relations is a value, and it is a value that schools should encourage students to adopt. This means that the school must commit itself in favor of integration. A desegregated school can no more be neutral or dispassionate on the value of desegregation than it can be on the value of education itself. Brotherhood must be sold using an ideological appeal which communicates to all students.

This is speculation, and it could be wrong. The only thing that is certain from these data is that merely well-intentioned programs do not work in teaching race relations, just as they do not work in teaching other subjects. One reason why we think our approach makes sense is that in the next section we see one example of a curriculum that is effective in promoting prointegration values among black students. This curriculum is a powerful one which effectively reaches the mass of black students.

THE LESSONS OF THE CIVIL RIGHTS MOVEMENT

All of us learn by doing and by example. This is true for the teaching of values as it is for the teaching of mathematics and is the reason why parents desperately say, "Don't do as I do, do as I say," knowing full well that such admonitions are futile.

For as long as anyone has bothered to notice, blacks have supported integration. No group ever naturally wants to associate with another. Such a response much be learned in opposition to the universal human desire for exclusiveness. The desirability of school integration was a lesson taught in the streets. The civil rights movement taught blacks a great deal. It taught them what they wanted—equality—and the means to get it—integration. It taught them that white schools were better than black schools and that by striving they could gain entrance to them. It taught them that blacks could be courageous and face the police and the nightriders unarmed.

The civil rights movement also provided a constructive outlet for the aggression that had built up as a result of centuries of mistreatment. For four decades black and white psychologists and anthropologists have written about the black need to express aggression. (The best known of these books is *Black Rage* [1968] by Grier and Cobbs.) Research psychologists from Johns Hopkins have shown that when mass civil rights activities occurred in southern towns, the number of physical attacks by blacks on other blacks declined sharply (Solomon et al. 1965).

The same pattern should surface when we look at the effects of civil rights activities on black high school students. A high level of civil rights activity should increase black student support for school desegregation as well as pride in its accomplishment. Civil rights activity and community opposition to desegregation should increase the value which black students attach to desegregation. (The general principle that goals which are difficult to reach are more highly prized has been demonstrated in laboratory experiments. Examples from everyday life abound. The fraternity member who has been hazed must either believe that joining the fraternity was a wise decision or admit he was stupid to undergo hazing. Hence, the more severe the hazing when pledging the fraternity, the greater the appreciation for the fraternity once admitted.)

In each community where our high schools were located, four community leaders were asked about civil rights activity, about superintendent and school board support for desegregation, and about community opposition. In some communities the school board supported desegregation, and there was little organized opposition. In others desegregation met with more resistance and, as Table 4–9 shows, it is in these cases that black students are more supportive of desegregation, more interested in associating with whites, and more in favor of attending desegregated schools (line 1). Attitudes apparently translate to action—communities with the greatest amount of opposition to desegregation now have black students who report the greatest amount of contact with whites (line 2). Finally, the same communities have a larger number of black students who say they are happy (line 3). We saw earlier that black happiness is very much a racial attitude—an overall sense of well-being is very much tied up with how one feels about being black and how one gauges the chances for success in a white man's world.

Table 4–10 shows the effects of a factor related to community

Table 4-9. Black student attitudes, by amount of civil rights activity in community.

| | Community Resistance to Desegregation | |
	Low	High
Percentage of Black Students with Favorable Racial Attitudes	56[a]	68[a]
Percentage of Black Students Who Report Friendly Interracial Contact	47	54
Percentage of Black Students Who Say They Are Happy	59	67

[a] $p < .05$.

Note: Schools matched on racial composition of school and neighborhood, duration of desegregation, school size, region, community urbanism and educational level, and black and white student socioeconomic status.

resistance, the amount of civil rights activity. Two of the results mesh with Table 4–9. The greater the amount of civil rights activity in the community, the more apt black students are to say they like school and to have higher academic self-esteem. While the results may seem intuitively unreasonable, they agree quite well with psychological and sociological theory. A person who feels good about one aspect of himself will tend to feel good about other aspects, so it is not surprising that academic self-esteem should be high when racial pride is high. Additionally, research on the theory of cognitive dissonance leads us to expect that the more obstacles put in the path of desegregation, the more strongly students will endorse desegregation and want to make it work. Finally, researchers studying the race riots of the 1960s noted their seeming cathartic effect so that most communities had exactly one riot; once the riot had occurred, the community was in effect immunized.

This helps us understand why schools which had great difficulty in initial desegregation often turn into superior schools later. For example, the *New York Times* (Sept. 8, 1976, p. 1) marked the twentieth anniversary of the bitter racial conflict at Little Rock Central High School by noting that the school has since become an outstanding example of good race relations. We think the school owes its success in part to the awful controversy it experienced. Table 4–11 supports this line of reasoning. Civil rights activity, community opposition, and a reluctance of district leaders to support desegregation initially are all associated with early difficulties but with lower racial tension later.

Table 4-10. Black student attitudes, by amount of civil rights activity in community.

	Level of Civil Rights Activity	
	Low	*High*
Percentage of Black Students Who Say They Like School	40[a]	50[a]
Percentage of Black Students with High Academic Self-Esteem	47	55

[a] $p < .05$.

Note: Schools matched on racial composition of school and neighborhood, duration of desegregation, school size, region, community urbanism and educational level, and black and white student socioeconomic status.

Table 4-11.   Level of racial tension, by three measures of community conflict over desegregation.

		Percentage Saying Racial Tension Is High[a]
Level of Civil Rights Activity	Low	48
	High	40
Amount of Community Resistance to Desegregation	Low	47
	High	40
Amount of School Board Support for Desegregation	High	49[b]
	Low	39[b]

[a]Based on black and white students, teachers, and principal.
[b]$p < .05$.

Note: Schools matched on racial composition of school and neighborhood, duration of desegregation, school size, region, community urbanism and educational level, and black and white student socioeconomic status.

IMPLICATIONS

Four of the analyses described in this chapter have clear policy implications. The best southern desegregated schools provide staff in-service training, use human relations materials, have effective student biracial committees, and incorporate black history into the school curriculum. All these activities require considerable leadership from the principal. Good in-service programs require a great deal of preparation, beginning with convincing the staff that an in-service program on race is important. Selection and use of special human relations materials requires a school-wide effort. The school needs to make sure that its human relations efforts are not undercut by a lack of support and reinforcement from the staff.

The principal will also have to work hard on the selection of a student biracial committee so that elements of a democratic process are combined with a selection procedure that guarantees that the committee includes a genuine cross-section of students rather than just the obvious student leaders. The elite represent only the elite and not the vocational students, the future dropouts. These students need to be heard too, and they need to have their rights protected just like everyone else. The biracial committee will need training perhaps through a series of special workshops. It will also take leadership to convey to students and faculty that the biracial committee must be taken seriously. Staff biases should not determine the fate of the committee's recommendations. The principal and faculty will have to lose some battles with the committee without losing their tempers in the process.

Incorporating minority history into the curriculum will also require leadership. The principal must prepare for the possibility of the history faculty's complaining about the additional work and about corrupting the classical curriculum for political reasons. The English and science faculty may also object when they realize that teaching the black experience means including black contributions in literature and science.

It is easy to make a school appear to be racially liberal. One can make sure that the pleasant, well-spoken, and studious black football player is included in the student council or that a light-complexioned girl who is popular with the white leadership, whose family is not too poor, and whose grades are good is made a cheerleader or a student council vice-president. This accomplishes little in itself. Bringing in human relations trainers to work with staff, incorporating human relations literature into the curriculum, establishing an effective (and powerful) biracial student committee, and incorporating black history into the curriculum are ways of reaching beyond the elite and the mainstream students and penetrating the entire student body.

One question remains. How can a school administration make the most of our finding that civil rights controversy contributes to an effective school? One is tempted to say that the school system cannot use controversy constructively—after all, what would the teachers union, the superintendent, the school board, and the community say?

Even if there seems to be no way for the school to organize a civil rights group without creating serious political problems for itself, let us consider the idea for a moment as a purely intellectual exercise to see what insights we can gain. Suppose that civil rights activity could be one of the worthwhile civic activities which the school sponsored just as it sponsored the Boy Scouts or held student-run conservation activities in celebration of Earth Week. Imagine a school-sponsored, rather conservative, civil rights group. We suspect a student group which limited its activities to fact finding and polite demonstrations for brotherhood could keep busy—there are usually some blatant examples of discrimination around, opposition to which would not be considered too controversial. We think the school would reap the benefits of such a group. First, it would focus a great deal of undirected aggression which might otherwise be aimed at the school. Second, endorsing desegregation as a school value presses both white and black students to support desegregation in their personal behavior.

Finally, it is not too unrealistic to look down the road to some future time when there might be considerable tension in the school. Then it would be a distinct advantage to have a moderate, sensible, and experienced civil rights group on hand. Without a moderate civil rights group, the school will find itself pressured to provide an open forum for militant groups on both sides. By giving these groups a forum, the school endorses radicalism and, in a very real sense, teaches radicalism. We suspect that a number of colleges lived through the 1960s by doing exactly the opposite—by encouraging the more tolerable opponents of the system in order to head off the less tolerable groups waiting in the wings. Instead of radicalism, these schools taught a reasonable and tempered American ideology.

This leads us to think that if a student civil rights group were politically possible, the school would derive some benefits from it. Some schools have organized such a group as an unofficial school activity, staffed by a teacher volunteering time after school. There are also some other possible applications for this idea. In some respects the school biracial committee is a kind of civil rights group. The group of black students who organize to protest some school policy can also be thought of as a civil rights organization. Biracial student groups who do service work in the community are a testimony to effective desegregation. In each of these cases the school has the opportunity to build student commitment to desegregation and to use these groups as an advertisement to the other students in the school that desegregation is valued and is worth fighting for. Students must be involved in the process of creating desegregation before they will value it enough to try to make it work.

APPENDIX 4A

Chapter 4 dealt with three major topics: the theory of "mainstream" schools, the effectiveness of various human relations activities, and the long-term effects of controversy over desegregation. This appendix reports some of the technical details of each of these analyses.

MAINSTREAM SCHOOLS, OBSERVER PERCEPTIONS, AND CLASSROOM DISCUSSION OF RACE

The reader will recognize our hypothesized mainstream bias of schools as being similar to what other researchers have called the middle class bias of schools. We do not believe that this bias is fundamentally class based. While social class and conforming behavior are correlated, they are not correlated so highly as to be synonymous; many students from working class backgrounds are good students who conform to the school rules and are popular and successful at school while many middle class students develop behavior problems and fall outside the mainstream of the school.

The senior staff person visiting each school was asked two questions: "If you had a child of the age of any of the children in this school, is this the kind of school you would like a child of yours to attend?" (The possible responses: I'd like it very much/I wouldn't mind, but I wouldn't be thrilled/I would not like it/I would not allow a child of mine to attend this school) and "Just your personal opinion—do you feel that the principal of this school is the kind of person you would like to have as a supervisor?" (The choice of responses: definitely would/probably would/probably wouldn't/definitely wouldn't). Both questions showed a similar pattern, correlating with white student responses but not with black. Although most of the staff responding were white, there is little correlation between their responses and the racial composition of the school. The equations linking observer opinion to white student attitudes are shown in Table 4A–1. The strongest relationship is between observer opinion and white student perception of staff racial attitudes, but this may be an artifact of the data collection: A large

Table 4A-1. Regression equations with standardized regression coefficients (betas) used to construct Table 4-8.

	White Students Like School	High White Self-Esteem	Whites Say Staff Favors Desegregation
Independent Variables:			
Mean White SES	-.093	.448[a]	.037
Mean Black SES	-.194	-.008	-.060
Black Students from Black Elementary/Junior High	.006	-.033	.009
White Students from Integrated Elementary/Junior High	.097	-.002	.162
High School in Black Neighborhood	-.025	-.001	.176
School Size	-.088	-.143	-.045
Region	-.117	.172	.235[a]
Community Educational Level	.002	.068	.128
Urbanism of County	.205	.042	.121
School Percentage White	.106	-.272[a]	-.123
Observer Rates School Highly	.187	.152	.237[a]
r^2	.112	.257	.289

[a] $p < .05$.

part of the observer's information about the school came from the principal's interview, which dealt heavily with his racial attitudes.

Since the observers do not favor white schools and do prefer schools with liberal staffs, the failure of the observer evaluation to correlate with black attitudes cannot be attributed to simple racial bias—which is why we think that a mainstream bias must be postulated. A school with a mainstream bias is one which provides unusually good educational and social opportunities to those black and white students who have sufficient intellectual and social prowess to take advantage of them. These opportunities are not constructed at the expense of the nonmainstream students; we do not have to hypothesize that it is necessary to make the plight of nonmainstream students objectively worse in order to make mainstream students happier. However, it may well be that the very act of providing a more attractive and rewarding educational environment for mainstream students will automatically subject nonmainstream students to relative deprivation. A strong student council which may be very effective in establishing good race relations within the school elite may simultaneously serve to alienate nonelite students. A school which provides opportunities for student self-expression and participatory democracy may in fact be providing mainstream students with the power to dominate the nonmainstream students. This may appear in our data as a racial bias in the school but only because nonmainstream students are considerably more likely to be black.

Table 4A–2 shows the equations relating student reports of classroom discussion of race to student attitudes and racial behavior. The independent variable is the response to "How often do you have class discussions about intergroup relations?" Twenty percent of whites and 23 percent of blacks say that discussions occur at least once per month. The general pattern shown here—positive correlations with white student attitudes and negative correlations with black attitudes—holds for a number of dependent variables in addition to those shown in the table. One alternative explanation is that the causal ordering is in the opposite direction; there is more classroom discussion when there is more tension and black students have more hostile attitudes toward whites or when blacks are more aggressive in raising racial issues. Our data do not permit us to test this hypothesis directly. However, discussion is not highly correlated with the presence of racial tension, and a tension hypothesis would predict worse racial attitudes for both whites and blacks.

A second alternative hypothesis is that classroom discussion is a liberating or consciousness-raising experience for blacks. Chapter 2 demonstrated that residing in the upper South and having higher family status are both related to stronger antiwhite attitudes and that these were indicators that such students had more freedom to express their feelings. If classroom discussion of race is a liberating force, why is it negatively related to self-esteem? Thus we think our mainstream bias hypothesis—that classroom discussion is an elite-dominated activity—is the only one that fits the data.

Table 4A–2. Regression equations with standardized coefficients (betas) used to construct Tables 4-6 and 4-7.

Independent Variables:	White Student Responses				Black Student Responses			
	Staff Likes Deseg- regation	Racial Attitudes	Racial Contact	Talk to Staff	Staff Likes Deseg- regation	Racial Attitude	Self- Esteem	Achievement Test Score
Mean White SES	.011	.099	-.053	.032	.151	.041	.034	.285[a]
Mean Black SES	-.073	.002	.060	-.176	-.137	-.073	.331[a]	.515[a]
Black Students from Black Elementary/Junior High	-.020	-.033	.000	.043	.185	.051	.083	-.130
White Students from Integrated Elementary/Junior High	.127	-.011	.121	.140	.074	.172	.089	.088
High School in Black Neighborhood	.158	.074	.052	-.045	.135	.049	.017	.101
School Size	-.051	.047	.156	.174	.058	.157	-.101	.044
Region	.236[a]	.209[a]	.249[a]	.000	.110	-.079	.005	.131
Community Educational Level	.116	-.035	.009	.199	.150	-.105	.123	-.217[a]
Urbanism of County	.154	.349[a]	.319[a]	-.065	-.008	.053	-.030	-.120
School Percentage White	-.033	.108	-.259[a]	-.045	-.182	-.058	-.152	-.019
Frequent Classroom Intergroup Discussions (White report)	.219[a]	.141	.123	.197[a]				
(Black report)					.039	-.116	-.253[a]	
r^2	.280	.354	.463	.161	.147	.075	.185	.472

[a] $p < .05$.

158

HUMAN RELATIONS LITERATURE, STAFF IN-SERVICE WORK

Table 4A–3 shows the impact of human relations literature and in-service programs for teachers on white and black student attitudes. The independent variables come from the principal's interview: He was asked, "During [this] school year, did this school receive any human or community relations literature? How about last year?" The principal was also shown a list of school programs, one of which was "programs to improve intergroup relations among teachers," and asked whether the school had such a program in the past two years. In both cases, the variable was coded 0 if not present, 1 if available for one year, and 2 if available for both years. The statistics given in Tables 4–4 and 4–5 in Chapter 4 show the apparent effect of having the program or materials supplied in both years as opposed to not having them at all.

As might be expected, the effects are stronger for blacks than whites; the strongest effect for whites is that which human relations literature has on their perception of the staff's racial attitudes. Whatever the staff's real attitudes may be, the fact that they use human relations literature should give the impression that they support integration. The use of human relations materials and in-service training for staff are not the sort of activities which create a mainstream bias. Well-prepared literature would be aimed at the entire student body, not just the elite or the most articulate, and effective in-service training would increase the staff's ability to communicate with nonmainstream students.

STUDENT BIRACIAL COMMITTEES

Teachers were asked, "If you have a biracial student committee, how effective has the committee been in solving intergroup problems and making desegregation go smoothly?" The responses range from "Effective: it has helped," to "It has definitely been harmful," and "no such committee." In schools where there is a biracial committee, only 36 percent of our teachers say unequivocally that it has helped; the rest say it has helped at most a small amount. The variable used in our analysis is the percentage of teachers who say that the committee

Table 4A-3. Regression equations with standardized regression coefficients (betas) used to construct Tables 4-1 and 4-2.

Independent Variables:	Percentage Whites Saying:				Percentage Blacks Saying:			
	Staff Favors Deseg-regation	They Like School	School Rules Are Fair	Staff Favors Deseg-regation	Like School	School Rules Are Fair	Like School	Staff Favors Deseg-regation
Mean White SES	.056	-.081	.107	.181[a]	.050	.098	.028	.159
Mean Black SES	-.083	-.211	-.044	-.144	-.221[a]	-.078	-.219[a]	-.144
Black Students from Black Elementary/Junior School	-.010	-.007	-.126	.172[a]	-.001	-.129	-.004	.170
White Students from Integrated Elementary/Junior School	.163	.099	-.016	.060	-.058	-.036	-.022	.090
High School in Black Neighborhood	.175	-.026	.020	.137	.284[a]	.231[a]	.254[a]	.104
School Size	-.033	-.079	-.248[a]	.063	-.015	.019	-.020	.044
Region	.212[a]	-.132	.171	.061	—[b]	-.070	-.019	.093
Community Educational Level	.130	.006	.105	.117	.113	.035	.141	.144
Urbanism of County	.138	.223	.076	-.056	-.081	-.071	-.059	-.029
School Percentage White	-.078	.140	-.023	-.168	-.006	-.037	-.020	-.187
Number of Years of Human or Community Relations Literature								
Teacher Intergroup Relations Programs Offered Two or More Years	.150	.100	.081	.200[a]	.163	.155	.128	.147
r^2	.260	.091	.093	.176	.130	.077	.122	.165

[a] $p < .05$.
[b] Indicates variable did not enter equation. The variable was not used in computing the r^2 for the equation.

Table 4A–4. Regression equations with standardized regression coefficients (betas) used to construct Table 4-3.

Independent Variables:	Whites Say Staff Favors Deseg-regation	Blacks Say Staff Favors Deseg-regation	Blacks Feel They Do Not Belong	Blacks Say School Rules Are Fair	Black Students Like School	High Racial Tension
Mean White SES	.040	.164	-.026	.088	.037	.051
Mean Black SES	-.088	-.143	.200[a]	-.078	-.221[a]	.186[a]
Black Students from Black Elementary/ Junior High	.031	.205	-.040	-.100	.032	.003
White Students from Integrated Elementary/ Junior High	.202[a]	.094	-.162	-.006	-.011	-.065
High School in Black Neighborhood	.151	.120	-.249[a]	.214[a]	.263[a]	-.120
School Size	-.071	.031	-.051	-.013	-.043	.432[a]
Region	.264[a]	.126	-.040	-.016	.018	-.038
Community Educational Level	.182	.175	-.199	.085	.177	.403[a]
Urbanism of County	.161	-.018	-.026	-.043	-.052	-.362[a]
School Percentage White	-.074	-.182	.251[a]	-.047	-.015	-.301[a]
Teachers Rate Student Biracial Committee Highly	.161[a]	.137	-.168	.137	.177	-.267[a]
r^2	.267	.164	.233	.077	.137	.405

[a] $p < .05$.

was effective. This makes it difficult to make unequivocal causal interpretations of a positive correlation between the presence of an effective committee and, for example, less racial tension since one would expect a school with good race relations to have staff who would say that most school institutions were helping. Certainly, if race relations were very bad, one would not expect teachers to give the committee much praise. The teacher questionnaire contains many other items which, like this one, invite teachers to evaluate some school programs. Very frequently, positive evaluations of programs do not correlate with lower tension or better race relations, and the coefficients are never as large as those shown in Table 4A–4. In addition, black and white students were asked similar questions about the biracial committee, and their responses also correlated strongly with favorable student attitudes and lower racial tension (data now shown). All this coupled with the strong favorable evaluation of such student groups by Forehand and Ragosta (1976) leaves us convinced that biracial committees are valuable.

MINORITY HISTORY/KNOWLEDGE OF THE BLACK EXPERIENCE

Table 4A–5 shows the equations which relate presence of a minority history course and general black knowledge of important black figures in history to various dependent variables. The two independent variables work in generally opposite directions; a minority history course makes black racial attitudes worse while knowledge of black history increases sense of belonging and makes attitudes toward school more favorable. Knowledge of black history is strongly correlated with general peformance on the achievement test, so achievement has been added as a control variable in the black knowledge equations. Black knowledge is apparently not simply a surrogate for general achievement. In the case of feelings of belonging in the school and feeling that the rules are fair, black knowledge and general achievement work in opposite directions. General achievement is weakly correlated with attitudes toward school and perceptions of staff racial attitudes, both of which are correlated with black knowledge.

Table 4A-5. Regression equations with standardized regression coefficients (betas) used to construct Tables 4–4 and 4–5.

	Black Student Dependent Variables							
	Positive Racial Attitudes	High Racial Contact	Mean Achievement	Students Feel They Do Not Belong	Staff Favors Desegregation	Students Like School	School Rules Are Fair	High Self-Esteem
Independent Variables:								
Mean White SES	.045	-.101	.276[a]	-.007	.112	-.024	.039	-.105
Mean Black SES	-.094	-.139	.504[a]	.162	-.194	-.286[a]	-.154	.101
Black Students from Black Elementary/Junior High	.055	-.020	-.154	.024	.193	.026	-.075	.096
White Students from Integrated Elementary/Junior High	.146	.084	.078	-.153	.071	-.042	-.038	.040
High School in Black Neighborhood	.080	.138	.110	-.250[a]	.111	.257[a]	.216[a]	-.023
School Size	.202	.222	.028	-.078	.051	-.015	.013	-.129
Region	-.049	.079	.144	.001	.080	-.035	-.050	-.046
Community Educational Level	-.079	-.082	-.244[a]	-.088	.155	.168	.134	.156
Urbanism of County	.070	.148	-.102	-.052	.009	-.023	-.031	.053
School Percentage White	-.065	.428[a]	.000	.244[a]	-.181	-.016	-.055	-.122
Black Student Achievement	—	—	—	.164	.077	.126	.213	.359
Minority History for Two or More Years	-.202[a]	-.178[a]	.047					
Black Students Score High on Black Knowledge				-.237[a]	.089	.056	-.102	.132
r^2	.097	.294	.444	.243	.159	.123	.080	.236

[a] $p < .05$.

163

CIVIL RIGHTS ACTIVITY AND COMMUNITY RESISTANCE TO DESEGREGATION

In each community, four community leaders, balanced by race and sex, were contacted by phone and asked the following questions:

1. How much civil rights activity has there been in (name of city or county) in the past ten years? Would you say a great deal, a moderate amount, or relatively little?
2. In some communities civil rights activity has resulted in trouble—meaning either very bitter feelings or many arrests, violence on the part of police or demonstrators, or property damage. Has there been in your judgment a great deal of trouble here in the past decade, some trouble, or almost none?
3. What has been the public position of the school superintendent about desegregation? Has he generally strongly supported desegregation, mildly supported desegregation, avoided taking a stand, or been opposed to it?
4. What about the present school board members? Has the board as a whole strongly supported desegregation, mildly supported desegregation, been divided, avoided taking a stand, or been opposed to it?
5. Some southern school districts put up a great deal of resistance to desegregation by appealing decisions, making public statements, and so forth. Others made only token resistance. Thinking back over the past three or four years, would you say that compared to other southern school systems (name of school district) put up a great deal of resistance, a moderate amount, or relatively little resistance?
6. How have the local political leaders responded to the desegregation issue in the past few years? Did they strongly oppose desegregation, mildly oppose it, not take a stand, or did they support desegregation?
7. What about the white business leaders here? Did they strongly oppose desegregation, mildly oppose it, not take a stand, or did they support desegregation?
8. Would you say there was a great deal of organized white opposition to desegregation, a moderate amount, or relatively little?

The first two variables measure the amount and intensity of civil rights activity in the community; the next two measure the amount of school board and administration support for peaceful desegregation; and the last four measure the amount of community resistance to desegregation. The three scales correlate strongly with each other: The more the community resisted desegregation, the less the school leaders said about the virtues of peace and the more the civil rights movement demonstrated. No doubt the three variables work together with leadership timidity, community resistance, and civil rights activism each both a cause and an effect of the other two variables.

We assumed that peaceful desegregation was an unmixed blessing for a community. However, we can now see that this view was biased by our personal fondness for peace and quiet. A thoughtful reading of sociology and some of our own research would have led us to expect something different. Lewis Coser (1964; and before him, George Simmel 1955) argued forcefully that conflict has the effect of creating group solidarity. The experience of going through a tense confrontation should have welded the black population into a cohesive unit, reducing alienation, enhancing self-esteem, and building support for the subcommunity's norms and values (which include nonviolence and integration). Coser has also argued that conflict helps a community learn. In this case, he would argue that the difficult shift from segregation to integration as a social value is more easily done if it is assisted by ample opportunity to fight it out in the open. In a sense, segregation without conflict is a bit like changing presidents without an election: The change has less legitimacy, the people have not thought very much about it, and the losing side cannot retire feeling they have lost in a fair fight.

Coser also points out that conflict creates new coalitions. Desegregation in the South was not simply a black versus white issue. The white community was divided into liberals, moderates, conservatives, and the Klan, and the conflicts among these four groups were intense. Although the teachers in our survey do not appear as liberals in absolute terms, their views are certainly more liberal than those of their communities. Many teachers were likely to take offense at the outrageous behavior of the extremists in their community. If their school board and superintendent succumbed to political pressure and spoke out against desegregation, many teachers would be likely to be angry about this as well—if only because such statements would make teaching more difficult. All this would work to push teachers into taking more liberal views.

The net effect is that conflict may not only produce a shift in opinion within one of the sides and an increase in solidarity among those who agree with their group's position; it may also produce polarization as those who do not wholeheartedly agree with their group's position move away from the rest of the group. This sort of polarization appears in an unpublished survey by Crain (1969) of white attitudes toward desegregation. He found that in communities which had more controversy over desegregation, white opinion showed no shift in mean opinion but a higher amount of variability.

Finally, conflict has a cathartic effect. On both sides, a bitter controversy should have the effect of persuading some school people to work harder to prevent conflict from occurring again. Students might be afraid of renewed conflict, but some of their need to express aggression might be worked out vicariously in the memory of civil rights confrontation.

Taken together, all this leads us to predict that if a community has controversy over desegregation, the community will later have:

1. Teachers who are more favorable to desegregation.
2. Black students who are more prointegration.
3. Higher black self-esteem.
4. Less racial tension and hostility toward school.

These predictions agree with the regression equations shown in Table 4A–6 and with the finding (in the appendix of Chapter 3) that teachers in high-conflict communities were more accepting of desegregation.

Table 4A-6. Regression equations with standardized regression coefficients (betas) used to construct Tables 4-9, 4-10, and 4-11.

	Positive Black Racial Attitudes	High Black Racial Contact	Black Students Are Happy	Black Students Like School	High Black Self-Esteem	High Racial Tension	High Racial Tension	High Racial Tension
Independent Variables:								
Mean White SES	.070	-.090	.147	.049	.045	.050	.049	.042
Mean Black SES	-.093	-.135	.182	-.230[a]	.296	.190[a]	.186[a]	.199[a]
Black Students from Black Elementary/Junior High	-.016	-.065	-.053	.007	.050	.051	.069	.066
White Students from Integrated Elementary/Junior High	.205	.122	.176	-.006	.090	-.037	-.039	-.041
High School in Black Neighborhood	.009	.092	.078	.239[a]	.004	-.132	-.134	-.143
School Size	.171	.189	-.172	-.011	-.111	.371[a]	.364[a]	.346[a]
Region	-.147	.019	.012	-.108	-.054	.042	.021	-.003
Community Educational Level	-.024	-.065	.111	.164	.109	.434[a]	.407[a]	.470[a]
Urbanism of County	-.095	.056	-.104	-.145	-.086	-.327[a]	-.322[a]	-.357[a]
School Percentage White	-.073	.430[a]	-.029	-.030	-.139	-.275[a]	-.265[a]	-.236[a]
High Community Resistance to Desegregation	-.280[a]	-.153	-.199			-.119		
High Level of Civil Rights Activity				.245[a]	.203		-.102	
Low School Board and Administration Support for Desegregation								.165
r^2	.135	.283	.116	.145	.149	.348	.346	.362

[a] $p < .05$.

167

5 EXTRACURRICULAR ACTIVITIES

Many teachers and administrators see extracurricular activities as incidental to, if not in direct conflict with, the main purpose of the school. As something extra to the curriculum, they serve to pacify students and to garner parental support for bond issues. Our data show a different picture. It is no exaggeration to say that extracurricular activities seem to be the single most effective device the high school has for reducing alienation, improving race relations, boosting achievement scores, and even increasing the number of students going to college. This chapter documents these effects; it also shows that if a high school administrator had funds to add one additional teacher to the school and wanted to make the maximum improvement in the school, that administrator should probably hire either another gym teacher or a teacher specializing in the teaching of music, drama, or art.

The successful high school treats extracurricular activities not as a palliative but as an institutional resource, a way of effectively organizing students. Unfortunately, administrators do not learn organization tactics in schools of education. Schools of social work offer organizing as an area of concentration, schools of city planning teach the theory of neighborhood improvement groups, and urban

168

studies departments study the organizing tactics of the Poverty Program. Education is the one people-helping profession which does not understand the idea of organizing client groups to accomplish its end.

In this chapter we will compare schools which offer many opportunities for participation in extracurricular activities to schools that offer fewer. We will see that sports and clubs are not an unmixed blessing; there are some problems in high participation schools, especially for black students. Nevertheless, a well-run extracurricular activities program is one of the most effective educational tools a high school can have.

A school superintendent we know claims that the secret of successful desegregation is football. While we are inclined to be somewhat more conservative about the value of football, we can think of five reasons why extracurricular activities might help a school fulfil its mission. First, activities provide an alternative means of achievement for the many students who are not academically gifted. Without these other forms of achievement, the school winds up teaching most students how to fail rather than how to succeed. Second, extracurricular activities provide a tension release—a way of blowing off steam which is especially functional for students who find academics frustrating. Third, they provide nonacademic channels for students to establish relationships with teachers and for teachers to establish relationships with parents. Fourth, such organizations help establish a bond between students and school. Membership in the high school glee club is a way of being a member of the school. Fifth, the activities of extracurricular groups help define the school. School is not simply lectures, homework, and grades. It is also working with one's peers to make music, win track meets, bake casseroles, and honor academic achievement. Since these extra-academic activities are usually better known than the school's classroom activities, they play an important public relations role; they are the school's main form of advertising. There are two ways in which extracurricular activities can be harmful. They can work to reinforce the informal status structure in the student body by reserving the rewards of leadership for the students who are bright, middle class, popular, and white. At the same time, sports and clubs can become a way of labeling groups of students—blacks may participate in sports, for example, but be tagged as "dumb jocks" as a consequence.[1]

THE EXTENT OF EXTRACURRICULAR ACTIVITIES

Most students participate in extracurricular activities to at least a limited degree. In 1972 (the same year our survey was done) a national survey of high school seniors found that over a third (42%) had taken part in school athletics; a sixth (17%) were involved in cheerleading, team managing or other activities supporting the athletic teams; and a third (32%) had been active in expressive activities—music, art, or drama groups. Thus, while we are recommending increased extracurricular involvement, we are aware that participation rates are already fairly high (see Appendix 5A). In our study we asked each student, "Are you a member of any school clubs or sports teams?" Around 60 percent of the tenth graders in our sample said yes.

Racial bias in total school opportunity to participate does not appear to pose a serious problem.[2] Students of both races find it a bit more difficult to participate when they are in the minority in their school, but the differences are not very large. Sixty-five percent of white students participate in predominantly white schools compared to 58 percent in black schools; 61 percent of black students participate in predominantly black schools compared to 57 percent in predominantly white schools.[3]

Looking further into differences between black and white students, we found that black females have the lowest participation rates. Black female participation also varies more than black male

---

[1]This can undercut nearly all the benefits of the extracurricular program. If the football team is thought of as a group of dumb jocks, team members may feel that they have to live up to their reputation by publicly advertising their unwillingness to do school work. The same thing can happen to a segregated black club, which may develop a group image of being victims of the school rather than members of it. It is usually, but not always, the case that membership in a school group implies membership in the school as a whole.

[2]We do not have data on the degree of segregation in the school's activities.

[3]These are the participation rates after statistically correcting for differences between schools in student social status, region within the South, school size, and the urbanism and educational level of the community.

participation. We suspect that sports alone will guarantee a moderate amount of black male participation. The best test of a school's extracurricular program will be black female participation rates; they are likely to be quite low unless the school makes a conscientious effort. Schools with low and high participation rates show important differences. The most important difference is school size—more students participate in small schools. A high school with only 500 students typically involves two-thirds of its black students and three-quarters of its white students. A very large high school, on the other hand, involves only half of either group. One might expect lower participation in rural areas since students often live miles from school, but this is not the case: 65 percent of blacks and 71 percent of whites participate in rural schools, compared to 52 and 56 percent respectively in urban schools. Participation also varies by region; rates are higher in the deep South (62 percent for blacks, 71 percent for whites) than in border states (54 percent for blacks, 56 percent for whites).[4] Finally, low status schools have higher participation rates—mostly because low income schools tend to be located in the rural deep South.

If the backward schools of the rural deep South have higher participation, this implies a deemphasis on extracurricular activities in the more progressive schools of the urban border states. Extracurricular activities are old-fashioned, and the schools which provide the greatest opportunity to participate are those which cling to a traditional style of high school education. This would explain why high status urban schools (which usually lead in educational innovations) have lower participation rates. Schools in the North, being more progressive, should have less participation. The survey of high school seniors referred to earlier found lower participation rates in northern schools.

If extracurricular activities are unprogressive, participation rates should have declined in the last twenty years. We routinely hear of school districts cutting frills from their budgets either to save money or to focus more attention on basic skills. A comparison of the 1972 high school senior survey with a survey of the class of 1957 seems to indicate that participation rates have declined. For example, 57

---

[4]Unlike most other statistics given in this book, these participation figures are not for schools matched on other characteristics. This means, for example, that deep South schools have more participation partly because they are smaller.

percent of the 1957 seniors reported participating in drama or music; by 1972 the percentage had dropped to 32.[5]

THE EFFECTS OF EXTRACURRICULAR ACTIVITIES

There is a great deal of variation in extracurricular activity from one school to another, apparently because schools vary in the opportunities they provide for student participation. Ranking schools from the lowest level of participation to the highest, we find that schools in the bottom fifth typically involve about 44 percent of their white students while those in the top fifth involve 83 percent. Ranked by level of black participation, the bottom fifth of the schools involves 38 percent of the black students, compared to 78 percent for the top fifth. Even in the worst schools, nearly half of the students participate; a strong extracurricular program involves the hard-to-reach half as well.

In the tables that follow we will ask, "What is the impact of an extracurricular program which involves four-fifths of all the students rather than something less than half?" Of course, participation can be racially biased, so a school may have a high participation rate for one race but not for the other.[6]

Table 5–1 shows that in high participation schools more parents visit the school, more students and teachers interact about personal matters, and more students say that a teacher has encouraged them to attend college. This is not because high participation schools are smaller or more rural; this table and those that follow control for such differences. Instead, it seems that parents are more likely to visit high participation schools to see their child perform in various activities. In the case of activities which do not lend themselves as easily to a public showing (such as the radio club), the involved students may encourage their parents to visit because they feel more positively about the school. Better parent-teacher contact should

[5]The appendix contains more information about the 1957 to 1972 comparisons of extracurricular activity.

[6]We looked into the question of bias and found both a race and a sex bias. For example, if white female participation is high, white male participation will tend to be high also, reflecting a white participation bias; there is also a chance that black female participation will be high, reflecting a feminine participation bias. There is only a tendency for black male participation to be higher when white female participation is high.

Table 5-1. Effects of low and high extracurricular participation on parental school visits, student-teacher talk about personal matters, and teacher encouragement to attend college.

	Percentage of Tenth Graders Participating in Extracurricular Activities			
	White		Black	
	Low 44	High 83	Low 38	High 78
Percentage Whose Parents Visited School This Year	23[a]	30[a]	27[a]	35[a]
Percentage Who Talked to a Teacher About Personal Matters	59[a]	69[a]	50[a]	57[a]
Percentage Saying a Teacher Has Encouraged Them to Attend College	43[a]	51[a]	47	51

[a] $p < .05$.

Note: Schools are matched on racial composition and size, region, urbanism and educational level of the community, and white and black student socioeconomic status.

result; a parent who visits the school for a band concert will find it easier to come back to talk with a teacher (or may even meet the teacher at the concert).

Greater extracurricular involvement means more opportunities for students and teachers to talk about nonacademic matters. The faculty adviser of a student association is often in a position to talk with students about personal matters. Being active in a club or sport means the student is around the school more, and a conversation with a teacher that begins with, "I liked your concert" can easily move to more personal matters. Any faculty-student conversation provides an opportunity for talking about the student's school work and particularly about going to college.

The faculty adviser to a club has an additional advantage in talking to students because he typically does not grade students on their academic work and hence can avoid an adversary relationship. The adviser is also likely to have student respect because he will be helping students achieve their own goal, whether it is a successful party or a winning football game. One study, which conducted in-depth interviews wtih students over considerable time, concluded:

> The teachers who were respected most by faculty and students alike were the coaches and the leaders in sports activities. . . . As far as the students were concerned, the athletic coaches were almost the only teachers in the high school environment who treated them as individuals. The coaches often serve as confidants, helping many students overcome emotional hurdles. One student told us, "If it hadn't been for Mr. A (the basketball coach) I don't know whether I could have stayed in school. He was able to present me with the hard facts and convince me that it was for my own good to stay in school. Also, staying on the team was important for me. . ." (Offer, Sabshin, and Offer 1969:42).

All of the differences in Table 5–1 are reasonably large, except that a high participation school is only slightly associated with a greater number of black students saying that a tacher has talked to them about attending college. Apparently, conversations with faculty about college occur more for white students in high participation schools than for blacks.

Table 5–2 shows that students, particularly blacks, tend to like high participation schools. For those students, white or black, who are having academic difficulties, an extracurricular program can offer

Table 5-2.   Effects of low and high extracurricular participation on liking school, time on homework, and acceptance of school rules.

| | Percentage of Tenth Graders Participating in Extracurricular Activities | | | |
| | White | | Black | |
	Low 44	High 83	Low 38	High 78
Percentage Who Say They Like School (scale)	44	48	42	50
Percentage Spending at least Thirty Minutes/Night on Homework	42[a]	50[a]	62	63
Percentage Feeling School Rules Are Fair (scale)	55[a]	61[a]	45[a]	51[a]

[a] $p < .05$.

Note: Schools are matched on racial composition and size, region, urbanism and educational level of the community, and white and black student socioeconomic status.

an alternative route to a sense of achievement. Extracurricular activities also provide opportunities to make friends, to develop interpersonal skills, and to talk casually with teachers. Under these circumstances, attitudes toward school should improve.

White students do more homework in high participation schools (line 2). Our data do not bear out the common assumption that extracurricular activities and homework compete for the student's time. Of course, minimum grade eligibility requirements for extracurricular participation may explain why some students study more. We think other students do more homework because they spend more time with other students and particularly with student leaders, who set a good example academically. One of the bits of conversation when students get together is, "I can't go. I've got to study for the test." The student leaders in extracurricular activities are more likely to say this and set the norm for the others in the group. The network of extracurricular activities thus reinforces the school's academic standards and socializes the nonconforming students into meeting these standards. This apparently applies only to whites. Blacks (who report doing more homework than do whites) do not increase their amount of homework in high participation schools. This, along with the earlier finding that blacks in high participation schools are not urged toward college much more than blacks in low participation schools, again suggests that there is less academic payoff from extracurricular activities for black students.

If students like school, accepting school regulations should follow naturally (line 3). Because they are in more frequent contact with conforming school leaders, students in high participation schools are themselves more likely to conform. If they do not and are punished for some rule violation, they are in a better position to talk with other students about what the rule means, recognize that it has been enforced against others (that it is being applied fairly), and even in some admittedly rare instances learn how to appeal an unjust punishment. (Of course, if many students believe the rules are unfairly administered, then the student who has many friends as a result of extracurricular participation will realize he is not alone. In this case, a high level of extracurricular participation may encourage students to organize and fight the administration.)

It makes sense that students in high participation schools, having more relationships with both teachers and students, will like school more and consider school rules fair. Teachers have often pointed out

Table 5-3. Effects of low and high extracurricular participation on self-esteem and happiness.

| | Percentage of Tenth Graders Participating in Extracurricular Activities | | | |
| | White | | Black | |
	Low 44	High 83	Low 38	High 78
Percentage Having High Self-Esteem (scale)	53[a]	66[a]	49[a]	55[a]
Percentage Saying They Are Not Happy	24[a]	18[a]	39	35

[a]$p < .05$.

Note: Schools are matched on racial composition and size, region, urbanism and educational level of the community, and white and black student socioeconomic status.

that the real problem students are the outsiders—the social isolates who go through high school alone and unhappy.

Participation in extracurricular activities often nurtures a sense of accomplishment which should carry over into positive feelings about academic ability. Table 5-3 shows that in high participation schools, more students rate themselves as successful in their academic work. Since we have matched high and low participation schools on community characteristics and student socioeconomic status, we doubt that high participation schools have more intelligent students. They simply have more confident students. The bottom line shows high participation schools have fewer unhappy students. This seems a natural consequence of better attitudes toward school, greater academic self-confidence, and closer relationships with teachers.

Since extracurricular activities provide a basis for making friends, high participation schools should have more interracial friendships. Table 5-4 shows that black and white students in high participation schools more often say they have opposite-race friends, that they contact these friends outside of school, and that they work together on their homework. (These items are combined to form the scale shown in line 1.) The black students in high participation schools tend to say the school staff favors desegregation. Finally, white students have slightly more favorable attitudes toward black students and toward desegregation. Apparently, extracurricular activities help to establish good school race relations. This is ironical. We earlier suggested that an emphasis on extracurricular activities reflects a traditional approach to education, one which presumably would not include an emphasis on good race relations. This is true. For example, whites in high participation schools have less contact with blacks and have more conservative racial attitudes and perceive the school staff as less sympathetic to desegregation. When schools are matched on region, community characteristics and size, some of these differences reverse—whites in high participation schools have more favorable attitudes on race than do their compatriots in similar schools (i.e., other smaller, deep South, rural schools). Whites in high participation schools still do not see the staff as more prointegration after schools are matched (line 2 of Table 5–4). We also see that blacks in high participation schools do not have much more favorable attitudes toward desegregation.

Students in high participation schools like school more, have greater self-confidence in their school work, and do more homework. Do they score higher on standardized achievement tests? The answer seems to be yes. Table 5–5 indicates that high

Table 5-4.   Effects of low and high extracurricular participation on racial contact and racial attitude measures.

| | Percentage of Tenth Graders Participating in Extracurricular Activities | | | |
| | White | | Black | |
	Low 44	High 83	Low 38	High 78
Percentage Reporting High Inter- racial Contact (scale)	33[a]	38[a]	46[a]	53[a]
Percentage Reporting That Principal and Teachers Favor Integration (scale)	15	15	15[a]	23[a]
Percentage with Positive Racial Attitudes (scale)	35	40	60	63

[a] $p < .05$.

Note: Schools are matched on racial composition and size, region, urbanism and educational level of the community, and white and black student socioeconomic status.

Table 5-5.   Effects of low and high extracurricular participation on achievement.

	Percentage of Tenth Graders Participating in Extracurricular Activities			
	White		Black	
	Low	High	Low	High
	44%	83%	38%	78%
Achievement Test Performance	455[a]	476[a]	340[a]	351[a]

[a] $p < .05$.

Note: Schools are matched on racial composition and size, region, urbanism and educational level of the community, and white and black student socioeconomic status.

participation schools have higher achievement test scores—twenty-one points higher for white students, eleven points for black students. We cannot tell from our data whether these students have actually learned more or whether they simply approached the test with greater confidence and motivation. Whatever the reason, improved achievement is welcome news.

HIGH SCHOOL EXTRACURRICULAR ACTIVITIES AND COLLEGE ATTENDANCE

White students from high participation schools more often attend college—at least in the North. Several studies have shown that students who participate in extracurricular activities are more likely to go to college. This proves little; every teacher knows that the bright and ambitious students are more likely to be joiners. These students would probably attend college whether or not they participated in extracurricular activities. Our analysis, which goes considerably further, shows extracurricular participation increases the probability of college attendance for students who would not normally go. Using data from the National Longitudinal Survey of 1972, we found that northern schools which provide ample opportunity for extracurricular participation send more white students on to college.[7]

Imagine two white students of average social status, achievement performance, and grade point standing. Imagine that they both attend northern schools of average size but that one school has an unusually low rate of extracurricular participation and the other an unusually high rate. In the low participation school, the probability of a male student attending college is 66 percent; for a female the corresponding figure is 62 percent. In the high participation school, the probability of attending college increases 6 percent for each sex (72 percent and 68 percent, respectively).[8] This cannot be due to the more ambitious students' choosing high participation high schools; typically, high participation schools are small and rural, not the sort to attract college-bound students. Besides, our analysis has already taken this argument into account—we have applied controls for student and school background factors. We have already seen that extracurricular activities provide informal opportunities for faculty members to sell the idea of college. In addition, students in high participation schools like school better, have greater confidence in their academic abilities, and score higher on standardized tests. Finally, extracurricular activities provide a continuity between levels of schooling. Junior high school students know whether the high school football team has won or lost, and they know that when they get to high school they will be able to try out for the team or go to the games. Students in high school talk about enjoying the social life of colleges, but they can only say this because they know a pep rally is fun from first-hand experience. High school extracurricular activities are thus a sort of advertisement for college life.

These results apply to northern whites, and a majority of high school students are northern whites, so this is important. We think that high participation southern schools also send more white students to college although our analysis doesn't show this. (The problem is that the National Longitudinal Survey does not provide data on the type of community the school is in.) High participation

[7]"Ample opportunity" is defined by the number of other students in the school who participate. This analysis thus relates the college attendance of each student to the extracurricular participation of the other students in his high school, not to his own extracurricular participation.

[8]The tabulation is shown in the appendix. These college attendance rates are high because they include any form of postsecondary school entered within three years of high school graduation.

schools are concentrated in the rural deep South; extensive extracurricular activities programs would probably show a beneficial impact on college attendance if one could compare high participation schools to low participation schools which were also concentrated in the rural deep South, where college attendance rates are normally low. (Our data do show that southern white students who themselves participate in extracurricular activities are more likely to go to college, but as we earlier said this cannot be considered strong evidence that a school which increased opportunities for participation would be likely to increase the total number of students going to college.)

The failure of high participation schools to send more blacks to college is a more serious problem. Earlier we saw that blacks in high participation schools did not report doing more homework or talking more to faculty about college. Perhaps participation does not pay off academically for blacks as much as it does for whites. Perhaps activities have a different psychological meaning for blacks, who are understandably less attracted to experiencing fraternity life at state U. Perhaps black participation is restricted to activities like sports, which reinforce stereotypes of blacks as nonacademic. (Perhaps even in predominantly black schools, extracurricular activities are too closely tied to social status, excluding the low income students who need encouragement to attend college.[9]

It may be that the explanation is one that has already been noted—that extracurricular activities are part of a conservative mode of education and consonant with a belief that college should be reserved for the elite.

These speculations about the meaning of extracurricular activities for blacks alert us to one of the difficulties the desegregated high school faces. Certain types of extracurricular activity may create or maintain sterotypic roles for blacks. Racial integration through extracurricular activities must extend to the honor society, the radio club, the service organizations, and the orchestra, as well as the football team and the dance band. Experience in truly integrated extracurricular activities might encourage blacks to go to college or would at least reduce the discomfort of attending an overwhelmingly white university for those who did go.

---

[9]One major problem is that in this one analysis we used total school participation rates, and, of course, blacks do not benefit from a system of extracurricular activities which does not involve them.

RACIAL BIAS IN OPPORTUNITIES
TO PARTICIPATE

We do not have information about racial bias in extracurricular activities in our 200 southern high schools, but the failure of extracurricular activities to benefit blacks as much as whites makes us suspect that this is an important issue. We examined the data we have, constructed an analysis which at least touches on this issue, and wound up convinced that these data do contain one warning—fraternities and sororities, while they may increase extracurricular participation, do more harm than good. By fraternities and sororities we do not mean only greek-letter social organizations. Most schools have banned such clubs, considering their exclusiveness improper in a democratic society. But equally exclusive organizations operate under other names. By an exclusionary club is meant one in which students are elected to membership by other students on diffuse grounds—the student is the sort of person who would make a good member. Of course, if the group has a very specific purpose, a French club, for example, then anyone who has done well in French would presumably qualify for membership. If the club's goals are much more general—to serve the community—then how does one decide who would be a good member? The answer usually boils down to popularity or status. The group then becomes a youthful country club, a way of barring the wrong people. When the definition of a fraternity or sorority is expanded to encompass any school-sanctioned group which elects its members on the basis of vague or diffuse criteria, most high schools today can be said to sponsor sororities and fraternities.

Such groups often operate under the auspices of service organizations. Certainly everyone benefits when young people become involved in community service; we do have reservations, though, about clubs which implicitly teach that only the worthy may serve. The lesson may not be intentional, of course, but guaranteeing equal opportunity to participate requires a certain self-consciousness on the part of school administrators. Every group's charter should specify procedures for insuring equal opportunity. Informal understandings are not enough.

Unfortunately for our analysis, we do not know how many of these exclusive clubs exist in each school nor how much weight they carry in the informal status ranking game that occurs in every school. We assume that exclusive clubs most often have white female members; if so, then a school which has a disproportionately high white female participation rate probably has more exclusive clubs. We do not have counts of the number of sorority-type organizations in each school and can only approach this problem in a very indirect manner. Up to now we have focused on the way a group's participation rate affects that particular group. Now let us see how the participation rate of one group (e.g., white females) affects another group (e.g., blacks).

To do this four indices of participation per school were computed—one for each race/sex combination. Our argument is that if a school has many organizations which elect their members on the basis of diffuse criteria (e.g., popularity), the school will tend to have a disproportionately high level of participation by white females. Male participation, which is primarily in sports, will not be affected as much, and black female participation will not be high in these schools because of their exclusion. Hence, the differences in the apparent effect of high levels of white female participation as opposed to high levels of participation by other groups will give some clues about the possible harm done by fraternity-sorority type clubs.

Table 5–6 summarizes the effect of high participation rates for the four race-sex combinations. High male or black female participation has the expected positive effects on white student racial attitudes, on black student perceptions of school race relations, and on black student happiness and self-esteem. Of the eighteen differences (six each for white males, black females, and black males), sixteen are positive. High white female participation has negative effects five times out of six: Whites indicate less favorable attitudes toward school integration and less often say their teachers like desegregation while blacks more often characterize the student leadership as anti-integration, more often say they are unhappy, and more often have low self-esteem. The differences are usually small (only two of the eighteen differences are statistically significant), but the consistency in this pattern (which holds for a number of other student outcomes as well) is disturbing.

In some of these schools, administrators must recognize the discriminatory nature of their school extracurricular policy. Our data indicate that principals and teachers tend to have less sympathy for desegregation in schools with high white female participation rates, which implies, conversely, that some liberal school staffs are not

Table 5-6. The effect of high and low male and female participation on white and black attitudes toward desegregation and on black feelings of happiness and self-esteem.

	White Girls		White Boys		Black Girls		Black Boys	
	Low 40	*High* 89	*Low* 40	*High* 81	*Low* 28	*High* 79	*Low* 38	*High* 86
Percentage of Whites Preferring an Integrated School	44	40	42	42	40	44	40[a]	44[a]
Percentage of Whites Desiring More Friends of Another Race	49	49	47	51	47	50	47	51
Percentage of Whites Reporting Pro-integration Teachers and Principal	15	14	13	15	13	15	12	17
Percentage of Blacks Reporting Pro-integration Student Leaders	22	19	20	21	18	22	19	21
Percentage of Blacks Saying They Are Happy	64	63	60	66	62	65	63	63
Percentage of Blacks Having High Self-Esteem	52	50	49	52	48[a]	54[a]	49	52

Percentage of Tenth Graders Participating in Extracurricular Activities

[a] $p < .05$

Note: Schools are matched on racial composition and size, region, urbanism and educational level of the community, and white and black student socioeconomic status.

willing to tolerate exclusive groups. Presumably, these schools transform diffuse groups into clubs catering to special student interests and which are more easily integrated.

A school's extracurricular policies can be discriminatory in other ways. In *A Handbook for Integrated Schooling,* Forehand and Ragosta (1976) observe that scheduling extracurricular activities for after-school hours can limit opportunities for participation, particularly for bused students. The same idea appears in *Update: A Desegregation Resource Handbook* of the Delaware Committee on the School Decision (n.d.) which proposes the incorporation of extracurricular activities into the regular school day and the running of a late bus as possible solutions to the problem.[10] One suburban school asked for municipal bus service to the school to provide the equivalent of several late buses.

Forehand and Ragosta (1976) suggest eliminating restrictive eligibility requirements such as grades, requirements which often preclude minority student participation. This rule makes sense even in nondesegregated schools since the alienated and the academically poor students stand to gain the most from participation. The simplest way to insure equity is to monitor the extracurricular program. Are there enough groups to serve everyone? Does one race or one type of student predominate in any of the groups? If so, why? What is necessary to change this?

WHAT CAN THE SCHOOL DO?

How does a school go about increasing extracurricular participation? We can suggest four general guidelines. First, and most critical, the school must set a goal of high participation, meaning nearly every student's active involvement in a club or team. The fact that a school

[10]Another manual, *Contingency Planning for a Unitary School System* (Conley, et al. 1977), observes that teachers may resent having extracurricular activities held during the school day. It stresses the importance of staff involvement in overcoming this resistance: "Staff involvement at the planning, implementation, and evaluation levels as opposed to being called in only to monitor or chaperone provides opportunity for joint decision-making which can result in a strong extracurricular program that is educationally beneficial to the students and supported by the faculty" (63). Well grounded in the desegregation experience of Jefferson County (Louisville), Kentucky, the manual offers specific useful suggestions on many aspects of desegregation.

is very large should not be an acceptable excuse for low participation rates. While it may seem obvious that a small school offers more opportunities for involvement, this is not really necessary. A small school provides greater opportunity to participate in football, for example, because every school, regardless of size, has only one football team. Yet private schools regularly field teams in several leagues for the same sport, thus greatly increasing participation opportunities for the individual student. In addition to offering a wider variety of sports, a large high school can also develop intramural sports in the way that colleges do. The large school can duplicate most of its organizations—even the honor society can be remade into several separate societies (to reward excellence in physical science, social science, humanities, social service, etc.). In the case of expressive and subject-matter clubs the possibilities are endless—a group can be organized around almost any topic.

A successful extracurricular program requires strong principal and teacher support. Can one reasonably expect further contributions from already overburdened teachers? The benefits of extracurricular activity justify the additional effort. A traditionalist can point to the achievement gains associated with extracurricular participation. Others will see the greatest merit in the social learning that comes from extracurricular participation. Regardless, facilitating extracurricular activity is time well spent.

Schools of education rarely teach groupwork theory, and one can hardly expect teachers to assume the role of club adviser without adequate training. Because teachers already have highly practiced interpersonal skills, training can focus on the fundamental strategies and theories of group organization. In many districts, school social workers could act as trainers. Schools often make mistakes with extracurricular activities because of this lack of knowledge of groupwork theory. For example, the first rule of groupwork is that both the structure and the goals of the organization must come spontaneously from the group. A teacher-adviser to a club will need training in the use of nondirective methods. Working with groups should not mean simply waiting patiently for the group's leadership structure and goals to evolve, however. The faculty adviser must encourage the group to write an agenda of activities which will involve and excite group members.

Another common error is that of ignoring the groupwork rule of starting from where the group is. For example, a service club adviser may steer the group into a rather abstract social service activity—raising funds for blind children—only to find that the group members quickly become bored. Altruism is learned gradually; it cannot be assumed. In groupwork with delinquent gangs, social workers often begin with a fund-raising activity to provide jackets or sweaters for all group members. The group then has a mission, which helps establish a group identity. School athletic teams recognize the importance of identity by awarding school letters. There is no reason why they should monopolize this clever idea. Letters, jackets, scarves, bookbinders, and so forth, could be used to give identity to participants in various school activities.

If the school has enough well-organized groups, only imagination will limit the number of useful activities they can undertake. These activities range from running a school dance to an ecology day to clean up the banks of a neighboring stream (ending of course in a bonfire and wienie roast). Many of these activities can deal explicitly with human relations issues. Some colleges operate special discrimination days when obscure and inane rules are enforced—no red heads are allowed on the stairway in the center of the building, and no one over five feet ten inches tall is allowed in the boys' gym. All these activities take work and adult time. Some schools have made a serious effort to recruit parents to assist in advising these clubs. In almost any community there is an enormous amount of talent available if only the effort is made to tap it.

In designing an extracurricular activities program in a desegregated high school, one must give attention to the relative attractiveness of different types of activities to different ethnic groups. In a predominantly white, high SES school an academically oriented program will not reach low SES minority students. Conversely, in a predominantly black school, basketball may become a black activity. The problems of tailoring activities to the ethnic and social class mix of the school are analogous to the problems a school district has in developing magnet schools as part of a desegregation program; a school with a certain curriculum emphasis may attract whites more than blacks and hence would succeed in a district where whites are in the minority, but it would fail to attract enough blacks in a predominantly white system. (Some school administrators try to overcome this problem by placing programs that attract whites in buildings in minority neighborhoods and vice versa.)

Finally, the key to the success of the extracurricular activities program lies in the way that students are encouraged to join.

Recruitment should not be left to chance. In one Delaware high school, teachers keep a record of which students participate and make a special effort to recruit the inactive ones. Clubs should take advantage of every special interest in the student body.

The most difficult task is organizing meaningful extracurricular activities for hard-to-reach youth. The C student is not going to join the honor society, and the shy or unpopular student is not going to participate in student government. These students can be reached with auto clubs, sewing groups, bowling leagues, electronic game clubs, after-school work groups, and so on. The advisers of these clubs must understand that clubs should not be ghettos, catering to an isolated group; they should not be segregated by race, class, social skill, or academic achievement. If the advisers understand this, they can succeed in finding the brilliant French major who is also interested in bowling, and the bowling club will be better able to integrate its members into the school. In most schools, exracurricular advisers can use as a model the football team, which usually includes all ethnic groups, good students as well as weak ones, and shy students as well as popular ones. If it does not, it is probably losing more games than it should.

There still remains the problem of how to set up diffuse-purpose organizations in such a way that they cannot become "sororities." The most common diffuse organizations are the service clubs. These might be organized on a homeroom basis, so that each homeroom becomes a social organization with its own name, identity and agenda of activities. Teachers with a special interest might recruit students with similar interests into their homerooms. (Mayer's *The Schools* [1963] describes the way one high school turned its homerooms into clubs by taking out the announcements and paperwork and keeping the same students and teacher together through all four years of high school. Of course, some teachers found groupwork difficult; the solution used was to allow other teachers to handle two such clubs, with a corresponding reduction in teaching load.) All this takes effort, but it should pay off—in happier students, better race relations, and higher achievement.

FINE ARTS TEACHERS AND GYM TEACHERS

The fine arts teacher is the one staff member in the high school whose duties consist mainly of extracurricular activity. In a sense, the same thing can be said about gym teachers since they spend a good deal of their time coaching intraschool sports and organizing intramural athletics; in addition the gym class itself functions almost as an extracurricular activity. Thus, it should come as no surprise that our analysis shows that these two types of teachers are among the most important academic resources in the high school.

There has been little research on the role of fine arts classes in school desegregation. One study of a magnet school designed to encourage voluntary integration in a northern city finds a striking contrast between the amount of segregation occurring in math and science classrooms and the success of integration in music, drama, and art classes. The authors suggest three explanations: The black-white achievement gap may hamper integration in science class; the art and music classes, on the other hand, seem to lend themselves to whole-group instruction with considerable opportunities for student

Table 5-7.   The effect of one additional music, drama, art, or gym teacher on self-esteem, and achievement.

	Number of Music, Drama, Art Teachers		Number of Gym Teachers	
	0.5	1.5	1	2
Male				
Black				
Self-Esteem	44%[a]	54%[a]	45%[a]	54%[a]
Achievement	340	339	333[a]	347[a]
White				
Self-Esteem	50%[a]	60%[a]	53%[a]	58%[a]
Achievement	445[a]	463[a]	451	460
Female				
Black				
Self-Esteem	52%	54%	53%	53%
Achievement	357	346	348	354
White				
Self-Esteem	59%	63%	61%	62%
Achievement	473	469	471	470

[a] $p < .05$.

Note: Schools matched on racial composition of school and race of school before desegregation, school size, region and urbanism of the community, and black and white student socioeconomic status.

interaction; finally, music, drama and art teachers may be more skillful at creating good interpersonal relations, or perhaps they simply have a stronger commitment to desegregation.

A southern high school of 1,000 students with below-average staffing in fine arts and gym would have a half-time music/art teacher and one gym teacher; a school with high resources would have one more of each—1.5 music and art teachers and 2 gym teachers. These two extra persons can make impressive differences in the school.

Table 5–7 shows the impact of adding either one music, drama or art teacher or one extra gym teacher per thousand students in a high school. For male students, whether white or black, self-esteem is higher by at least 5 and usually 10 percentage points if an extra one of these teachers is present. The difference for female students is small. (Perhaps female students at this age have less trouble academically and so have less need for alternative areas of achievement.) Although self-esteem supposedly measures feelings about academic performance, we have already seen that students do not make very clear distinctions between the different areas of their lives. Students who feel good about themselves will feel good about their academic work and vice versa. An opportunity to perform and achieve in any area is likely to enhance academic self-esteem.

Moreover, the arts and athletics provide a physical outlet, an opportunity for self-expression, and, for many students, an opportunity to be creative. These physical and creative outlets lead to a tension reduction which spills over into the rest of the school day. We also see improved achievement scores for males—for blacks as a result of additional gym instruction, for whites due to an additional fine arts teacher. While not as large as the effects we have seen for self-esteem, these achievement gains certainly cannot be ignored—the differences are fourteen and eighteen points on an SAT-like scale. This implies that the presence of a single teacher is sufficient to raise the performance of all 500 male students in a typical high school by these many points on the SAT—this without teaching any academic subject! Of course, this gain is no more remarkable than the achievement effects that we attribute to extracurricular activities—indeed it is all part of the same story.

If the average fine arts or gym program pays off, improving program quality should pay off as well. We suspect there is room for improvement in many schools. Gym in particular seems to alienate students unnecessarily. One school in California was forced into reform because of student opposition to physical education. That school eliminated many mickey mouse requirements, abandoned Victorian era girls' gym suits, and greatly expanded the number of electives within the gym program. (The school now offers credit in thirty-five sports.) The results look good; gym attendance has improved and with it attendance in other classes as well.

CONCLUSIONS

Every teacher knows that what he or she is able to accomplish in class depends more than anything else on student receptivity. Students who want to learn will learn; students who do not want to learn will not. While a good teacher can do a great deal to motivate students, much lies beyond the scope of the individual teacher. The mood that students bring into the classroom cannot easily be changed in fifty minutes. This is why the school as a social organization plays such a critical role in determining what each teacher can accomplish and why the mood of the whole school matters so much. Providing students with the opportunity to blow off steam, to express themselves, to take leadership roles, to obtain the highly visible rewards that go with winning a ball game or painting a picture or playing in a concert can change their feelings about themselves and about school. As the mood of each student changes, the feeling tone of the entire school begins to change. The school that emphasizes such activities will find a large percentage of students entering each class ready to learn. When that happens, teachers can teach.

APPENDIX 5A
TECHNICAL APPENDIX

This appendix gives the details of the school-level analysis of the effects of extracurricular participation rates on student attitudes and behavior, and presents an individual-level replication of that analysis. It also presents details of the comparison of extracurricular participation rates found in high school surveys done in 1955 and 1972, and analyses the effects of extracurricular participation on college attendence using the data of the National Longitudinal Study (NLS).

DATA ON CHANGE IN EXTRACURRICULAR ACTIVITY RATES SINCE THE 1950S

A 1955 survey of high school sophomores by the Educational Testing Service was the basis for a longitudinal follow-up survey by Bruce Eckland and his colleagues in 1970.[11] Fifteen years later, the students of 1955 were asked whether they had participated in various kinds of high school extracurricular activities.

These data may be used to compare participation in high school extracurricular activities in 1955 to the participation rates in the NLS of the High School Class of 1972. The NLS is a large scale longitudinal survey conducted by the National Center for Education Statistics and designed to provide information on high school alumni as they move into early adulthood. In the spring of 1972 a baseline survey was conducted on a nationally representative random sample of 16,683 high school seniors drawn from 1,061 high schools. The first follow-up survey was done in October 1973, a year and a half after these students graduated from high school, and added 257 more schools to the original sample. Additional follow-ups were undertaken in the fall of 1974, 1976, and 1978 and are still being conducted.

The baseline questionnaire asked, "Have you participated in any of the following types of activities either in or out of school this year?" Nine types of activity such as debating, drama, band, and chorus are listed with the following possible responses: have not

[11] A paper by Hanks and Eckland (1976) uses a different methodology to study the effects of extracurricular participation on college attendance in this longitudinal data set.

participated, have participated actively, and have participated as a leader or officer. Although question wording differed, the data seem to indicate considerably higher participation rates in 1955. The Eckland survey asked, "About how much did you participate in each of the following activities in high school...?" Responses were "I participated in.... (dramatics or music) a lot, some, none, or (the opportunity was...) not available."

Varying response categories pose one difficulty in comparing the Eckland and the NLS survey. Given a choice between a lot and some, an Eckland respondent with only minimal involvement might choose some. The same respondent, had he been given the NLS question (possible responses: participated as a leader, participated actively, and did not participate), might say he did not participate. On the other hand, one might argue that in a fifteen-year follow-up survey many students who participated to a trivial degree might not remember it at all.

Different activity categories also hamper comparison of the two surveys. The drama and music, student government, and publications categories are comparable, however. In these cases, the Eckland data show higher participation in the fifties than in 1972. For example, 57 percent of the Eckland sample said that they participated in drama and music (25% a lot, 32% some) compared to 21 percent participating actively or as a leader in the NLS; 35 percent of the Eckland sample said they participated in student government (9% a lot, 26% some) compared to 21 percent in the NLS sample. On balance, the data indicates that the level of participation in extracurricular activities has declined in the last fifteen years although additional evidence is needed on this point.

EFFECTS OF SCHOOL EXTRACURRICULAR PARTICIPATION RATES

Tables 5A–1 through 5A–4 show the regression equations relating school level of participation to various student outcomes. The seven scales used as dependent variables appeared earlier: racial contact, racial attitudes, liking school, acceptance of school rules, self-esteem, staff seen as prodesegregation, and achievement. However, the individual items used as dependent variables include several not used before:

- Parents visit school—"Have either of your parents come to school this year for PTA, Parents' Days, or for parents' conferences?"
- Talk to teachers—"Have you ever talked to any of your teachers or other adults here at school about things you are doing outside of school—your job, a hobby, or something you are really interested in?"
- Staff urges college: "Have any adults here at school ever told you personally that you should go to college?"
- One-half hour or more per night of homework: "How much time do you usually spend doing homework after school?" Categories are none, less than one-half hour a day, about one-half hour, about one hour, about two hours a day or more. The scale is standardized so as to reflect the percentage of students who do thirty minutes or more of homework per day.
- Student leader feelings: "What about the student leaders and popular students at your school? How do they feel about black and white students going to the same school together?" Responses are the following: most of them like it; most of them don't like it; some like it; some don't; and don't know.

Finally, the analysis of the impact of white female participation uses two individual items from the racial attitudes scale: "If you could choose the kind of school you could go to, would you pick one with: all white students, all black students, a mixture of different kinds of students, other?" and "Would you like to have more friends who are of a different race?"

Notice that in a large number of the equations in Tables 5A–1 through 5A–4 the extracurricular participation rate is the strongest factor in the equation. Betas in excess of .25 for white students and .20 for black students are uncommon in this data set. Since betas for our control variables are lower than the betas for the extracurricular participation variable, this reduces the likelihood that some unknown additional variable could have an effect sufficiently powerful to erase the impact of extracurricular participation. The extracurricular participation effect could be washed out only if a control variable more powerful than any we had included had been overlooked.

Table 5A-1. Regression equations with standardized coefficients used to predict white outcomes in Tables 5-1, 5-2, and 5-5.

	Dependent Variables (White Student Responses)						
Independent Variables	Parents Visit School	Talk to Teachers	Staff Urges College	Students Like School	One Half Hour or More/Night Homework	School Rules Are Fair	Mean Achievement Performance
White SES Scale	.174	-.015	.055	-.149	.111	.012	.622[a]
School Size	-.156	-.058	.112	-.006	.169	-.185	-.081
School Percentage White	.009	-.096	-.200[a]	.123	.089	-.002	-.076
Community Educational Level	.181	.244[a]	.115	.037	-.356[a]	.144	-.097
Black SES Scale	.130	-.096	-.061	-.188	-.039	-.027	.209[a]
County Percentage Urban	.148	.029	-.247[a]	.263[a]	.198	.118	-.033
Region (0 = deep South, 1 = border)	.025	.051	-.165	-.051	-.044	.241[a]	.154[a]
White Extracurricular Participation Rate	.228[a]	.377[a]	.284[a]	.113	.241[a]	.215[a]	.191[a]
r^2	.181	.144	.230	.080	.146	.096	.440

[a] $p < .05$.

Table 5A-2. Regression equations with standardized coefficients used to predict white outcomes in Tables 5-3, 5-4, 5-6.

	High Self-Esteem	Students Are Not Happy	High Racial Contact	Positive Racial Attitudes	Staff Is Proseg-regation	Prefer Biracial School	Want More Friends Other Race
Independent Variables							
White SES Scale	.324[a]	-.183[a]	-.127	.033	-.010	.106	.057
School Size	-.006	.145	.228[a]	.105	-.019	.043	.097
School Percentage White	-.276[a]	-.222[a]	-.397	.001	-.115	.062	-.001
Community Educational Level	.139	.063	.050	.009	.100	-.004	.022
Black SES Scale	.019	.215[a]	.100	.040	-.030	.036	-.028
County Percentage Urban	.137	-.197	.330[a]	.377[a]	.192	.363[a]	.366[a]
Region (0 = deep South, 1 = border)	.273[a]	-.178[a]	.306[a]	.238[a]	.287[a]	.225[a]	.217[a]
White Extracurricular Participation Rate	.407[a]	-.269[a]	.147	.131	.014	—	-.013
White Girls' Rate					(-.044)	-.081	-.013
White Boys' Rate					(.085)	(.011)	(.110)
Black Girls' Rate					(.102)	(.108)	(.097)
Black Boys' Rate					(.206)[a]	(.104)	(.140)
r^2	.317	.194	.443	.314	.163	.400	.325

[a] $p < .05$.

Note: Parentheses indicate the beta if this variable were to be entered in the equation following Region. This variable was not used in computing the r^2 for the equation.

195

Table 5A-3. Regression equations with standardized coefficients used to predict black outcomes in Tables 5-1, 5-2, and 5-5.

	Dependent Variables (Black Student Responses)						
	Parents Visit School	Students Talk to Teachers	Teacher Urges College	Students Like School	One Half Hour or More/Night Homework	School Rules Are Fair	Mean Achievement Performance
Independent Variables							
Black SES Scale	.127	-.145	.074	-.210[a]	.056	-.100	.474[a]
School Size	.061	.078	.064	.032	.030	.079	.101
School Percent White	-.133	-.209[a]	-.081	-.106	.069	-.093	-.018
Community Educational Level	.031	.083	.005	.043	-.288[a]	.042	-.248[a]
White SES Scale	-.031	.169[a]	-.005	.062	.078	.088	.316[a]
County Percentage Urban	-.038	.085	-.102	.028	-.079	.005	-.056
Region (0 = deep South, 1 = border)	-.142	.225[a]	.038	.011	-.299[a]	-.001	.190[a]
Black Extracurricular Participation Rate	.234[a]	.233[a]	.122	.227[a]	.006	.159	.157[a]
r^2	.101	.138	.027	.087	.223	.032	.417

[a] $p < .05$.

Table 5A–4. Regression equations with standardized coefficients used to predict black outcomes in Tables 5–3, 5–4, 5–6.

Independent Variables	Dependent Variables (Black Student Responses)					
	High Racial Contact	Teachers, Principal Prodesegregation	Positive Racial Attitudes	Student Leaders Prodesegregation	High Self-Esteem	Students Are Not Happy
Black SES Scale	-.104	-.117	-.100	.120	.317[a]	-.182
School Size	.195	.149	.243[a]	.066	-.013	.087
School Percentage White	.506[a]	-.328[a]	-.077	-.221[a]	-.147	.063
Community Educational Level	-.179	.011	-.130	.129	.065	-.011
White SES Scale	-.071	.158	.032	.085	.008	-.069
County Percentage Urban	.157	.089	.076	-.048	.032	-.048
Region (0 = deep South, 1 = border)	.118	.135	-.013	.110	.067	-.132
Black Extracurricular Participation Rate	.191[a]	.228[a]	.088	—	.225[a]	-.110
White Girls' Rate				(-.061)	(-.071)	(.030)
White Boys' Rate				(.022)	(.098)	(-.156)
Black Girls' Rate				(.075)[a]	(.223)[a]	(-.081)
Black Boys' Rate				(.045)	(.100)	(-.008)
r^2	.320	.145	.044	.116	.171	.070

[a] $p < .05$.

Note: Parentheses indicate the beta if this variable were to be entered in the equation following Region. This variable was not used in computing the r^2 for the equation.

197

In order to economize on space, the regression equations predicting white student outcomes from extracurricular participation rates are presented in Tables 5A–1 and 5A–2. Tables 5A–3 and 5A–4 contain the equations for black student outcomes. In addition, Tables 5A–2 and 5A–4 give the effects of the four sex-specific participation rates on black and white students. The sex-specific regression coefficients appear in parentheses indicating that the complete equation is not given. For example, the first parenthetical number under white girls' rate in Table 5A–2 indicates that the beta for white girls' participation on white perception of staff racial attitudes is –.044 when this variable is substituted for the overall white extracurricular participation rate in the equation. This changes the coefficients of the control variables, but the changes are not shown to save space.

When sex-specific participation rates are used, the regression coefficients are small. One reason is that the number of students who provide data is halved, reducing the variable's reliability. A good example is the impact of black participation rates on black perception of the staff's attitude toward integration which is .228: the betas for the two sex-specific rates (which are not used in this chapter) are each .15. In general, using the overall mean will increase the beta by about one-half, compared to the betas for the sex-specific rates.

THE NATIONAL LONGITUDINAL STUDY

The National Longitudinal Survey asked seniors to indicate if they had participated in nine different sorts of extracurricular activities. These responses were scaled with two points for participation as a leader or officer and one point for each type of active participation. Thus the student who acted as a leader in all nine types of activity would receive the maximum score of eighteen.

In our analysis of the NLS, we constructed individual-level regression equations to determine what kinds of students participated in extracurricular activities, and what effects participation had on later college attendance. Table 5A–5 shows that high participation students tend to have better grades (although not necessarily higher achievement test scores) and higher socioeconomic status. However, in every case but one the strongest predictor of an individual student's participation rate is the participation level of the

Table 5A-5. Standardized regression coefficients (βs) from equations predicting individual-level extracurricular participation by region, race, and sex.

	South				North			
	White		Black		White		Black	
	Male	Female	Male	Female	Male	Female	Male	Female
Dependent Variable								
Individual Participation $\bar{x}$	11.49	12.22	12.02	12.14	11.11	11.46	11.52	11.94
σ	1.97	2.31	2.14	2.21	1.87	2.14	1.93	2.32
Independent Variables								
Individual Achievement	-.005	.007[a]	-.048	-.072	-.006	.031	-.042	.065
Individual Class-Rank	.229[a]	.157[a]	.102	.220[a]	.255[a]	.265[a]	.147	.282[a]
Individual SES	.150[a]	.253[a]	.178[a]	.142[a]	.190[a]	.169[a]	.179[a]	.271[a]
School Size	.034	-.043	-.036	-.073	-.017	-.052[a]	.011	-.080
School Mean Participation	.321[a]	.349[a]	.416[a]	.269[a]	.327[a]	.351[a]	.307[a]	.196[a]
School Mean SES	-.150[a]	-.152[a]	.067	.015	-.079[a]	-.040	-.129	-.146
School Mean Achievement	.038	-.020	-.160	-.022	.001	-.065[a]	.063	.067
School Percentage White	.118[a]	.098[a]	.123	.054	-.001	.061[a]	.341[a]	.102
r^2	.175	.270	.219	.143	.234	.272	.175	.228

[a] $p < .05$.

Source: National Longitudinal Study.

199

other seventeen sampled students in the same school. This variable, called "school mean participation," is always significant, and in six of the eight equations it is the strongest single predictor. This seems to us convincing evidence that participation is more a function of opportunity than of individual desire.

Table 5A–6 shows the relationship of individual and school mean participation to college attendance. This table is based on a path model which argues that the school level of participation influences the probability of attending college. The first column of the table contains the standardized regression coefficients for four control variables—individual achievement, class rank, SES, and school size. The standardized and unstandardized regression coefficients are shown when either individual participation or school mean participation enters the equation after the first four variables. The table indicates that both variables are significantly related to the probability of white male college attendance although individual participation is the stronger. In the second column of the table both individual and school mean participation enter the equation simultaneously. When both variables enter the equation, the effect of school mean participation drops almost to zero while the effect of individual participation remains strong. This is consistent with the path model shown below:

Model 1:

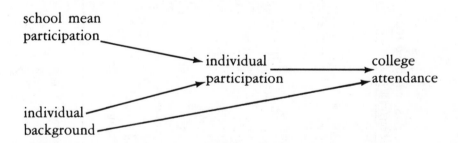

Thus school mean participation has an indirect effect on college attendance for white males. If participation did not encourage students to attend college, a different model would be appropriate as shown above:

Model 2:

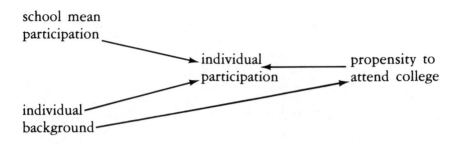

(We measure propensity to attend college by using its surrogate, actual college attendance.) Model 2 does not fit the data because it requires first, that the participation of the other students in the school be unrelated to a student's propensity to attend college when individual participation is not in the equation, and hence, second, when individual participation and school mean participation are both entered in the equation, the coefficient for school mean participation would be reduced from zero to a negative value. If Model 2 were correct, a regression equation with both individual and school mean participation as predictors of college attendance would be incorrect since neither in fact causes college attendance. It is the use of an incorrect regression equation that creates the negative coefficient for school participation. However, if Model 1 is correct, then the regression equation is a proper one, and the fact that school mean participation drops from a positive coefficient when it is in the equation without individual participation to a near-zero relationship when individual participation is in the equation means that school mean participation has an indirect but not a direct effect on college attendance. This is what the tables for northern whites show, indicating that Model 1 is correct.[12]

Model 1 does not fit the Southern data. The b for southern white male college attendance is only .005 before individual participation enters the equation and drops to -.007 afterwards. These data provide no evidence that participation in extracurricular activities influences the chance of a southern student attending college. We

[12]The reader may have noticed that this verbal argument is essentially the same as that which one would make statistically if a model was stated as a set of structural equations, allowing for reciprocal causation, and they were solved using two-stage least squares. See Duncan (1975) for an introduction to this method.

Table 5A-6. Regression equations used to predict college attendance in NLS data from individual and school-level extra-curricular participation.

		College Attendance							
		North				South			
		White Males		White Females		White Males		White Females	
Independent Variables		Equation with Control Variables Only	Equation with Two Participation Variables Added	Equation with Control Variables Only	Equation with Two Participation Variables Added	Equation with Control Variables Only	Equation with Two Participation Variables Added	Equation with Control Variables Only	Equation with Two Participation Variables Added
Individual Achievement	β	.235[a]	.239[a]	.258[a]	.257[a]	.200[a]	.201[a]	.227[a]	.215[a]
Class Rank	β	.192[a]	.157[a]	.145[a]	.104[a]	.193[a]	.171[a]	.086[a]	.050
Individual SES	β	.225[a]	.206[a]	.244[a]	.222[a]	.261[a]	.252[a]	.328[a]	.293[a]
School Size	β	.018	.048[a]	-.008	.027	.014	.026	-.008	.033
Individual Participation	β	(.121)[a]	.117[a]	(.138)[a]	.137[a]	(.088)[a]	.088[a]	(.180)[a]	.184[a]
	b	(.030)	.029	(.031)	.031	(.021)	.021	(.038)	.039
School Mean Participation	β	(.051)[a]	.018	(.052)[a]	.005	(.005)	-.007	(.008)	-.023
	b	(.033)	.021	(.030)	.003	(.003)	-.004	(.005)	-.013
r²		.254	.267	.244	.260	.255	.262	.260	.288

[a] $p < .05$.

Note: Parentheses represent the coefficients if this variable were to be entered in the equation immediately after school size. The r^2 for the equation was computed using only the first four independent variables. For individual and school mean participation, the unstandardized coefficient (b) is shown below the standardized coefficient (Beta).

Source: National Longitudinal Study

suspect that the coefficient for school-level participation would be positive if we could control on urbanism, community educational level, or region within the South since data from our own study shows that participation is highest in rural, low SES communities in the deep South, where college attendance rates would normally be low. Tables for blacks (not shown) look much like the tables for southern whites and again give no indication that participation would encourage black students to attend college. We are measuring school-level participation rates for white and black students combined, which may or may not explain why school-level participation does not relate to black college attendance.

MUSIC, DRAMA, ART AND GYM TEACHERS

Table 5A–7 shows the regression equation relating number of arts teachers to race- and sex-specific self-esteem and achievement. The table indicates that the apparent impact of arts teachers on self-esteem is quite strong—for white males, as strong as school-level SES. All four self-esteem coefficients are positive, but only the male coefficients are large. Achievement is significantly related to number of arts teachers only for white males.[13]

Table 5A–8 gives the regression equations for per capita number of gym teachers. Again the coefficients for male self-esteem are large and positive, and the coefficient for black male achievement is also statistically significant. The effects of music teachers and gym teachers on male self-esteem and achievement seem sufficiently strong to discourage one from believing that either an additional control variable or a different statistical model would wash out these results. Since the number of arts teachers and gym teachers is a skewed distribution, several tests were run transforming the distribution. In Tables 5A–7 and 5A–8 we used the natural log of the number of arts teachers per thousand students plus one, thereby reducing the scores in the schools with very high numbers of

---

[13]In these equations percentage white is entered as a quadratic term. Since the impact of percentage white is curvilinear, the addition of the square of the school racial composition increases the total variance explained. (Black self-esteem is highest not in all-black schools, but in schools approximately two-thirds black and one-third white, dropping sharply from this point to a low in all-white schools. White self-esteem and achievement are highest in schools which are virtually all-black, next highest in all-white schools, and lowest in mixed schools.)

Table 5A-7. Regression equations predicting black and white sex-specific self-esteem and achievement from per capita number of music/drama/art teachers (Table 5-7).

	Black Males		Black Females		White Males		White Females	
	Self-Esteem	Achievement	Self-Esteem	Achievement	Self-Esteem	Achievement	Self-Esteem	Achievement
Black SES	.257[a]	.495[a]	.193[a]	.364[a]	.193[a]	.542[a]	.422[a]	.637[a]
School Percentage White Squared	-.275	.061	.574	.389	.309	.317	.345	.487
Urbanism of County	.097	-.289[a]	-.012	-.128	.103	-.027	.056	-.136
School Size	-.045	.081	.019	.028	-.035	-.175[a]	-.145	-.063
School Percentage White	.094	-.077	-.699[a]	-.481[a]	-.392	-.373	-.533	-.589[a]
Individual White SES	-.044	.187[a]	.063	.351[a]	.038	.247[a]	-.021	.124
Prior School Racial Composition	-.038	.065	.018		-.018	-.127[a]	-.081	-.089
Region (0 = deep South, 1 = border)	-.044	-.012	.026	.234[a]	.106	.088	-.014	.016
Number of Music, Drama, Arts Teachers/1,000 students	.203[a]	-.008	.040	-.107	.261[a]	.146[a]	.123	-.044
r^2	.136	.270	.094	.362	.185	.385	.182	.323

[a] $p < .05$.

204

Table 5A-8. Regression equations predicting white and black sex-specific esteem and achievement from per capita number of gym teachers (Table 5-7).

	Black Males		Black Females		White Males		White Females	
	Self-Esteem	Achievement	Self-Esteem	Achievement	Self-Esteem	Achievement	Self-Esteem	Achievement
Independent Variables								
Black SES	.274[a]	.502[a]	.194[a]	.362[a]	.226[a]	.560[a]	.441[a]	.629[a]
School Percentage White Squared	-.293	.095	.562[a]	.432	.188	.249	.288	.507
Urbanism of County	.105	-.291[a]	—	-.134	.122	-.017	.064	-.138
School Size	-.032	.113	—	.055	-.044	-.180[a]	-.155	-.057
School Percentage White	.161	-.082	-.683[a]	-.518[a]	-.264	-.301	-.478	-.608[a]
White SES	-.053	.174	.065	.341[a]	.045	.251[a]	-.019	.123
Prior School Racial Composition	-.014	.073	.021	—	—	-.116[a]	-.073	-.091
Region (0 = deep South, 1 = border)	-.032	-.051	.041	.188[a]	.150[a]	.113	.013	—
Number of Gym Teachers/1,000 Students	.214[a]	.154[a]	-.002	.056	.152[a]	.087	.045	-.013
r²	.141	.292	.093	.355	.147	.374	.171	.322

[a] $p < .05$.
Note: Dashes indicate that coefficient was too small to enter equation.

teachers and making the distribution less skewed. The natural log transformation slightly strengthens the relationship.

THE EFFECTS OF EXTRACURRICULAR PARTICIPATION: AN INDIVIDUAL LEVEL REPLICATION

In discussing the effects of school extracurricular participation rates on the attitudes of students, we sometimes argued that individuals who were active in sports and clubs should change their attitudes because of this experience. This is an individual-level, not a school-level, explanation, so we interrupt our school-level analysis to present individual-level regression equations linking an individual's participation to his own attitudes. The effects, based on 3000 black students and a sample of 2000 whites, are shown in table 5A–9. The coefficients are taken from equations which control student SES, school racial composition and duration of desegregation, the average SES of the opposite-race students in the school, and the urbanism of the community. Region was not available and hence was not controlled. The results are very difficult to interpret, since we know that students who participate in clubs and sports probably differed from nonparticipants before they joined, and it is impossible to know how much of the differences in table 5A–9 are the result of participation. For example, the table shows no difference in the racial contact scores of white students who do and do not participate in extracurricular activities. If the whites who go out for sports and clubs are initially more isolated from blacks, then participation has had a positive effect. If they initially had more black acquaintances, then participation has reduced their racial contact.

Although the table is difficult to interpret, we are reassured to find that none of the coefficients are negative, and those for self-esteem and various staff-student and school-parent contact variables are sizeable for both races. In some cases—for example, racial contact,— it is clear that had we been able to add region as a control variable, the coefficient would become more positive, since extracurricular participation is greater in the deep south, where there is less racial contact.

Table 5A-9. Individual-level regression of extracurricular participation on student outcomes.

	Regression Coefficients Relating Extracurricular Participation to:			
	White Student Outcomes		Black Student Outcomes	
	Unstandardized (b)	Standardized (β)	Unstandardized (b)	Standardized (β)
Dependent Variables:				
Parents Visit School	16	.17[a]	10	.11[a]
Talk to Teachers About Personal Matters	10	.11[a]	15	.16[a]
Teachers Encourage College	22	.21[a]	11	.11[a]
Amount of Homework Done	10	.10[a]	3	.04[a]
Achievement Test Scores	34	.17[a]	16	.11[a]
Believe Staff Likes Desegregation	3	.03	3	.04[a]
Racial Attitudes	0	.00	6	.06[a]
Racial Contact	1	.01	8	.08[a]
Happiness	7	.10[a]	3	.04[a]
Like School	10	.11[a]	8	.09[a]
Think Rules are Fair	6	.07[a]	3	.03
Self-Esteem	19	.21[a]	15	.18[a]

[a] $p < .05$.

Note: regression equations control on SES, community urbanism, school percentage white, duration of desegregation, and mean SES of other race. Dependent variables are standardized to percentage units, except achievement, which is in SAT units.

6 STRUCTURES TO HELP TEACHERS TEACH

The first task of the school is of course academic instruction, and the social responsibilities of the school do not make this job easier. American schools are by design "common schools"— serving students of all classes, races, and ability levels; serving would-be delinquents as well as serious students. Most Americans want common schools. At least, one does not hear very many people arguing for the traditional European educational system in which most students were written off as early as age eleven, given a minimal education, and sent into the factories at age sixteen. Perhaps such a system is better, but it runs contrary to the American ethic of equality of opportunity.

We are still learning how to make common schools work. Until very recently most young people did not go to high school, and high schools could be, as their name implies, school for an elite. Today most students graduate from high school, and many educators think the most difficult task of the school is coping with heterogeneity.

This chapter will look at several modifications of the structure of school. One promising technique for dealing with heterogeneity is having students work cooperatively in teams. Ability grouping is another strategy for dealing with student heterogeneity. Most desegregation experts disapprove of tracking, but the evidence suggests that it has advantages as well as disadvantages. Creating

208

either cooperative teams or ability groups will affect the reward system of the school—its grading policy. A third strategy is the use of electronics—computer-assisted learning and audio-visual materials along with the professional support staff to enable the school to use media. Finally, we will comment on the other side of the heterogeneity problem—the control of disruptive behavior.

HETEROGENEITY AND COMPETITION

The last bastion of cutthroat competition, of every man for himself, and the devil take the hindmost may well be the public school classroom. Each day students are evaluated against the performance of the other students in the same class. Some one does the best, some one else the worst. Sometimes grades are publicly posted, but always grades from A to F are given, telling the student where he places in relation to others. We subject children to a form of competitive grading which we would not tolerate for ourselves as adults. Teachers grade students, but they bitterly resist outside evaluation of their own work. Almost nowhere in the economy does one earn a higher or lower wage at the expense of a fellow worker.[1]

We evaluate children but not adults in this manner simply because adults have more power to resist. It is no accident that the older students get, and hence the more powerful, the more lenient the grading system. As students have grown more aggressive in dealing with faculty, grade averages have steadily risen to the point where college admission officers complain about grade inflation. High school students rebel against competitive grading in a variety of ways—some pretend not to study very hard; many cooperate in cheating; and all create their own status systems by honoring athletics, popularity, ability to get dates, or even delinquency as alternatives to the status system created by the report card.

Student attempts to subvert the system are not without a certain logic. Clearly, there can only be one best student. The others, regardless of their relative performance, are not best. To be consistently regarded by others and, ultimately, by oneself as forever

---

[1] One might even argue that classroom competition poorly prepares a student for the more muted competition of adult life; a modern economy requires cooperation as much as competition.

falling short can damage even the sturdiest ego. Under such circumstances it would not be unreasonable to conclude, "Since I can't be the best, I won't want to be the best." The reward structure leads students to justify the inevitable not best by downplaying the importance of doing well academically.[2]

Equally disturbing, particularly in a desegregated school, is the fact that competition-based reward structure works against cooperation. It takes little insight to realize that helping another student decreases one's own chances for success. The every man for himself philosophy diminishes the community. When the community is a desegregated school, racial attitudes and behavior will suffer.

USING A TEAM APPROACH

Organizing classrooms into small groups or teams can remove some of the sting of competition. Students can also gain additional motivation by working in a supportive small group. Slavin and Madden (1979) analyzed data from seventy-one schools, using data similar to ours in each school. They found two factors which predicted good race relations: more students playing on integrated athletic teams and students saying that their teacher had assigned them to work with a student of the opposite race. Without a careful structure for selecting team members and dividing work among those members, team projects can work against a favorable classroom climate. For example, allowing newly desegregated students the freedom to choose their groupmates will almost certainly result in segregated groups. Loosely structured projects also invite domination by the more aggressive and articulate team members.

Researchers at the Johns Hopkins University have tested three teamwork strategies applicable to the desegregated classroom. All the systems use a cooperative reward structure, that is, rewards are given to groups based upon group performance. Thus, they can eliminate unequal motivation, the pitting of students of unequal ability against one another, and the unfavorable connotation associated with doing well academically, all of which operate to some extent in the traditional classroom. At the same time they effectively encourage competition and peer tutoring.

[2]The grading system also places the teacher in an awkward position, not unlike that of an employer who gives no paycheck to most of his employees.

Johns Hopkins has developed kits mainly for elementary and middle school students. A few of the kits are for use in high school classes, and a number of high school teachers have used the junior high math packages in remedial classes. (As this is written, an experiment is being done in an entire junior high school using each homeroom as a team to maximize both attendance and performance in all classes.) It is not difficult for teachers to prepare their own materials, and we are convinced the techniques will work in most high school classes. Let us describe the three main techniques, and the reader can decide if they can be adapted to high school subjects.

The first technique, Teams-Games-Tournament (TGT), can be used for any material which involves short-answer exams—except that instead of the usual exam system, students compete in teams against other teams in tournaments. The key to TGT is the team—students are assigned so that each team reflects the race, sex and ability-mix of the classroom. Each team competes against other teams in a tournament, which typically lasts ten weeks with one game played each week. In a game, three students representing three different teams play at each table. The game is simply a short-answer test; each student answers a question in turn, with the other two students free to challenge answers they think are wrong.

The winner at each table gains six points for his team, the student in second place four, and the last student two. The scores of all the team's members are totalled to give a team score. Initially students are assigned to game tables on the basis of past performance—the best student from one team competing with the best students from two other teams and so forth. This means that every student, regardless of ability, has a roughly equal chance of earning six points for his team. After each game the winning and losing student from each table are moved to harder or easier tables to make the competition as equal as possible.

Each week the teacher prepares a newsletter to announce the outcome of the previous tournament. The newsletter emphasizes weekly team performance but also recognizes individual table winners and keeps a record of cumulative team standings. In addition to the newsletter, many teachers use bulletin boards, special privileges, or other rewards to emphasize the point that doing well as a team is important.

With elementary students, the tournaments have generated tre-mendous enthusiasm—with teams staying after school to prepare for next week's big game. The special pay off in a desegregated school is that every student has an incentive to work with the other members of his team—regardless of differences in sex, race, or ability level. A series of evaluations of TGT show that it has a positive influence on both a student's liking of others and his feelings of being liked. Mutual concern grows as does a sense of group membership. TGT also helps create favorable attitudes towards school and academic success. Further, students involved in TGT felt that they were more likely to succeed, and, consequently, success became more valuable to them. The effects of TGT on race relations alone provide a convincing argument for its implementation in racially mixed classrooms. (DeVries and Slavin 1976: 68).

TGT is based on sound principles of social psychology. First, the probability of a student's achieving has no relation to overall ability level—poor students can help their teams as much as brilliant students. Nor do rewards depend on relative performance, so poor students no longer find themselves in an adversary position with their brighter peers. Further, interdependent work with students of another race, sex, or ability level fosters mutual respect and friendship. Finally, each student has the happy experience of belonging to and being accepted by a group.

There is a less combative version of TGT in which team members do no compete with other teams face to face at game tables but take individual teacher-graded quizzes. Students receive points for their team depending on how well they score compared to other students of the same ability level. (Only the teacher knows who each student is competing against.) Like TGT, the emphasis is on total team score over a period of several weeks with weekly newsletters keeping everyone posted on their team performance; the difference is that there is no face-to-face competition.

The "Jigsaw" teaming approach developed by Elliot Aronson (1975, 1978) is also less competitive than TGT in the sense that the groups do not need to play against each other. Jigsaw was designed to improve student attitudes and reduce racial tension in the newly desegregated Austin, Texas school system. The underlying premise of the Jigsaw strategy is that the competitive reward structure of the traditional classroom fails to produce healthy social attitudes. The traditional classroom revolves around the teacher as power figure, resource person, and divine determiner of the one and only correct answer, a combination which guarantees that students will regard each other as opponents in their battle for recognition, thus, preventing the development of friendly and cooperative relationships and aggravating racial tensions.

In Jigsaw, students form five- or six-member groups with each member receiving a portion of the total assignment. Each member masters his own material which he then teaches to the group. Students depend on each other for the total picture. Whether the teacher chooses to hold team tournaments or grade students in the traditional way, individual success literally depends on group cooperation.

In studying the method, Aronson (1975) observed that although students initially tried to compete, they quickly realized the inappropriateness of their old habits in this new situation. At that point, attitudes and behavior began to change. In a controlled experiment Aronson examined the impact of the Jigsaw method at the elementary school level. After only six weeks, the members of the Jigsaw groups—

- Showed a stronger liking of their peers,
- Believed they could learn from their classmates,
- Liked school better,
- Had more positive self-concepts,
- Improved academically, and
- Showed improved racial behavior.

Commenting on the potential utility of the Jigsaw technique in racially mixed classrooms, Aronson wrote, "It is not so clearly a solution, by itself, to racial tension, but it is an important adjunct to desegregation. 'Separate but equal' didn't work as a cure for prejudice. Perhaps, in time, 'equal and interdependent' will"(1975:49).

GRADES

Team learning and tracking both raise the issue of grading. In most high schools the grades given are based on both ability and effort. To the extent that they are based on ability, they represent nothing more than the frequent repetition of the same old news—some students are brighter than others. One of the major differences with a team approach is that grades are relative to ability. The same amount of improvement leads to the same grade, regardless of starting point. Similarly, a tracked school provides the opportunity to grade students in comparison to others of the same ability level. (This is not always the case. Some schools have a policy of not permitting A or B grades for students in the lower tracks.) We think that grading students on the basis of performance rather than ability would reduce student discontent and motivate more students to achieve.[3]

High schools are trapped by the need to produce transcripts for college admissions decisions. Presumably college admissions officers wish to know about the student's ability. Ability-based grades also made sense when high schools consciously discouraged weaker students from staying in high school. Now when every effort is made to help everyone finish high school, such a grading policy seems harmful. It seems that two sets of grades are needed—one to advise colleges on the student's strengths and weaknesses, the other to reward the student immediately for the work he has done in the past few weeks. Schools should experiment with new grading procedures.

TRACKING

Civil Rights leaders have long denounced tracking as a way of bringing segregation back into desegregated schools. True, prejudiced teachers can use tracking to channel white students into some classes and blacks into others. Even impartial student assignment on the basis of test scores would result in some classroom segregation. Obviously, allowing individual classes to remain segregated defeats the purpose of school desegregation.

A careful look at our data has convinced us that the story is more complicated. Desegregation should lead to integration—to black and white students working and playing together and learning about citizenship in a biracial society. We know one thing for certain about race relations—the best antidote to prejudice is equal status contact. Team learning succeeds in part because it creates equal status contact. Each member of the team, regardless of ability level, can contribute as much as any other to the group's total score. All team members thus have the same status. Regular classwork, on the other

[3]Unfortunately, our study contains no data on grading practices.

hand, results in unequal status. The traditional classroom revolves around studying, homework group discussion, and tests, activities which ensure that students of drastically unequal levels of achievement will have little to say to each other and will not easily overcome the differences between them. Tracking, which restricts the ability range of the classroom, provides one solution to the problem of unequal status.

We arrive at a difficult tradeoff. Is it better to accept status inequalities in the classroom in exchange for maximum desegregation, or should we allow classrooms to differ in racial composition so that the racial contact which does occur will be between students of more equal status? The answer may depend partly on the kind of staff in a given school. An ideologically conservative principal and staff may use tracking in ways which penalize low ability and minority students. They may consistently underestimate minority student ability so as to create substantial segregation. They may treat the low ability tracks as holding tanks, or they may regard all tracking assignments as immutable. Practices such as these convey a message not likely to be lost on the students. If little is expected of the students in the lowest track, they will achieve little. Staff attitudes will thus determine the type of effect tracking will have. Specifically, one might predict that tracking in conjunction with a conservative staff will make a bad situation worse. With a liberal staff, however, one would expect tracking to have a favorable impact.

We asked principals the number of different ability levels used in tenth grade English classes, the proportion of tenth grade academic subjects using ability grouping, and the degree to which their students had been ability-grouped in junior high school. Combined responses to the three questions form our measure of tracking. In the analysis that follows, the schools are divided into two equal groups, those with less tracking and those with more, and then these groups are divided on the basis of the staff attitudes towards school desegregation (i.e., liberal or conservative) presented in Chapter 3. This separates the 194 schools into four categories: liberal untracked, liberal tracked, conservative untracked, and conservative tracked. If, as one might expect, the combination of tracking with liberal staff attitudes is beneficial, positive effects will occur for this one type of school in comparison to the other three. As usual, the analysis matches the schools on student, school, and community characteristics.

Table 6-1.   Percentage of students reporting high interracial contact by race, presence of tracking, and staff racial attitudes.

	Percentage of Students Reporting High Interracial Contact			
	(White Students)		(Black Students)	
	School Is:		School Is:	
Staff Is:	Untracked	Tracked	Untracked	Tracked
Liberal	36	38	44	51
Conservative	30	32	42	49

Note: Schools matched on racial composition of school and neighborhood, duration of desegregation, school size, region, community urbanism and educational level, and black and white student socioeconomic status.

Table 6–1 shows that percentage of students reporting friendly interracial contact. We know that tracked schools have more racially imbalanced classes. Hence, it is surprising that both black and white students report more interracial contact in tracked schools.

In an earlier chapter, we concluded that liberal teachers encourage interracial contact, and Table 6–1 shows this again. Both blacks and whites should find racial contact easier in a tracked school because their opposite-race peers will be performing at a comparable achievement level, thus removing one potential source of strain. Staff racial attitudes are not as important as tracking in predicting the amount of contact blacks will have with whites. For whites, tracking plus a liberal staff is the best combination.

Table 6–2 presents the percentage of black and white students who feel they belong in each type of school. For whites, neither tracking nor staff racial attitudes seem to make a difference—the four percentages are essentially the same.[4] For black students, the differences are large and exactly as predicted. A conservative school staff will make black students feel unwelcome irrespective of ability grouping. In an untracked school, a liberal teaching staff will make blacks feel somewhat more at home. The ideal situation occurs in

[4]There may be a slight tendency in Table 6–2 for whites to be more uncomfortable when the staff is more liberal. The differences are too small to pay attention to but are not surprising; many white students are uncomfortable with desegregation and would be more at ease in a school where the teachers favored white students, and where they felt less faculty pressure to associate with blacks.

Table 6-2. Percentage of students who say they "belong" in tracked and untracked schools with liberal and conservative staff.

	Percent "Belonging" in School			
	(White Students)		(Black Students)	
	School Is:		School Is:	
Staff Is:	Untracked	Tracked	Untracked	Tracked
Liberal	73	74	72	82[a]
Conservative	76	76	67	69

[a]This cell significantly different from other cells, $p < .05$.

Note: Schools matched on racial composition of school and neighborhood, duration of desegregation, school size, region, community urbanism and educational level, and black and white student socioeconomic status.

schools with both ability grouping and liberal teachers. Under these conditions, 82 percent of the black students say they belong in the school. The 18 percent who feel they do not belong is only one-half the percentage who say this in untracked, conservative schools. We assume that in ability-grouped schools with sensitive teachers blacks will find that they can compete academically and will not view integration as a threat.

It follows that when a black student feels a part of the school, he will like school. The pattern for blacks in Table 6–3 is similar to what we saw in our analysis of sense of belonging. Ability grouping makes no difference when the staff is conservative. Black students more often say they like school when the staff is liberal. Again, the combination of ability grouping and liberal staff works best. Fifty-two percent of the students in liberal, tracked schools say they like school, the highest percentage of the four cells in the table. For white students, tracking and staff racial liberalism make little difference. White students do show a slight tendency to prefer tracked schools, but the differences are nominal.

Table 6–4 presents the effects of tracking on achievement test performance. Since Chapter 2 showed sex differences in achievement, male and female scores were computed separately. Both whites and blacks tend to have higher test scores in liberal schools although the differences are generally quite small. Of eight possible comparisons, the schools with liberal staffs have higher achievement in six cases. One of the remaining cases (white males in untracked

Table 6-3.   Percentage of students who like school, by race, presence of tracking, and staff racial attitudes.

	Percentage of Students Who Like School			
	(White Students)		(Black Students)	
	School Is:		School Is:	
Staff Is:	Untracked	Tracked	Untracked	Tracked
Liberal	45	49	48	52
Conservative	44	47	42	41

Note: Schools matched on racial composition of school and neighborhood, duration of desegregation, school size, region, community urbanism and educational level, and black and white student socioeconomic status.

schools) shows no difference; the other (white females in untracked schools) shows lower scores for liberal staff. The generally higher achievement in liberal schools may result from better teaching. Faced with a heterogeneous classroom, liberal teachers may work harder with the minority students, thus slighting the white students. This may explain why white students do not seem to perform better in liberal, untracked schools.

The table also indicates that tracking is associated with lower minority scores but not lower white scores. In all four possible cases for blacks, tracked schools have lower achievement. In one case (black girls in conservative schools) the difference is sixteen points. For white students, tracked schools have marginally higher scores in three cases out of four. The remaining case, however, (white girls in conservative schools) shows a sizeable difference favoring untracked schools. Thus, we cannot conclude that tracking helps white students, but it clearly hurts blacks in terms of test scores.

A recent review of the voluminous literature on tracking, including reanalyses of four school surveys, led Jencks and his colleagues (1972) to conclude that tracking does tend to widen the achievement gap between blacks and whites but not enough to be considered important educationally. Our data seem to support this view. The black-white achievement gap is on the order of one hundred points in these schools. Tracking increases that gap by an average of seven points.

We have arrived at a difficult decision point. It seems clear that in terms of race relations and student attitudes, newly desegregated

Table 6-4. Mean achievement of students, by race, sex, presence of tracking, and staff racial attitudes.

	Mean Achievement							
	(White Females)		(Black Females)		(White Males)		(Black Males)	
	School Is:		School Is:		School Is:		School Is:	
Staff Is:	Untracked	Tracked	Untracked	Tracked	Untracked	Tracked	Untracked	Tracked
Liberal	466	474[a]	354	347[b]	453	459	344	340
Conservative	474	459	348	332[b]	453	456	341	336

[a]Combined effect of staff liberalism and tracking is significantly positive, p < .05.

[b]Effect of tracking is significantly negative, p < .05.

Note: Schools matched on racial composition of school and neighborhood, duration of desegregation, school size, region, community urbanism and educational level, and black and white student socioeconomic status.

219

high schools benefit by ability grouping. On the other hand, the data provide some evidence that tracking harms black achievement test performance. Ability grouping need not have negative effects on achievement, but teachers will need to push the students in their low ability classes to achieve just as they would push heterogeneously grouped students.

INDIVIDUALIZATION AND ELECTRONIC HARDWARE

In the long run, the answer to eliminating the evils of classroom competition lies in individualization—a curriculum for each student and grading which depends solely on mastery of that curriculum. (See Bloom [1976] for an argument in favor of mastery learning.) In the last few years we have learned a great deal about individualization in elementary schools, and thousands of teachers now have the necessary skills for teaching students of widely varying abilities. High school teachers face greater difficulties when it comes to individualization since they typically see a hundred or more students daily. Computerized instruction thus seems especially promising as a way to individualize the secondary curriculum.

Computer costs have dropped dramatically in the last decade, making individually tailored programs of instruction financially feasible for the first time. Researchers at the University of Illinois have developed and tested a system called "Plato," and have found it effective with high school students. Another system operates in four Los Angeles elementary schools and is being evaluated by ETS. Students work at computer terminals, studying language arts, reading, and mathematics for five to twenty minutes each day. The student solves problems presented by the computer and receives instant feedback on his performance.

Immediate feedback, plus the capacity to tailor the level of difficulty to the students' needs makes the computer an excellent tool for remedial instruction. Students with a history of academic frustration will appreciate receiving work geared to ability. The designers of Plato found that many students who had previously shown little interest in class work routinely stayed after school to play on the terminal. Finally, machines have the infinite patience most teachers lack, so computer-assisted instruction can provide a welcome relief for everyone.

Unfortunately, few schools made instructional use of computers at the time of our study, so we cannot evaluate their effectiveness. We will consider instead a seemingly more mundane innovation—the use of electronic media. Most schools underutilize electronic media. In the average classroom, media usage refers to the movie which occasionally interrupts the normal flow of events. Often, expensive equipment goes unused because teachers have no one to ask for technical assistance. Shifting to a multimedia curriculum can entail substantial money and time. However, many of the schools in our sample have made the transition and have found it worthwhile.

We asked our principals to list the different kinds of personnel in their schools, ranging from music teachers to truant officers. In comparing school achievement, we found only one type of educational specialist that seemed to make a difference—the audio-visual coordinator. Only 21 of the 200 schools had such a person, but these 21 showed consistently higher test scores for both black and white students. As Table 6–5 indicates, the presence of an audio visual specialist is associated with mean achievement gains of thirty-nine points for whites and twenty-three points for blacks.[5]

Audio-visual equipment can mean many different things. It may mean two teleivison sets for an entire school, or a large collection of films, slide projectors, record players, and tape recorders. All of our schools had some equipment, but those with an audio-visual coordinator had more elaborate arrangements. Two had their own television production operation in which students and staff worked together to make video tapes for classroom use. One school used a series of films for their minicourses in Asian and African studies. A number had equipment for individualized instruction—language laboratories with headphones, individual carrels with teaching machines, microfilm viewers, phonographs, and tape recorders. Many of our schools used teaching machines for remedial work, particularly in reading. One school staff developed a programmed instruction course in remedial math. Two of the schools turned much of their regular class time over to individualized instruction. Another

---

[5]We considered the possibility that the audio-visual specialists did not really bring about increased achievement and that the 21 schools were peculiar in some way. A variety of statistical checks on our data revealed no abnormalities. See the technical appendix for details.

Table 6-5.   Achievement test scores of black and white students, by presence of an audio-visual specialist in the school.

| | Does School Have Audio-Visual Specialist? | |
	Yes	No
Mean Black Achievement	364	343
Mean White Achievement	498	459

Note: Schools matched on racial composition of school and neighborhood, duration of desegregation, school size, region, community urbanism and educational level, and black and white student socioeconomic status.

had a media center housing a wide range of equipment for individuals or small groups. Teachers and students made frequent use of the center for work on a one-to-one basis.

Higher achievement seems a logical consequence of media usage mainly because it requires greater student involvement than most kinds of classwork. Cusick (1973) found that the average high school student spends only a few minutes of each day actively involved in learning. Most devote their time to thinking about more interesting things and pay the minimal amount of attention necessary to avoid detection. Students often claim, not unjustifiably, that school is boring. It is also true that we hold rather high expectations for our teachers. Not even Bill Cosby could deliver ever more entertaining monologues to the same audience five days a week, nine months a year. We think a sound media program could combat much of the boredom and frustration which affects students and teachers alike.

By awakening student interest, good media material enables the teacher to do a better job. Media usage also frees the teacher to spend additional time in one-to-one relationships with students. As Table 6-6 indicates, more students report speaking with teachers about personal matters in schools with an audio-visual specialist.

The entertainment value of media, coupled with its great potential for individualization, should have a dramatic impact on student morale. We found, for example, extremely low levels of racial tension in the two most highly individualized schools in our sample. We suspect that a strong media program also makes for better morale among faculty members. Media can relieve the tension caused by continual lecture-discussion, thus enabling teachers to develop a more satisfying blend of teaching methods.

Table 6–6. Percentage of black and white students reporting personal conversations with school staff, by presence of an audio-visual specialist.

	Does School Have an Audio-Visual Specialist?	
	Yes	No
Percentage of Black Students Reporting Personal Conversations with School Staff	58	53
Percentage of White Students Reporting Personal Conversations with School Staff	69	63

Note: Schools matched on racial composition of school and neighborhood, duration of desegregation, school size, region, community urbanism and educational level, and black and white student socioeconomic status.

MAKING AN INNOVATION WORK: THE NEED FOR AN AUDIO-VISUAL SPECIALIST

Implementing a complicated innovation such as electronic media involves a major bit of social reorganization. One Los Angeles principal planned with his staff for nearly two years before installing computer-assisted instruction. He realized that adopting such an innovation would make little sense without a staff commitment to broaden their teaching methods. For example, the computer program the school adopted used somewhat unconventional mathematical symbols. Teachers needed to explain the same symbols in class. They also had to understand how the program functioned so they could coach their students when necessary. They had to learn how to read the computerized evaluation of each student in order to tailor classwork to individual needs. Perhaps most important, teachers needed to overcome their natural animosity to a machine which in one small way could teach more effectively than they.

The school will face an even greater challenge in moving toward a multimedia curriculum. Computerized instruction has its own internal logic and structure. A media program, on the other hand, will have no order beyond that which staff members impose. Converting discrete pieces of material into a coherent curriculum will require substantial effort from each teacher. In addition, a media program encompasses all aspects of the curriculum, making it one of the more complex educational innovations.

Our statistical analysis shows that the audio-visual specialist, not the equipment itself, raises achievement. We asked principals whether they had audio-visual materials, and, or course, the vast majority said they did. We found no evidence that materials alone affected achievement. The point is an obvious one—media do not help unless put to proper use. Merely setting up a budget for equipment purchases will not work; too many storage rooms contain expensive, unused equipment financed by Title I. Teachers have neither the time nor the experience necessary to screen large amounts of material, select usable pieces, and incorporate them into the curriculum. The school desiring widespread media usage will allocate these responsibilities to the audio-visual specialist. Some schools employ an additional librarian for this purpose; others release a teacher from classroom duties. A genuine commitment to a media program involves assigning a full- or half-time person to coordinate materials and to train teachers in their use.

A successful media program will also require space for carrels so students can work with equipment on an individual basis. Often, the daily schedule will need revision to allow students ample time to use the media. Finally, teachers will need an opportunity to express their preferences concerning both the type of materials and their integration into the curriculum.

Any educational innovation, however uncomplicated it appears, requires this same kind of school and staff reorganization. The Rand Corporation study of federally funded innovations makes this point more generally (Berman and McLaughlin, 1978). In many schools, the researchers found newly instituted reading or bilingual programs which limped along, never truly accepted by the school. When federal funds ceased, these programs collapsed. The Rand study developed an interesting rule of thumb to predict program success. The researchers focused on two general questions: Was the program modified to fit the school's needs? and Did the school change its policies and practices in any way to accommodate the program?

Unsuccessful programs failed to recognize that any significant change affects and is affected by what happens throughout the school. The authors found unsuccessful innovations in two kinds of schools. One type of school, for example, might install teaching machines for individualized instruction but continue to base grades on the same tests as before. In such a situation, the teaching machines would rapidly become irrelevant, used only when they perfectly fit the existing curriculum. Simply corrupting the innovation to fit the school will not bring educational change. At the opposite extreme lies the school which borrows intact an innovation that worked well someplace else. Attempting solely to adapt the school to the innovation invariably fails also. Successful educational change meets two criteria: first, a tailoring of the innovation to the school's needs and second, an adjustment in staffing and organization on the part of the school. The Rand authors term this process "mutual adaptation" and argue that it alone leads to successful innovation. (Berman and McLaughlin 1978:16)

The success of an audio-visual program depends on this same adaptive process. If we went to two high schools and found identical media materials in each, we would feel fairly certain that the program did not meet the needs of at least one of those schools. We would expect to find, for example, one school emphasizing the type of remedial math teaching most consistent with its classroom instruction practices. Or we might find that one of the schools had special media material developed by the social studies faculty to fit with a unit on city life. We would conclude that each school had modified the innovation to fit its own special needs. At the same time, a school must alter its own structure to make the innovation work. At a minimum, our successful schools have added an additional staff person to manage the media program. In the extreme case, schools have drastically cut back on classroom instruction so students will have ample time to work in media centers.

Our successful schools have in common this mutual adaptation, a process that goes well beyond purchasing equipment or hiring a coordinator. The media specialist must function as part of a school-wide program. Some school procedures will have to be changed. Teachers will need opportunities to work out problems as they arise and to modify the program when necessary. Ideally, teachers should receive funding to visit media programs in other schools. In effect, the staff must make a group decision to intensively use media. The process of arriving at that group consensus may take a year or more and will require active support from the principal even after the media specialist is hired. The implementation of an innovation is a school-wide process. Successful educational change requires nothing less.

HELPING TEACHERS TEACH: THE INSTRUCTIONAL SPECIALIST

The idea of the audio-visual or computer specialist can be expanded further. Everything a teacher does uses technology: Books, lesson plans, tests and blackboard diagrams are all technical projects which someone must design. We normally give teachers textbooks and expect them to find the time to design everything else they use. This is obviously ineffecient. Staff time is too valuable to be spent inventing the wheel anew each day. In addition, teaching is a lonely business. There is no one with whom to share decisions except department chairmen and the principal, who cannot easily step out of their positions of authority and become colleagues. Some schools have developed instructional materials coordinators, teachers with no classroom responsibilty who help other teachers locate materials and can serve as colleagues. It seems to us that the argument we have made about the need for audio-visual and computer specialists can be applied to instructional materials coordinators as well. Schools are peculiarly hierarchical institutions—the classroom teacher interacts with very few other professionals at the same rank. More thought should be given to the creation of staff positions which are not superordinate to teachers.

HETEROGENEITY AND DISRUPTION

Discipline and the control of disruptive behavior have always been problems for schools, but the school pranks of the nineteenth-century have become more serious as schools have become more heterogeneous. We have not written a chapter entitled "School Discipline" because this entire book is in a sense about controlling disruptive behavior. Prevention is the most effective form of medicine, and because the school plays such an important role in a student's life, it plays an important role in delinquency prevention.

One statement of the origins of delinquent behavior (Hirschi

1969) argues that students conform to social rules for four reasons: (1) Because of their attachments to adults, they conform to avoid displeasing their parents and teachers; (2) because they are committed to career goals and do not wish to jeopardize their chances; (3) because they are involved in satisfying personal activities; and (4) because they believe in the rules of the society. Obviously the school plays an important role in promoting student conformity. School is a place to which one can become attached; it is an avenue to an adult career; it can provide involvement in all sorts of activities; and as it does each of these things, it strengthens the student's belief in the correctness of the rules of the society. Or, as Gottfredson writes:

> So, school rewards are central to this theory of delinquency. The bonds of social control are strengthened for youth who find school rewarding, and they are weakened for youth who do not. Weakened restraints produce a cycle of continuing school failure and delinquency and disruptive behavior. On the other hand, experiences of school success result in a cycle of continuing academic achievement and vocational or career success(1980:12).

Schools can create a climate of prevention by establishing a grading system which rewards immediate performance rather than general ability, and by encouraging attachment to others through extracurricular and community service activities. Effective schools also increase student-teacher attachment by creating more opportunities for teacher-student interaction. The most effective schools are either small or are organized so that teachers interact intensively with a small number of students (for example, by assigning teachers to the same students for more than one class period each day, or by having homeroom teachers assigned to the same students throughout the four years of high school).

Preventing disruption also means dealing effectively with student misbehavior. Congress recently commissioned a major study of school violence. The original report issued by the National Institute of Educational (1978) and a secondary analysis of the data (Gottfredson and Daiger 1979) both conclude that the rules for classroom behavior must be clear to all parties and must be consistently enforced. This in turn means that teachers and administrators must be in agreement and must work together. This recommendation seems obvious, but it is our impression that few schools really follow it. Rules are not always written down, the rules may vary considerably from one classroom to the next, and whether infractions will be punished is often an open question. In many schools, for example, students know that certain teachers do not agree with the administration about what students are required to do. In addition, students should have some share in setting the school's discipline policy (although both reports make it clear that schools should not become enamored with participatory democracy, which seems to be harmful). Once the rules are set, students need to know they are not negotiable and that their enforcement is the same for all students. This applies to the minor rules of the school as well as the major ones; schools which do not control minor problems are the schools that have major problems with violence.

CONCLUSIONS

If a desegregated school is to work, it must teach its black and white students mutual liking and respect. A single-minded concern with academic performance which pits students against each other teaches a different lesson. Successful desegregation demands equal status racial contact; black and white students must come together as cooperating equals.

Many schools have met this challenge. It requires dealing sensitively with the complex problems created by achievement differences. Simply telling students to form teams and then friendships will accomplish little. Team assignments and activities need a tight structure to prevent the more verbally aggressive students, those accustomed to being classroom stars, from dominating the group. The implementation of ability grouping presents more severe problems. Ability grouping has enormous potential for abuse. It can result in unnecessary segregation or in the stigmatizing of lower track students. School staff will need to devote special attention to the lower track classes, making sure that these students do as well as they would under a heterogeneous system. Unfortunately we cannot advise teachers and administrators on how to tackle this difficult assignment. We can, however, point to the substantial noncognitive benefits of tracking newly desegregated students, and we remain convinced that a good ability grouping system merits the effort required to set it up. Finally, we have spoken at length about the problems of implementing a sound media program. Given a strong commitment on the part of school staff, this innovation too can bring impressive results.

APPENDIX 6A
TECHNICAL APPENDIX

The assumption underlying much of this chapter is that competitive grading is socially very harmful. We have found no literature which directly tests this assumption. Our own questionnaire contains no questions about grading practices, and there is little written on the topic. Two brief but cogent discussions are by Coleman (1961: 317–324) and McPartland and McDill (1977).

The longer we thought about this the more puzzled we became. If grading has such harmful effects, why has it received so little attention in the education literature? We can only speculate, but two rather cynical hypotheses came to mind. First, we use grades because we always have. We need a system of rewards and sanctions to motivate students, and no one has suggested a better system. Or (and more to the point, we think) grades exist because the people involved in education, including those who preach radical school reform, made good grades. The people who did not learn to read well, the people who made a poor showing in school, do not write books or give speeches.

COOPERATIVE GAMES

The major work on cooperative games is presently being carried out at Johns Hopkins University. In addition to Teams-Games-Tournament, researchers at Hopkins have developed a new version of cooperative learning curricula, Student Team Learning. They have written a number of reports, and articles and brochures describing the available materials can be obtained from the center for the Social Organization of Schools at Johns Hopkins. Jigsaw, a teaming approach used in Austin, Texas, has been described by Aronson in both article (1975) and book (1978) form, and is also distributed by Johns Hopkins.

TRACKING

Tables 6A–1 and 6A–2 show the regression equations used to analyze the effects of tracking. These equations use the same ten control variables used in the preceding chapter: region, urbanism and educational level of community, black and white student SES, school size, racial composition of the school and its neighborhood, and two measures of duration of desegregation. As the upper panel of Table 6A–1 shows, black student morale and racial contact rates are higher if black students attend school in a black neighborhood. The same pattern was found in the data shown in Chapter 2. Tracking, teaching liberalism, and the interaction term between the two serve as independent variables. All three variables are coded as dichotomies.

Table 6A–2 shows the regression equations for the achievement of the four race-sex groups in each school. Note that black female students benefit the most from comprehensive classes and, con-

Table 6A–1. Regression equations with standardized regression co-efficients (βs) used to construct Tables 6–1, 6–2, 6–3.

	Black Like School	Black Racial Contact	White Like School	White Racial Contact
Independent Variables:				
School Percentage White	−.099	.721[a]	.166	−.397[a]
Black SES	−.230[a]	−.119	−.182[a]	.096
Black Elementary/ Junior High	−.032	.019	−.011	−.027
Always Integrated	−.060	.060	.054	.126
School in Black Neighborhood	.224[a]	.189[a]	−.016	−.026
School Size	−.008	.095	−.096	.124
Region within South	−.090	.037	−.143	.158[a]
White SES	.092	−.158[a]	−.147	−.081
Community Education Level	.167	−.022	.048	.061
Urbanism of County	−.106	.058	.192	.254[a]
Tracking	−.014	.137	.130	.073
Tracking + Liberal Teachers	.200	.079	.032	.022
Liberal Teachers	.060	−.034	.033	.160
r^2	.170	.497	.097	.717

[a] $p < .05$.

Table 6A-2. Regression equations with standardized regression coefficients (βs) used to construct Table 6-4.

	Black Achievement		White Achievement	
	Male	Female	Male	Female
Independent Variables:				
School Percentage White	-.044	-.119	-.043	-.067
Black SES	.522[a]	.373[a]	.241[a]	.134
Black Elementary/				
Junior High	-.168	-.114	.003	.047
Always Integrated	.150	.073	-.020	.037
School in Black				
Neighborhood	.032	.015	.015	-.050
School Size	.095	.073	-.197[a]	-.054
Region within South	-.052	.177[a]	.122	.007
White SES	.149	.305[a]	.543[a]	.581[a]
Community Education				
Level	.287[a]	-.153	-.046	-.157
Urbanism of County	-.080	.018	.003	.007
Tracking	-.050	-.173[a]	.022	-.138
Tracking + Liberal				
Teachers	-.009	.169	.053	.349[a]
Liberal Teachers	.065	-.033	-.025	-.250[a]
r^2	.345	.382	.355	.360

[a] $p < .05$.

versely, benefit the least from tracking. These results seem consistent with our findings in Chapter 2 that black girls adjust more quickly to desegregation and tolerate assignments to schools with large numbers of high social status white students more easily. Our findings can be explained by a general proposition: Female students can better tolerate being surrounded by academically superior students or students who claim social superiority.

Much of the analysis shown here was done by Jean Jenkins, an analyst working on *Southern Schools*. (NORC 1973) She found that tracking increases classroom segregation, which in turn reduces student racial contact. However, Jenkins also found a direct positive effect of tracking on contact which more than offset the negative effect of increased segregation.

THE USE OF COMPUTERS AND ELECTRONIC MEDIA

The National Institute of Education (NIE) has contracted with the ETS and the Los Angeles Unified School district to carry out a major study of the effects of computer-assisted instruction. Four elementary schools now have computer terminals. The contractors have developed an elaborate randomization procedure for assigning students to terminals which will allow an experimental test of their effectiveness. A final report has not yet been written; interim reports are available from NIE.

Researchers at the University of Illinois have developed a sophisticated computer program known as "Plato," appropriate for

Table 6A-3. Regression equations with standardized regression coefficients (betas) used to construct Tables 6-5 and 6-6.

	Mean Black Achievement	Mean White Achievement	Black Students Talk to Teachers	White Students Talk to Teachers
Independent Variables:				
School Percentage White	-.008	-.006	-.108	-.095
Black SES	.544[a]	.236[a]	-.065	-.144
Segregated Elementary/ Junior High (Blacks)	-.150	.042	.151	.063
Always Integrated (Whites)	.078	.051	.071	.193[a]
School in Black Neighborhood	.115	-.028	-.045	-.038
School Size	.041	-.168	.255[a]	.189
Region within South	.105	.050	.210[a]	-.034
White SES	.259[a]	.652[a]	.176	.085
Community Education Level	-.271[a]	-.157	.194	.198
Urbanism of County	-.091	-.027	-.049	-.038
Presence of Audio- Visual Specialist	.156[a]	.223[a]	.096	.146
r^2	.463	.476	.318	.149

[a] $p < .05$.

use with elementary- through college-level students. Information about Plato and evaluations of its effectiveness can be obtained from the University of Illinois.

Table 6A–3 presents the regression equations linking the presence of an audio-visual specialist to black and white achievement and black and white reports of informal contact with school staff. *Southern Schools* (NORC 1973) contains a detailed discussion of the role of audio-visual media. That analysis shows that the audio-visual specialist variable was the only variable which consistently affected the achievement of both black and white high school students. A related elementary school variable, the principals' report that the school had received equipment such as reading machines, tape recorders, and video tape machines, for student use, also showed a positive relationship with achievement test performance.

We telephoned the twenty-one schools which claimed an audio-visual specialist in order to test our finding in two ways. First, if the presence of an audio-visual specialist truly increased achievement, correcting any reporting errors about the presence of such a specialist should increase the correlation between specialist presence and achievement. Second, among those schools with audio-visual specialists, we should find a positive relationship between the extent to which the specialist is used and achievement. Since our second test would apply only to those schools with a specialist, it would be statistically independent of the overall correlation between presence of the specialist and achievement. Both statistical tests supported our conclusion: First, we found several schools where the principal explained that either the school did not have an audio-visual specialist or that the specialist's duties were very limited. These schools, as predicted, did not have high achievement. Second, among those schools that did have a specialist, the greater the amount of media used the better the race relations and the higher the achievement.

7 THINKING ABOUT MAKING DESEGREGATION WORK

Chapters 3, 4, 5, and 6 have shown us some specific things schools can do to make desegregation work. We are not going to summarize those chapters in detail here. Instead, we are going to pause and try to pull together the findings in those chapters to see if they point to some general maxims about desegregated schools. Up to now we have been leery of sweeping general statements. It seems to us that there are too many books about schools which make general pronouncements, in effect telling school administrators and teachers to do good things without saying much about how to do them or what exactly to do. We have tried to be specific.

We have also tried to stay as close as we could to the facts—we have not tried to argue for our own personal biases. Of course, every book does have a point of view. Chapter 1, in setting the stage for the book, does show the reader the philosophical biases we brought to this project. Our portrait of City High School shows what kind of school we like, and our description of the research we did showed what we value in a school. For us, a good school is one in which students like school, get along with other students, want to do school work, score well on tests, and want to go to college; it is a school where black and white students are friends and there is little racial conflict. No one of these goals is of highest priority—a school in which test scores are sky high or there are no racial problems may not be the best school overall.

Given that philosophical approach, the analysis was an effort to discover what characteristics of a school seem to increase its chances of success. Chapter 2 looks at the effect of different kinds of desegregation plans. The evidence, which is mainly negative, mostly shows that the kind of desegregation plan does not matter very much. Busing, for example, seems to have little effect on how well the school functions although it is true that students who are bused do not feel as at home in the school. The racial composition of the school makes a difference, and it looks as if schools which are 40 to 80 percent white are more able to provide a good education. (Even this is debatable since these schools do have more racial tension.) Chapter 2 shows some surprises—for example, schools with middle class black students have more racial tension than schools with low income students. Since Chapter 2 deals with matters which are out of the control of the school—the kinds and number of students are fixed by the desegregation plan—it does not contain any specific advice to school administrators and teachers—except perhaps to reassure them by showing that schools desegregated in different ways all have about equal chances of becoming good schools.

Chapters 3 to 6 do contain specific advice for schools. Chapter 3 showed that the racial behavior of teachers is critical to the school's success. It is the teachers' behavior, not their personal attitudes, which seems to be most important, and the school (and especially the principal) can strongly influence teacher behavior. In particular, it looks as if simply the principal's public commitment to establishing good race relations will influence teachers' behavior. In-service programs for staff and human relations programs in the school curriculum can also help.

In Chapter 4, the main conclusion is that trying to improve intergroup relations will pay off. Using curriculum materials on race relations, teaching black history, and providing special training in race relations for teachers will work. The data also suggest that the school must deal with race relations through a carefully structured program. Chapter 5 showed, first, that high rates of participation in extracurricular activities are a positive force for the school, and, second, that employment of additional staff to teach music, drama, art, and gym will produce positive results for the school. Finally,

Chapter 6 showed that team approaches to teaching are successful; that tracking, done by a sympathetic staff, is beneficial for race relations but makes it more difficult for black students to score high on achievement tests; and that employment of a staff media specialist will raise achievement scores for both black and white students.

THE SCHOOL AS A PLACE FOR ADOLESCENT DEVELOPMENT

There is a pattern to this list of recommendations. First, the schools that do these sorts of things are recognizing the emotional needs of their students and trying to meet them. A perhaps obvious point is that students cannot concentrate on learning if they are preoccupied with personal problems. If the school wants to help its students to become useful and happy adults, it should help them deal with adolescence.

Douvan and Adelson (1966) talk about the four basic issues adolescents must deal with: sexuality, identity, achievement, and interpersonal relations. We have not talked about sex; perhaps we assumed that helping students deal with this (in a more extensive way than simply providing sex education) would be too radical for the schools. It is true that if the students overcame some of their fears and anxieties about the opposite sex, they would have more energy to focus on their studies. No one can look at today's divorce statistics without concluding that these students will need all the help they can get if they are to cope with marriage better than their parents.

More obviously related to the function of the school is the establishment of adolescent identity. The need to answer the question, Who am I? pervades much of the teenager's daily life. Fifty years ago, a sociologist used the expression "looking glass self" to make the point that we form opinions of our own self-worth from the way others treat us. One crucial part of identity grows out of the way that parents respond to the child; another from the way that peers react; a third from the way authority figures behave toward him. These last two elements of adolescent identity are largely formed in school. Many of the school characteristics which this research has found to be effective are effective because they help students arrive at a positive sense of identity. This is most clear in the finding that black students are more highly motivated and have higher self-esteem if they can identify important black historical figures. The need for a positive sense of identity is also part of the explanation of why extracurricular activities, the arts, and gym are important—students have the opportunity to interact in constructive ways with teachers and other students in these settings and to reveal aspects of themselves.

Extracurricular activities also play a role in Adelson and Douvain's (1966) dimensions of adolescent development: achievement and interpersonal relations. They conclude that these dimensions are sex linked: males are more concerned with achievement, females more with relating to others. Certainly throughout adolescence boys seem to be struggling with the need to achieve—in competitive sports for example—and to obtain status in the eyes of their peers. At the same time, girls become intensely involved with peer groups, with dating, and with close relationships with best friends. The adolescents who do not do this successfully have trouble growing up, and they have trouble in school.

High school is where many of these adolescent needs are met. Admittedly the teenager brings to these problems his own personal background, strongly influenced by physiological and home environment factors, but it is in high school that the student is first given the opportunity to work out his relationship to the opposite sex, his sense of self, his need to achieve, and his need to develop interpersonally. The way the school meets these needs is heavily influenced by the structure which the school provides for the adolescent. In short, schools socialize the young as well as teach them. High schools have always resisted the notion that they should be responsible for, or even concerned with, the emotional development of their students. School psychologists, if they are present at all, are mainly concerned with specialized intelligence testing. Counselors are concerned with helping students choose among academic courses or with helping students apply to college. The good high schools in our study have taken at least a small step away from this model of the high school as a purely academic institution.

Educators must come to terms with the fact that schools do influence the emotional development of students. The school which attempts to ignore affect is at the very least creating an environment of emotional deprivation which is akin to the inanimate environments created for raising laboratory monkeys. The school cannot avoid being a large part of the adolescent's emotional environment.

The only choice the school has is in deciding what kind of environment it will be.

THE TWO SOCIAL ENVIRONMENTS OF THE HIGH SCHOOL

The typical high school creates two environments—one adult controlled, another student controlled. Each is both helpful and destructive. The adult-controlled environment is one which teaches the values of hard work and achievement. Unfortunately, this is often done in a boring fashion in which nineteenth-century novels irrelevant to the emotional development of teen-agers are mixed with even more irrelevant classes in science and math and leavened by classes in poorly equipped shops in obsolete trades. In many cases this adult-controlled environment has the sort of mindless authoritarianism portrayed in Wiseman's documentary film *High School* (1969). This situation is changing for the better; what has not changed, however, is the status system in which A's are better than C's, college preparatory classes better than remedial classes, and Dickens and chemistry better than current events and woodworking. It is an environment of constant rewards and punishments in which diligence, docility, and native intelligence are rewarded and laziness, rebellion, and lack of native cognitive skill are punished. It is an environment with many more punishments than rewards.

The reason why schools are unable to meet most students' need for achievement is that the adult-controlled part of the school defines achievement in a peculiarly one-dimensional way. Achievement means grades, and a handful of students wind up with all the honors. Sociologists have pointed out that schools perform a sorting function—finding the brightest students and making sure they go to college. Unfortunately, this means structuring the school so that most of the honors and rewards go to this group while everyone else gets a sort of second-class citizenship. There are ways around this: Mastery learning, tracking, and individualization are methods of eliminating these invidious comparisons with other students so that each student is urged to measure his achievement against an absolute standard rather than in comparison to other students. The team learning techiques described in Chapter 6 take a different tack by rewarding cooperative behavior. Slower students are rewarded for their contributions to the team's effort, and no one's grades are at the expense of another.

Competitive grading may do great psychological damage. The student who has been told at six-week intervals for most of his life that he is not as good as others should be angry. By high school many students will have realized that they have little chance of success. If rewards go exclusively to the diligent, the docile, and the intelligent, many students may decide that the odds against them are simply too great. They are likely to define the school's adults as punitive as well as controlling and rebel against them. It is this rebellion which is at the core of juvenile delinquency, and it is not limited to the lower classes. The NIE's safe schools study (1978) found high rates of violence and property damage in suburban and middle class schools. Pamela Richards studied delinquency among students in a middle class school and concluded that delinquency is often a result of students' being angry at the adults with whom they have to deal. She also noted that this kind of anger is surprisingly common: 22 percent of junior high school students and 26 pecent of senior high school students are often or always angry at their parents; 38 percent of the seventh and eighth graders and 26 pecent of the high school students are often or always angry at school officials (Richards 1979: 493).

Some of these students have a safety valve because the school tacitly consents to the operation of a second environment—that of football, cheerleading, clubs, and dances in which students themselves define the criteria for status. This environment also teaches valuable lessons in interpersonal relations, cooperation, and nonacademic kinds of achievement. Twenty years ago James S. Coleman (1961) discussed this second environment in his book, *The adolescent society*. In those postsputnik days, his main concern was that the adolescent culture was anti-intellectual, undermining the academic values of the school and seducing potentially brilliant students away from their studies. We see it differently. For many students the adolescent society is a therapeutic defense against the punishments of the adult status system; the adolescent society makes school bearable. We have argued, for example, that extracurricular activities are valuable, because they provide the emotional support and opportunities for nonacademic accomplishments which make school more tolerable.

Organized, school-sponsored extracurricular activity can also be more humane than the alternative, a student-controlled environment of laissez-faire brutality where rewards and punishments are given out according to the rules and manners of a not very civilized teenage society. In this world the physically strong and beautiful dominate the puny and the plain, and exclusive positions of honor are reserved for the popular students while others strive for acceptance and are rebuffed. The school's two reward structures both offer more punishments than rewards, and work together to create a large group of students whose self-images are built on adjectives such as lazy, stupid, unathletic, clumsy, ugly, or shy. Those who are most excluded drop out of school, get married, or turn to cars, liquor, dope, religious evangelism, or sexual promiscuity. Many of these students spend precious years as adults trying to rid themselves of the self-images derived from their teenage behavior.

Cusick's *Inside High School* (1973) points out that there is a symbiosis between adult culture and the teen culture. He gives examples of the principal's using the leaders of the teen status system to help him carry out school activities. By leaving the adolescent society alone and assuming that it cannot be controlled, the school allows its excesses—fraternities and sororities which structure teenage aggression into hazing and cliquishness.

Seldom does anyone attack the symbiotic relationship between the two reward structures. One person who did was Carl Bernstein, the Washington Post reporter, who delivered a different kind of commencement address:

The ultimate revenge in this life, I think, is to come back to your high school as its commencement speaker. Imagine. Me. Not the president of my class, not the former chairman of the Latin Scrabble Club, not the head of the Keyettes (I think it was Nancy Immler, who would never go out with me). Not Goldie Hawn, with whom I once rode to the Hot Shoppe after the Bethesda-Chevy Chase game in the back seat of Pete Oldheiser's chopped-and-lowered Buick. Not Bob Windsor, the football player. But me, from the very bottom of my class.

So it would be presumptuous of me to preach at you from the usual list of topics for graduation speeches—patriotism, national service, leadership, these-are-the-best-years-of-your-life, etcetera. I'd rather get back to basics. Which is to say that I'd like to share with you some of my feelings about Montgomery Blair, about high school, about the educational process in this country, and about the "real world" that is something quite apart from what most teachers and parents would have you believe.

I think the best way to do this is to tell you about my own stay at Blair now that—after some fifteen years—I seem to have overcome the pain.

My own graduation from Blair is a memory so vivid that I continue to have nightmares about it. I was never able to send out invitations and those little white cards with your name engraved in script because Mr. Adelman, with good reason, had refused to pass me in chemistry. And I was also flunking gym. The explanation had less to do with my scores on tests or physical dexterity than with the fact that I wasn't in class very often. In those days we had a free fourth period to work on the school paper, *Silver Chips,* of which I was circulation and exchange manager. That free period would be spent at Jim Myers' recreation center on Thayer Avenue—the pool hall. Somehow the fourth period stretched into the fifth and sixth, which was the same time I was supposed to be in gym and chemistry classes.

I was also working evenings at the time—I started as a copy-boy at the *Evening Star* in my junior year—and working for a newspaper seemed to me a lot more interesting than doing homework at night.

So when it came time to order caps and gowns in 1961, Mr. Shaw, then the principal of Blair, told me not to bother. There followed some intense lobbying by me and my parents. And there was a big discussion among members of the faculty, who finally reached a decision to get me out of Blair rather than put up with me for another year. The night before graduation, Mr. Shaw called my parents with news of this dispensation; the Bernstein family escaped disgrace, at least for a little while.

Then came the University of Maryland, which, despite my hopeless grades, accepted me on probation...And much to the amazement of my family, my friends and former teachers at Blair, I finished the first semester at Maryland with a better-than-decent average.

That didn't last for long, however. I started working at the paper five days a week, stopped showing up for classes unless there was an exam and flunked out the next semester. It went on like that for a couple of years—readmitted on probation, middling grades, up and down—and then came the final straw. The university suspended me for having too many parking tickets. I never went back...

I concentrated on my work at the *Star* and became a reporter. I started to find a satisfaction in my life that had been lacking at school. And I tell you this not to recommend that anybody here follow the same course or to extol the virtues of starting at the bottom but to make a slightly different point—and it's the only thing I want to pass on to you today:

Your life isn't over if you're not at the top of this class. You've been graded and you've been tested and you've been ranked and I'm here to tell you that it really doesn't mean a thing. The die isn't cast yet, the final scores aren't in. And that goes for the top of the class, too. The fact is that easy passage through Blair, through high school, doesn't mean that the wheels of success are somehow permanently greased.

One of my most intense memories is of my 10th reunion of the Class of '61. For reasons that sociologists and educators and psychiatrists could spend lifetimes analyzing, what happened to that class contradicts all the old myths about success in high school. A disproportionate number of those judged in our yearbooks and in the hallways of Blair as "most likely to succeed" seemed to have had the most difficult time of it—trouble adjusting to college, to professional life, to personal relationships. And, to generalize again, many of those who had the roughest time at Blair—the kids regarded as troublemakers by the faculty, the students with obvious difficulties of social adjustment, the ones who often seemed so aimless—a disproportionate number of them seemed to have moved on in their lives to real satisfaction—professionally, educationally, emotionally.

Which brings me finally to the idea rattling around in my head since I first received your invitation to speak. Quite simply: The real world is a lot more tolerant, a lot more interesting, a lot more fun, a lot more sensible really than the cocoon that is high school. Wherever you stand in this class, you've gotten through the worst part—high school—and you deserve to feel really good about that. Now comes the opportunities, whether you're headed for university, a job, the military, marriage. Now you get to be your own person, not what your teachers want you to be, not what your parents expect you to be. At last you're not going to be compelled by others to do anything. And that really is what that piece of paper—the diploma—is all about. It's a ticket—out of this place and into life.

I think that the most acute observation I've ever heard about high school was made by Mike Nichols, the producer-director. He was 16 when he was admitted to the University of Chicago, and he started working with Elaine May about the same time and got his start in the theater. And he said in an interview:

"It was the first time I realized that life wasn't frozen in that high school pattern forever. You know, in high school you think, 'Mike Tenzer can beat me up and I can beat up Dave Halpern. And Lenore Lichtenstein will go out with me and Laura Firestein will never! And life will be like this forever.' "

As Nichols found out, life won't be like high school. Enjoy it.

The job of the high school is to look more like the real world—to look like a place where there are many ways to express one's need for friendship, individuality and achievement.

RACE RELATIONS

In the desegregated school we must add to the burden of dealing with adolescent development the problem of dealing with race. Most schools handle both these problems in the same way—by ignoring them. For most school people the ideal solution to the race problem would be one in which race was never mentioned—where race did not exist. The idea that this can be done in the 1980s in an American high school is far fetched. Outside the school, students live in a segregated world where neighborhoods, clubs and churches are segregated and where even popular music comes in two distinctly different forms. At most, schools throw a sop to minorities in the form of a black studies program which is itself likely to be segregated and which our data suggests makes things worse as often as it makes them better. We have seen that communities where desegregation was traumatic have less racial tension perhaps because they have been made aware that race cannot be ignored.

Black and white students cannot be expected to know by instinct how to interact or how to overcome their fears—they must be taught. There is little natural opportunity for interracial contact when out-of-school life is so highly segregated. Students will assume that they have nothing in common with students of another race. Opportunities for contact must be created by the school and structured in such a way as to maximize mutual respect—which is why tracked schools may have one advantage since they bring students together on a more equal basis. Of course, academic similarity is only one basis for friendship—students may find mutual interests in sports, hobbies, organizational work. The good school provides opportunities for equal status interracial contact based on these similarities of interest. When real racial problems appear, they must be dealt with straightforwardly. The good high schools in this study have anticipated racial problems and developed staff and student capabilities for dealing with them. We cannot specify a neatly detailed blueprint for doing this; we suspect that for any school it involves some trial and error. The good schools have worked to obtain the staff's commitment to racial equality and have involved students in the job of facing the race issue.

When this survey was being done, we invited students to comment on our questionnaires. One student suggested we add this item about school race relations: "This school pretends it doesn't have any problems." A school in which students check this response fails to realize that for many blacks in America, race is the central concern of their lives. There is an old New York City joke about the all-encompassing way Jews define themselves: The student is asked to write an essay about elephants, and he writes one entitled "The Elephant and the Jewish Question." The joke prompts us to ask whether we can realistically expect black students to divorce their school experience from their skin color. For blacks, race is not a part-time concern. Many people believe that segregated schools are better for blacks because they can openly espouse the values of black excellence. Cannot integrated schools do that as well? More bluntly, cannot integrated schools at least openly espouse the values of brotherhood?

CHANGING A SCHOOL

Can one create a successful integrated school? Some writers are pessimistic, assuming that gulfs of race and class will not be overcome and that desegregation will necessarily fail. In this study we have found schools which have succeeded, and we can disprove the pessimists by citing economist Kenneth Boulding's law: "That which exists, is possible."

We do not mean to imply that successful integration is easy or that it can be accomplished overnight. Most importantly, we think it requires a wholehearted, even single-minded commitment. Janet Schofield and her colleagues studied one school which did make an effort at integration. There was little superficially wrong with the school; students did not dislike it, and there was little racial tension. There was also little in the way of positive race relations, and Schofield describes the progress toward true integration as glacial:

> Although this school did make many provisions to meet its special responsibilities as an interracial school, its experience underlines the problems associated with approaching interracial schooling with even a remnant of the "business as usual" attitude. (Schofield, forthcoming)

The school which they studied is a newly integrated junior high school. A magnet school located on the boundary of a black neighborhood, it attempts to draw white students with a program for the gifted. (One might immediately question the practicality of this as a way to create an integrated school. What are the prospects for a desegregated school when the white students are recruited by appealing to parental desires for exclusive programs?) In the eighth grade, students must pass a competitive exam to be admitted to the gifted program. At that point, the school really becomes two schools: a white high ability school where students are admitted on the basis of test scores, and a black school where students are admitted because they live nearby. In the sixth and seventh grades, the school is not tracked, but often individual classrooms are. Schofield cites one teacher who divided the class into two groups by academic ability; with a single exception, one group was white, the other black. (In the preceding chapter when we argued that tracked schools seem to have somewhat better race relations, we did not have anything this extreme in mind.)

With such extensive classroom segregation, opportunities for interracial contact were limited to the lunch room and the halls; in the lunchroom, students voluntarily segregated themselves, and the halls and washrooms became areas of tension. The halls, cafeteria, and washrooms were problems in part because, in Schofield's words, the teachers' "lack of interest in and feeling of responsibility for what happens outside of the classroom is striking" (Schofield, forthcoming). This school is not a family like City High School; it is a hundred individual classrooms, separated by a no-man's-land where teachers have—and want—no responsibility.[1]

Many teachers in this school are described as taking an academics first orientation, defining their job as limited to teaching academic material. Although the school makes official pronouncements about brotherhood, it is not clear how seriously the administration and the school board mean these pronouncements to be taken (funds for the school extracurricular activities have been discontinued). Certainly most teachers in this school were still convinced that academics should come first. The result is an emphasis on traditional teaching and an intensely competitive environment in which both whites and blacks quickly learn which students are smart and which are not.

The school makes an effort to deal with race by setting aside part of the day for social activities, race relations work, and extracurricular programs. However, the teachers have great difficulty helping students deal with their racial feelings, for most of the staff are virtually paralyzed by their strong resistance to talking about race. One senses that many of the teachers feel that if race were brought up they would be unable to cope with the resulting racial conflict. The teachers pretend to be unaware of color so that the students in the class must also pretend to be color-blind. Pretending color blindness is not the same as learning to be unprejudiced. The nonacademic program of the schools also fails because teachers have little or no training in group leadership; even in a one-race school they would have difficulty running group social activities.

Schofield argues that this school is probably typical of many newly desegregated schools. Trained to teach academic subjects, teachers have no special skills to deal with the dynamics of a racially mixed group and are very much afraid of having the ugly aspects of race explode in front of them. This in turn limits their ability to teach their students to cope with race. Teachers, like most adults, have lived largely segregated lives, making it difficult for them to come to terms with their own feelings about race. More than anything else, this is the result of segregation.

[1] See Payne's (1979) description of the hall problems of a black high school as an abdication of school responsibility.

One school board member, a committed white liberal, told us that serving on the school board had been a great privilege because it had brought her in contact, for the first time, with educated blacks. She had taught high school for several years before becoming a board member. How could she have been effective in a desegregated classroom, having never met a black who was educationally her equal?

One of us interviewed the principal of a newly desegregated high school. He was young, bright, and articulate; but when forced to talk about race, he stumbled, finding complicated circumlocutions to avoid the words "white" and "black." Partly he had been taught, in college, that race was not the issue—that blacks were really the same as white people (except perhaps that they were culturally deprived). He had also been taught that race was not to be talked about in polite society. And he was scared. One researcher observed an elementary school teacher who, when asked by a student in her desegregated class what color a crayon was, stuttered before being able to say "black." Another example: A college physics teacher recalled that the first time a black student appeared in his class, he had difficulty talking about a principle known as "black body radiation."

If this sort of embarrassment is common, it is little wonder that so many educators believe that the best way to deal with the race issue is to ignore it and hope it will go away. The resut is that white and black students, thrown together in a desegregated school and needing help, find the staff refusing to even acknowledge their problem.

There is another factor involved; helping students deal with race is counter to the academics first definition of the school. Like color blindness, academics first seems widespread among educators. One of us listened to a big-city school administrator recalling his days teaching an experimental two and one-half hour "core" class covering English, history, and social studies. He had disliked it because as a social studies teacher he had difficulty teaching junior high school grammar. (Which does not raise a question, Why are we allowing someone to teach our children who does not know grammar? but rather, If an obviously intelligent college graduate has difficulty with these lessons, are we sure we should be teaching them to a mixed-ability class of fourteen-year-olds?) For this teacher, the main issue in evaluating the core curriculum was not whether it provided a better environment for the student making the transition from elementary to secondary school, but whether teachers would have to broaden their academic specialization.

This teacher is typical of secondary school teachers. An academic specialist, he knows little about adolescent development, has no training in group dynamics or in personality development, and places a low priority on helping adolescents develop the social skills they will need to live as adults. The root of problem is not to be found in any personal failing of secondary school teachers; the fault lies with the schools of education, which do not teach any of this, and with the education profession, which does not believe it should be taught.

The school will teach students how to live in the real world, whether we want it to or not; and it will certainly teach most students how to deal with race since it is very likely to be the first place where the student comes in contact with people of different races. There are some simple things teachers can do about race in their own classrooms. Schofield and Sagar (1979) cite two examples: One is to replace the individual armchairs of the classroom with tables since there is more interaction around a table than there is with individual chairs. The second thing is to seat the students at the tables in alphabetical order. We can add a third—teachers can use the new teamwork classroom techniques. These three are easy in the sense that one teacher can do these things without the cooperation of the administration or the other staff members. Our other recommendations require a cooperative schoolwide effort.

Consider, for example, the widespread use of electronic media or the expansion of the extracurricular activities program. Both require considerable staff preparation since teachers must learn new skills and the school administration must put up the needed funds. Both these projects appear feasible, but making them work well means taking the harder step of modifying the traditional education ideology: no more academics first; no more ignorance of race; no more defining the school as merely a group of individual teachers whose responsibilities end at their classroom doors; no more, in Schofield and Sagar's phrase, "business as usual"(Forthcoming).

Getting rid of business as usual means bringing the staff together to achieve a consensus that emotional growth and true integration are school priorities. The staff must agree to seriously evaluate its success in achieving these goals. One of the interesting things about the Schofield study is that most of the teachers she talked with said that race relations in the school were very good. They could say this because the school was allowing them to close their eyes to a reality which was quite obvious to the observers. By committing itself to good race relations and agreeing about what good race relations means, the school makes it impossible to kid itself. If the school really cares about race, the staff must ask at the end of the year: How many interracial friendships are there really in this school?

Finally, the principal and staff must ask the students to commit themselves openly to good race relations. They must force students to talk about race, and they must be willing to talk straightforwardly to students. Again, this implies an enormous amount of preparatory work. It means helping the teaching staff learn to talk about race among themselves and then learn to talk with students about it, and it means the teachers' learning a set of group management techniques which will enable them to present race without allowing the class to be taken over by the handful of articulate white and black students who can sabotage an unstructured situation. Thinking about this, one can imagine what an enormous effort is involved in helping an entire high school faculty come together on a common commitment to deal with race. This helps one to understand why Springfield City High School was able to do so only after a period of something close to a race riot. Many schools will make an effort like this only after they have been forced to the brink. We wish that more schools were foresighted enough to try to deal explicitly with race without being forced. After all, in a desegregated school race is the issue. Pretending that it is not does not fool anyone.

APPENDIX 7A
TECHNICAL APPENDIX

In writing this book, we were constantly aware of the question, How do we know this is true? As graduate students it was continually drummed into us: Correlation is not causation. We were most certainly not interested in writing a book which said that the presence of an audio-visual specialist is correlated with higher black and white achievement, and we have no way of knowing whether this means anything or not. We had to decide at every point in the analysis whether a correlation did indeed imply a causal relationship. We found that gradually over the rather long period of time that this analysis took we had developed some ideas about causation.

First, it was important to recognize that if a is correlated with b but does not cause b, then there are only three other possibilities: Either a and b are both caused by some other factor, or b causes a, or the result comes from sampling error. Sampling error we were generally comfortable with. All of the major conclusions in this book are based upon one or more correlations significant at the 5 percent level. In addition, the correlations are always part of a systematic pattern; not only does a correlate with b, but it also correlates with c and d in such a way as to make a sensible story. In one particular case we discarded a statistically significant correlation, one which was potentially very important, because it was not supported by a pattern of other correlations in the expected manner. We reminded ourselves that there is one chance in twenty that a meaningless correlation will be significant at the 5 percent level and decided that the correlation might be a fluke.

The question of the alternative hypotheses—that the dependent variable is really the independent variable or that the correlation is spurious—was dealt with in a couple of ways. First, we always prefer that a correlation be from one class of respondents to another. This is the main reason why the data were aggregated to the school level: When the dependent variable is the response of black students, the independent variable is almost always a response given by either white students, teachers, or the principal. If the respondents were students or teachers, the data was averaged across all the respondents in each school.

Making sure that the independent and dependent variables are supplied by two different classes of respondents eliminates the most common source of spuriousness—all the processes which are internal to a person which could influence his answers to two different questions. These mostly boil down to processes which create artificial consistency. The person who says one positive thing about his school will probably say other positive things as well (this is sometimes called a "halo" effect). Suppose we hypothesize that schools with prodesegregation staffs have black students who like school. We cannot test this hypothesis using only black student data. If black students say that they like school and also say that their teachers are prointegration, it is hard to say what this means. Maybe the teachers are more liberal than most, but maybe the students are just being kind as you would expect from students who like their school (in which case the dependent variable is the cause of the independent variable), or perhaps the black students in this school are inhibited, anxious to say the right thing (in which case the relationship between the "like school" response and the "teachers like integration" response is spurious, both caused by student inhibition). If white students say that the staff is sympathetic to desegregation at the same time that black students say that they like school, we can rule out all explanations based on the internal mental processes of the black students. This does not eliminate all counterhypotheses: It may be that when black students like school, teachers become more accepting of desegregation because of this, or it may be that in a conservative community, both white and black students are inhibited and will speak well of their school. By using aggregate responses from two types of respondents we cut down considerably on the number of alternative interpretations of a correlation.

It was not necessary to carry out our analysis at the aggregate level. We could have simply aggregated white student data, teacher data, principal data, and so forth to construct a profile of each school, attached this description of the school to the record of each individual black student, and carried out the correlations at the individual level. Mathematically, this would be no different from what we have done except that we would be explaining individual-level variance rather than between-school variance in our regression equations.

Incidentally, this also means that the issue of the ecological fallacy is irrelevant to this analysis. The ecological fallacy means that one cannot necessarily conclude that personal characteristics *a* and *b* are correlated simply because these two characteristics are correlated among grouped data. For example, if one found that neighborhoods which had high crime rates also tended to have many children under age five, one could not conclude from that information that children under age five were a major source of crime. Nowhere in this book have we said very much about individual-level correlations. Occasionally we have—knowing that schools with middle class black students have more militant student attitudes has led us to speculate about whether middle class blacks are more militant than working class blacks. Even there we remain aware of the possibility that it may be the working class blacks in a middle class school who are the militants.

Rejecting the counterhypothesis that *b* causes *a* instead of *a* causing *b* depends greatly on judgment. Generally, we have tried to structure our analysis in such a way that the major independent variable is a school characteristic which could not reasonably be assumed to be a response to student characteristics. For example, we cannot think of any reason why only schools with unusually bright student bodies should hire audio-visual specialists. So we are willing to interpret this relationship as meaning that audio-visual specialists affect student achievement. By the same token, using this criterion for interpreting relationships means that there are certain hypotheses which cannot be tested with these data. For example, there is a relatively strong correlation between the scores of the black students on the black knowledge scale and their scores on the achievement test. As far as we are concerned, it is simply not possible to conclude from this that a knowledge of black history inspired the students to score higher on standardized achievement tests, and no regression equation could convince us that black knowledge caused achievement. The hypothesis simply remains untested.

One way we tried to avoid correlations which were spurious was to study carefully the role of the control variables we used and to watch the relationship of the regression coefficient to the original zero-order relationship. We were most confident that a correlation was not spurious when the zero-order correlation and the regression coefficient in a multiple regression equation were similar. If they were, this meant that the control variables we were using were having little effect, which meant that better measurement of the control variables, or adding additional control variables correlated to the ones we did use, would not have much effect. This is no surefire defense against spuriousness, but it is a helpful rule of thumb.

We did one analysis which is logically different from the others and that has to do with extracurricular activities. Since our data do not contain a measure of the amount of resources that the school system devotes to extracurricular activities, we must create a surrogate measure by counting the number of students who participate in extracurricular activities. Here we are violating our rule, for if we ask, "Does extracurricular participation cause students to like school more?" we are using a student response on both the independent and dependent variables in an analysis. We solved this problem to our own satisfaction in two ways. First, we looked at all of the correlates of extracurricular participation and convinced ourselves that the pattern of correlations—increased number of parent visits, increased teacher-student informal contact, and so forth, all fit a general theory. In this case the conclusion that a causes b is deduced from a theory at the same time that it is supported by a correlation. Second, we embarked upon the most complex analysis in the book, in which aggregate and individual level data are used simultaneously to predict individual-level college attendance. Here we escape the problem by using the response of one student as the dependent variable and the response of every other student in the school except him as the independent variable. It should be noted that ordinary survey analysis does not use multiple respondent aggregate data and hence always uses the same respondent for both the independent and dependent variables. In this sense this analysis is methodologically quite a bit stronger than most.

A GENERAL COMMENT ON THE VALUE OF INPUT-OUTPUT ANALYSIS

It is no accident that this book begins and ends with a field case study. One of our continual complaints throughout this analysis is that there are not enough good case studies like those done by Forehand and Rogosta (1976) and Schofield (Forthcoming) which could be used to help us interpret our statistics. Several years of statistical analysis of school-level data have taught us more than we ever wanted to know about its limitations. We have also learned a lot about its strengths. The result is that we are now convinced that the right methodological answer is to let many flowers bloom. There are things that a case study can and cannot do, and there are things that laboratory experiments and statistical studies can and cannot do. The truth will emerge fastest if all these techniques are used in concert.

It is our impression that input-output analysis has fallen into bad repute in the past few years. While, as we said, we know more than we wish we did about its limitations, we are also convinced of its value. Some methodologists have argued that conclusions of causal influence cannot be drawn from cross-sectional data but require longitudinal data. Panel surveys cost a great deal more than one-shot surveys, and these critics are in some ways wishing for the moon since a large-scale panel is not likely to appear any time soon.[2] In addition, a longitudinal panel is not a cure-all. Many of the problems of causal inference remain with panel data. For example, the finding that a particular school resource is correlated with a change in achievement test scores between time one and time two is still subject to the counter-interpretation that having students whose test scores are going up inspires the school to adopt a particular resource use. The reason why so much attention has been devoted to the need for longitudinal panels is probably that such a heavy emphasis has been placed upon achievement as the dependent variable. Most school resources affect students during only a short period of their lives—a year or two at most. Most of the variance in their achievement test scores is determined outside of that period of time; most of the variance in high school achievement scores is a function of things that happened before the student even entered high school. School effects on achievement have to be very small, and only the most sophisticated panel designs can do the job of isolating them.

Input-output analyses have also been discredited in part because they have produced intuitively unreasonable results—of which the most unreasonable is the argument that school resources make no difference. In fact, school resources do affect achievement. School resources cannot be measured by simply counting the total number of tax dollars a school district gets and dividing by the number of

---

[2]The exception is "High School and Beyond" (National Opinion Research Center, 1981) which began with tenth graders in 1980, following them forward; but many hypotheses require that the members of the panel be first surveyed at age five before they start school, and then followed for the next twelve years. We are sure there will never be very many panels like that. One of the best (Rutter et al., 1979) is a result of clever reuse of data collected for other purposes.

students it has the legal responsibility to educate. To analyze what school characteristics affect achievement one must use variables derived from sound theories of learning and designs yielding good measurements of those independent variables which can reasonably be expected to affect achievement. When, for example, people correlate the actual amount of time spent in school learning a particular type of material with the proportion of students mastering the topic, there are reasonable correlations of nontrivial size. Not, perhaps, an earth-shattering conclusion, but it does make the point that schooling makes a difference. In the same manner a technically sound study of the effects of the duration of schooling, comparing students who receive only the regular nine months of schooling to those who receive that plus a summer term, has shown that more schooling produces more learning (Heyns 1979). When we cannot find a correlation between per capita expenditure on education and achievement and conclude that more schooling is not better than less, it is our interpretation that is at fault, not the method.

This study was weak in its ability to detect cognitive effects of school characteristics. The reason for this weakness is that the author of the questionnaire (Crain) is a sociologist, not an educator. Hence, he did not know what school characteristics needed to be measured. There is no place in the questionnaire for a description of the tenth grade curriculum or the methodology used in remedial instruction. Nor is this study alone in this omission; none of the input-output studies done so far have used a sophisticated theory of learning or collected complex data about school educational practice.

To our knowledge, this is the only large-scale input-output analysis which has used dependent variables other than achievement. The only similar analysis was done twenty years ago—*The Adolescent Society* by James Coleman (1961), but his study surveyed students in only ten high schools. We are frankly impressed with what can be done with noncognitive outcomes. For variables such as quality of race relations, the between-school variance is quite large, the sociological theory is well enough developed to give us some plausible hypotheses to test, and interesting variables can be measured with present day survey technology. Under those conditions we should get important results, and we do.

We think input-output analysis has a definite role as a way of testing most theory. Its weaknesses are that it cannot test theories which predict very small effects—these require panel studies—or test relationships in which the causal order could go either way—these require randomized experiments. It also cannot test hypotheses having to do with psychological or sociological characteristics of individual students; these require surveys or panel studies of students, usually limited to a single school. Finally, input-output analysis is a poor way to discover new things—it can look only at variables the researcher selected before the study began. Field case studies are the way to discover new concepts.

Given these important limitations, analyses like the one we have done are the best way to test the hypothesis that of two common ways schools teach, one is better than the other. This sort of analysis can then lead one to test theories about school organization and school culture. There is plenty of need for this kind of research. What we need is not to say that research of type x is bad; do not do it, but to say that type x has limits; it must be supplemented by work of types y, z, and w. Unfortunately, there seems to be a correlation between the research method advocated and the ideological bent of the researcher. Input-output analysis has tended to become the province of economists, sometimes with conservative political leanings, whose instincts lie in the schools do not make a difference direction. Observational case studies are more likely to be done by anthropologists and sociologists of left political views, who are inclined to see schools as examples of evil authority at work. The result is that input-output analyses will tend to show that schools can do nothing right, and field studies will show that they can do everything wrong. We suspect that educational research will be better off when conservatives spend more time visiting schools and liberals spend more time on the computer.

APPENDIX A
METHODOLOGICAL APPENDIX

National Opinion Research Center (NORC) staff conducted the survey in September 1972 under contract to the United States Office of Education, Office of Planning, Budgeting, and Evaluation. The survey was part of an Emergency School Assistance Program (ESAP) evaluation. The sample called for 200 high schools selected from districts receiving ESAP funds. In fifty districts, we asked school officials to identify pairs of similar high schools to receive funding. After they did so, one of the two schools (selected randomly) was deemed ineligible for funding that year. This was the first randomized experimental evaluation of a large-scale federal program. The analysis, conducted by Carlyle Maw (NORC 1973), found a statistically significant achievement gain for black male students in schools which received ESAP funds. Crain and York (1975) relate the story of that evaluation.

The randomized experimental method was subsequently used for the larger evaluation of ESAP (later ESAA) conducted by System Development Corporation (Coulson, et al. 1977). The interested reader should consult the series of annual project reports. (The SDC evaluation also found a significant achievement effect resulting from the presence of federal funds.)

Since the major objective of the study was program evaluation, we randomly selected schools from only those districts applying for

ESAP funding. This probably biases the sample toward those districts more aggressively seeking federal funds. Since the actual probability of receiving funding was quite high, it seems unlikely that funded districts had substantially more skill in developing special programs than unfunded districts; they may, however, have been more willing to put together a federal program proposal. We cannot say what bias, if any, resulted from our selection procedure. We assume that the schools in our sample do not differ from other southern high schools. The sample covers the entire South, from northern Virginia to western Texas, as far north as Tennessee and as far south as Florida. Two classes of schools are excluded: several schools in Texas with large Hispanic populations, and a few large, urban schools with extremely high absenteeism rates on the day of testing.[1] With these exclusions, the final sample contained 194 schools. An NORC supervisor visited each of the 194 schools and interviewed the principal. In a later visit, the supervisor and two assistants distributed questionnaires to ten teachers and to students in three classrooms. In order to get the most representative sample, we surveyed students in English classes on the assumption that virtually all tenth graders enroll in tenth grade English.

To minimize possible sampling error, we ranked tenth grade English classes by racial composition and selected one class from each end of the ranking and one from the center. Thus if classes were racially imbalanced due to ability grouping (which seems likely at the high school level), this system would increase the chances of getting a full range of ability levels in the survey. In sampling the ten teachers, we attempted to maximize the probability that surveyed students would have had these particular teachers in class. In addition to the three English teachers, we sampled mathematics and social studies teachers with several tenth grade classes. Thus we cannot guarantee that our students and teachers had common classes, but the likelihood is greater than if we had taken simple random samples from each group.

Students took an hour-long version of the Sequential Test of Educational Progress (STEP) of the ETS. Darrell Bock of the University of Chicago constructed the short version, called the Survey Test of Educational Progress. It contains five subtests:

[1]We eliminated the urban schools, assuming that the absent students would severely bias the school performance level upward.

reading, language, mathematical concepts, mathematical computation, and science. The English expression and social studies subtests were omitted because they required familiarity with both English usage and specific information which varies greatly among regions and ethnic groups in the United States. The fifty-seven-item test was normed for the ninth grade with a coefficient of generalizability (KR20) ranging from 0.84 for black female students to 0.91 for white male students. The students also completed an hour-long pencil and paper attitude questionnaire. Teachers were given a shorter self-administered questionnaire. Finally, the NORC supervisor filled out a questionnaire describing the school and interviewed both the principal and a district-level administrator to gather additional information about school resources and funding. Telephone surveys were conducted with four community leaders in each city in order to gain information about community attitudes toward the schools. In order to minimize the political dependence of these leaders on the school system, a snowball sample was used. We asked a black male who served on the ESAP citizens' advisory committee to nominate a white female respondent, who in turn nominated a black female, who nominated a white male. We felt that cross-race nominations would reduce the probability of sampling white racists and black militants. Thus the panel would more nearly represent the views of the liberal center of the community.

After data collection, editing, and coding, the data were aggregated to the school level. A single data file for each school was constructed, containing the following information. All surveyed schools from any one district would have identical district-level data. School-level data would, of course, vary by school.

District-level data included:
1. The adult median education level.
2. Percent of population living in urban areas.
3. Percentage nonwhite of the county.
4. Responses to community leader survey, averaged for the four respondents.
5. Responses from the district administrator in charge of federal programs.
School-level data included:
6. Responses from the principle interview.
7. Teacher responses, averaged for the ten surveyed teachers.

Usually these took the form of the percentage of teachers giving a particular response; for certain scales, mean scale scores were computed.

8. White student responses to the student survey. As with teachers, responses took the form of percentages (on single items) and means (on scales).

9. Black student responses to the student survey.

10. For selected scales, mean scores for all black male, white male, black female, and white female students.

11. Responses by the supervising interviewer to a short questionnaire describing the school.

VARIABLES

Tables A–1 presents the components of the seven scales which act as dependent variables for most of our analyses. Our eighth and ninth variables, individual items rather than scales, are: (agree/disagree) "Sometimes I feel I don't belong in this school" and "Everything considered are you very happy, pretty happy, or not too happy these days?" The tenth basic dependent variable is achievement. A factor analysis of these variables appears in the appendix to Chapter 1. Table A–1 also lists the variables used to construct the SES scale, the teacher racial attitudes and behavior scales, and the scale of degree of tracking.

AGGREGATION

We have normally aggregated the data to the school level from multiple individual responses. Most of the literature on aggregation deals with inferences about individual-level data which can be drawn from group-level results. This ecological fallacy literature states that simply because two variables correlate at an aggregate level of analysis does not mean they will correlate at the individual level. Since our interests lie primarily in schools as producers of social climates, it is appropriate that we analyze school-level data. In Chapter 2, for example, we argued that a school's racial composition affects its mean black achievement levels, that is, that

$$b_{\bar{y}\,\bar{x}} > 0, \qquad (A.1)$$

where b_{yx}^{--} is the unstandardized coefficient from the regression of $\bar{y}_j$

(mean achievement in school j) on $\bar{x}_j$ (% white of school j). Analyses of this type are not subject to aggregate bias, since there is no individual-level version of school racial composition. In other words, the regression of an individual-level trait (achievement) on a global trait (school racial composition) necessarily yields the same coefficient as the regression of the group mean of that variable on the same global property of the group (Lincoln and Zeitz 1980: 397).

However, when a school-level variable does have an individual-level counterpart (for example, the mean extracurricular participation rate of a school versus an individual's extracurricular participation or lack of it), one is often tempted to make an individual-level inference from a school-level result. The validity of such an inference rests on two issues. We will discuss each in turn.

First, the degree to which a school-level equation would yield the same result as its individual-level version depends on the amount of variance in the dependent variable which lies between schools. For example, in Chapter 5 we argued that a school's mean rate of extracurricular participation affects its mean achievement level. If all of the variance in achievement lay between schools, (that is, schools would differ in achievement levels, but students within a given school would not), then knowledge of a given school's mean achievement level would enable us to predict perfectly the achievement of any student within that school. At the other extreme is the hypothetical case where all of the variance in the dependent variable lies within schools (that is, students within a given school would have differing achievement levels, but all schools would have identical achievement means). Here, knowledge of a school's achievement mean would not enable us to predict with any accuracy an individual student's test score. In general, then, the amount of variance which lies between schools limits the extent to which one can argue for the presence of school effects. A discussion of the amount of between-school variance for the dependent variables can be found in the technical appendix of Chapter 1.

The second issue is one of model specification. If the school-level independent and dependent variables are correlated with other omitted school-level variables, then the school-level equation will yield coefficients which are biased upward. Referring again to our earlier example, if a school's mean achievement and mean extracurricular participation rate are both correlated with mean student ability, but mean student ability has been omitted from the equation, the influence of mean participation on mean achievement will be

MAKING DESEGREGATION WORK

Table A-1. Selected questionnaire items.

Socioeconomic Status Scale:

How much education does your mother have? (If you don't know, it's all right to guess.)
> Did not go to high school
> Went to high school but didn't graduate
> Graduated from high school
> Attended college

Do you live with both of your parents?
> Yes
> No

How many brothers and sisters do you have?
> One
> Two
> Three
> Four
> Five
> Six
> Seven
> Eight or more
> None

Does your family get a newspaper regularly?
> Yes
> No

Does your family own their home?
> Yes
> No

Does your home have an air conditioner?
> Yes
> No

Self-Esteem:

How do your parents feel about the grades you get in school?
> Very satisfied
> Somewhat satisfied
> Somewhat dissatisfied
> Very dissatisfied
> I don't know

Forget for a moment how teachers grade your school work. How do you rate yourself in school ability compared with those in your class at school?
> I am one of the best.
> I am above average.
> I am average.
> I am below average.
> I am one of the poorest.

Table A-1. (Continued).

Do you think you have the ability to complete college?
    Definitely yes
    Probably yes
    Probably no
    Definitely no
    Not sure either way

Racial Contact:
    Think for a moment about the three students you talk with most often at this school. Are they the same race as you?
        Yes, all same race as me
        No, one or more is from another race
    Have you ever called a student of a different race on the phone?
        Yes
        No
    This school year have you helped a student from another race with school work?
        Yes
        No
    This school year have you asked a student from another race to help you with your homework?
        Yes
        No

Racial Attitudes:
    If you could choose the kind of school you would go to, would you pick one with:
        All white student
        All black students
        A mixture of different kinds of students
        Other
    Would you like to have more friends who are of a different race?
        Yes
        No
    How uncomfortable do you feel around students of a different race?
        Generally very uncomfortable
        Generally somewhat uncomfortable
        Occasionally somewhat uncomfortable
        Not at all uncomfortable

Like School:
    Do you like the principal of this school?
        Yes
        No

Table A-1. (Continued).

In the morning, are you usually glad to go to school?
   Yes
   No
Do you usually hate school?
   Yes
   No

Rule Acceptance:
   At school, are you often blamed for things that just aren't your fault?
   Yes
   No
Do you think most of the rules in this school are fair?
   Yes
   No
Do you get really angry when teachers try to make you do thinkgs you don't want to do?
   Yes
   No
When you get punished at school does it usually seem it's for no good reason at all?
   Yes
   No

Delinquency:
   Have you been in any fights at school this school year?
   Yes
   No
In the past year, were you ever sent to the office because someone thought you were breaking some school rule?
   Yes, only once
   Yes, two or more times
   No
During this school year, did you ever stay away from school just because you didn't want to come?
   Never
   Yes, for 1 or 2 days
   Yes, for 3 to 6 days
   Yes, for 7 to 15 days
   Yes, for 16 or more days

Tension:
Black and white student items:
   Here is a list of things that have happened in some schools. Please indicate whether or not each of these has happened at your school this school year.

Table A-1. (Continued).

Groups of black students attacking white students
Groups of white students attacking black students
White students complaining that favoritism is being shown to black students[1]
Black students complaining about white racism—favoritism to white students
Tensions have made it hard for everyone
On the whole, how would you say things are working out with both blacks and whites in the school?
Almost no problems
Some minor problems
Some serious problems
Many serious problems
School does not have both black and white students

Teacher Items:
On the whole, how would you evaluate the way in which desegregation is working out in your school?
Almost no problems
Some minor problems
Some serious problems
Many serious problems
Does not apply
Here is a list of things that have happened in some desegregated schools. Please indicate whether or not each of these things happened at your school.
A greater amount of fighting than before desegregation[2]

Principal Items:
The amount of violence varies from community to community and school to school. Thinking about the entire current school year here at (name of school), how many instances of a student being hurt in a fight seriously enough to require hospitalization have occurred? (Codes 0,1,2,3,4+)
A student being hurt in a fight seriously enough to require hospitalization?
A student being hurt seriously enough in a fight to require attention by a doctor or nurse?
A student's locker being broken into?
How many instances of a student being robbed by a gang or group of other students have occurred this school year?
A teacher being attacked by a student?
A robbery of school property worth over $50?
During the schoolyear, has this school been kept closed any days or has it closed early because of racial (intergroup) tensions or problems?
Yes
No

Table A-1.   (Continued).

Teacher Racial Attitudes: Nonschool

Listed below are some statements other people have made. For each, please mark whether you strongly agree, agree somewhat, disagree somewhat, or strongly disagree.

The amount of prejudice against minority groups in this country is highly exaggerated.

I would like to live in an integrated neighborhood.

The civil rights movement has done more good than harm.

Blacks and whites should not be allowed to intermarry.

If you had to choose one factor which accounts most for failure of the Negro to achieve equality, which would you choose—a lack of initiative and drive, or the restrictions imposed by a white society?

Lack of initiative and drive

Restrictions imposed by a white society

Teacher Racial Attitudes: School Related

Some people say that black students would really be better off in all-black schools. Others say that black students are better off in racially mixed schools. What do you think?

Most black students are better off in all-black schools.

Most black students are better off in racially mixed schools.

(parallel item asks about white students)

Teacher Racial Behavior:

Black and white student items:

How about most of your teachers—how do you think they feel about blacks and whites going to the same school together?

They like it.

They don't like it.

It doesn't matter to them.

Don't know.

As far as you know, how do each of the following feel about desegregation? Most white teachers in this school:[2]

Like it very much

Like it somewhat

Do not care

Dislike it somewhat

Dislike it very much

Don't know

Does not apply

Principal Item:

As far as you know, how do most white teachers in this school feel about desegregation—do they like it very much, like it somewhat, dislike it somewhat or dislike it very much?

Table A-1. (Continued).

Extent of Tracking:

Principal Items:

When your present tenth graders were in seventh and eighth grades, approximately how many of them went to schools which had ability grouping? Would you say almost all, over half, less than half, or very few?

Approximately what proportion of the tenth grade academic classes—English, math, social students, and so forth—are separated by program so that students are in class only with students in their ability-group level or program? (Code all, more than half, about half, less than half)

Are the nonacademic classes, such as home room, gym, health, music, and art separated by ability-group levels or tracks? (code all, some, none)

How many different levels of tenth grade English are there in this school? (Code 1 to 7+)

---

[1] Black response to this item not used.
[2] Other items in this list were not used in this scale.

---

exaggerated. Lacking a measure of mean student ability, we have attempted to deal with this problem by controlling for the mean socioeconomic status of the student body. For purposes of statistical significance, the 194 schools are independently sampled tests of a hypothesis, not the 10,000 students. Estimates of the error due to sampling are thus based on the number of schools being analyzed and the variance of the distribution of school scores—the between-schools component of the individual-level variance.

We anticipated that white and black students might have very different experiences in the same school, so we have always aggregated responses separately by race. (Occasionally, as in the achievement analysis of Chapter 2, we also aggregated separately by sex.) The fact that each school has different numbers of black and white students creates problems of sampling bias. We may have only sampled one or two black students in a predominantly white school while in another school we may have sampled as many as fifty or sixty. In order to compensate for the error introduced by having only a few students represent certain schools, we assigned a weight to each school. In cases where black student responses are the dependent variable, schools were weighted according to the number of black students by the following formula:

$$W_i = \frac{n_i}{n_i + k} \qquad (A.2)$$

where n_i is the number of students in school i and k is the ratio of the percentage of variance that lies within schools to the percentage of variance that lies between schools. k is assumed to be three for all the variables used in this analysis. If there were only a very small amount of variance within schools—that is, schools were very homogeneous—k would be very small, and W would be close to one regardless of the number of students. In a homogeneous school, any one student would be a reasonably good representative of the school, and the data would be as reliable with one student as with many. Conversely, if the amount of variance between schools were small, then extraordinarily accurate estimates of each school would be needed in order to detect real differences between schools, k would be very large, and very large samples from each school would be needed in order to get weights near one.

In this particular case, the weight assigned is one if the number of students in a particular school is infinite and declines to one-quarter when only a single student is surveyed. This formula, taken from Armor (1972a), minimizes error due to the small samples in some schools and provides a somewhat conservative estimate of the number of schools for tests of statistical significance since it always assigns weights of less than one and hence always computes a total n less than the actual number of schools.

ESTIMATES OF SAMPLING ERROR IN SCHOOL MEANS

Two kinds of sampling error complicate our analyses. The first comes from our selection of schools. We may have chosen some very atypical schools and thus produce misleading correlations. For this reason we compute tests of statistical significance. Our selection of students, on the other hand, introduces a second type of error, error which exaggerates the differences between our schools.

Let us consider a simple example. Imagine that we randomly sampled n students from each of m schools, that students had a true mean of x and a true variance of σ^2 on some particular variable, and that the m schools in fact had identical student populations. The sampling of the students would guarantee that the measured school means would vary, however. The distribution of sampled students would have a mean of x and a variance σ_s^2 given by

$$\sigma_s^{\,2} = \frac{\sigma^2}{\sqrt{n}} \tag{A.3}$$

In order to estimate the true variation among the schools in our sample we had to estimate the amount that sampling error contributed to the between-school variance. After a number of efforts we found we were unable to arrive at a satisfactory estimate. Since we aggregate black and white student data separately, the number of students used to compute a school's means varies from one to sixty. If we did not use a weighting procedure, we would assume the between-school sampling error to be

$$\sigma_s^2 = \frac{\displaystyle\sum_{i=1}^{i=m} \frac{\sigma_i^2}{n_i}}{m} \tag{A.4}$$

where n_i and σ_i^2 are, respectively, the number of students sampled and the variance in school, i, m is the total number of schools, and σ_s^2 is the variance of the school mean due to sampling error. If we assume σ_i^2 to be constant, this can be written as

$$\sigma_s^2 = \frac{\sigma_i^2}{n_e} \tag{A.5}$$

where n_e is the effective mean sample size, and is estimated by

$$\frac{1}{n_e} = \frac{\displaystyle\sum_{i=1}^{i=m} \frac{1}{n_i}}{m}. \tag{A.6}$$

Weighting the data reduces the error considerably, since the between-school variance becomes

$$\sigma_s^2 = \frac{\displaystyle\sum_{i=1}^{i=m} \left(\frac{n_i}{n_i + k}\right)\left(\frac{\sigma_i^2}{n_i}\right)}{\displaystyle\sum_{i=1}^{i=m} \left(\frac{n_i}{n_i + k}\right)}. \tag{A.7}$$

Weighting is equivalent to increasing n_e, the effective mean sample size, from 9.99 to 12.3 for blacks and from 14.2 to 22.7 for whites.

This procedure results in inflated estimates of school-level sampling error. It seems likely that random sampling from some universe is not an appropriate model. One cannot assume that the students represent independent draws from an urn. First, we stratified the English classes before selection, reducing sampling error. Second, the students are in the same school and interact with each other. (For example, had we asked, "Are you the tallest in your English class?," we would presumably get little between-school variance, since each class has only one such person. Many student attitudes are formed either by using other students as a reference group or as a result of the status competition among students. Thus we would predict that there are no schools where every student says he is happy; every ladder has a bottom rung.)

After examining the data, we concluded that the effective n of the school is too small, and our estimates must be considered imprecise, yielding only rough conclusions about the absolute magnitude of the between-school variance. Even these rough estimates, however, are useful for drawing conclusions about the variance of one variable relative to the variance of another.

We estimated the true between-school standard deviations for various variables. Let us consider one variable as an example: the proportion of the white students reporting that they thought their friends would think badly of them if they went someplace after school with a black student. This variable has a mean of 0.44 and a between-school standard deviation of 0.215 (and hence a variance of $0.215^2 = 0.0464$). Since the variable is a dichotomy, the individual-level variance is $pq = (0.44)(0.56) = 0.2464$. Of this, about 85 percent or 0.2094 lies within schools. Since the effective sample size per school is 22.7, the between-school variance due to sampling error is then 0.2094/22.7. This means that the true between-school variance is $0.0464-0.0092 = 0.0371$, and the true between-school standard deviation is $\sqrt{.0371} = 0.192$, or 19.2 percent. Thus 15 percent (0.0371/0.2464) of the variance lies between schools, and 20 percent (0.0092/0.0464) of the measured between-school variance is really due to sampling error.

This variable has an unusually large amount of between-school variance. Partly this is because it asks students to describe their school environment rather than report their personal feelings, so students within each school should agree with each other more. Partly it is because racial climate varies greatly among schools. At the opposite extreme, the same analysis of white responses to the question, "Are you very happy?" shows that only 2 percent of the variance lies between schools, and 64 percent of the measured between-school variance (which is only 0.0110) is really sampling error. The estimates of the between-school differences of different types of variables are shown in Table 1A–2 in the technical appendix of Chapter 1. Since there are fewer blacks than whites in our schools, sampling errors for blacks are larger.

This exercise also helps prepare us for the analysis in Chapters 2 to 6, where we use multiple regression to analyze these variables. Knowing the proportion of between-school variance not due to error tells us how much can be explained by school factors. For example, the school mean response to white reports of peer resistance to interracial activities has a variance which is 20 percent sampling error and only 80 percent true, and thus 80 percent is the upper limit of what can be explained by a multiple regression equation using school characteristics. When the true variance is small relative to sampling error, the amount of variance to be explained is, of course, smaller. For example, we think the variance in black mean response to the happiness question may be as little as 19 percent true; this means that our regression equations cannot be expected to explain more than 19 percent of the variance. (In fact, our best equations for predicting happiness are able to explain about 10 percent of the variance with school-level variables.)

REFERENCES

Armor, David. J. 1972a. "School and Family Effects on Black and White Achievement: A Reexamination of the USOE Data." In *On Equality of Educational Opportunity*, edited by Frederick Mosteller and Daniel P. Moynihan, pp. 168–229. New York: Random House.

———. 1972b. "The Evidence on Busing." *The Public Interest* 28 (summer):90–126.

Aronson, Elliot. 1975. "Busing and Racial Tension: The Jigsaw Route to Learning and Liking." *Psychology Today* 8 (February):43–50.

———. 1978. *The Jigsaw Classroom.* Beverly Hills, Calif.: Sage Publications.

Benham, Barbara J.; Phil Giesen; and Jennie Oakes. 1980. "A Study of Schooling: Students' Experiences in Schools." *Phi Delta Kappen* 61, no. 5 (January):337–340.

Berman, Paul, and Milbrey Wallin McLaughlin. 1978. *Federal Programs Supporting Educational Change: Implementing and Sustaining Innovations.* Vol. 8. Santa Monica, Calif.: The Rand Corporation.

Bloom, Benjamin S. 1976. *Human Characteristics and School Learning.* New York: McGraw-Hill.

Brown v. Board of Education of Topeka et al. 1954. 347 U.S. 483.

Caplan, Nathan, 1970. "The New Ghetto Man: A Review of Recent Empirical Studies." *Journal of Social Issues* 26 no. 1:59–73.

Coleman, James S. 1961. *The Adolescent Society.* New York: The Free Press.

Coleman, James S.; Ernest Q. Campbell; Carol J. Hobson; James M. McPartland; Alexander M. Mood; Frederick D. Weinfeld; and Robert L.

York. 1966. *Equality of Educational Opportunity.* Washington, D.C.: U.S. Government Printing Office.

Collins, Thomas W. 1977. "From Courtrooms to Classrooms: Managing School Desegregation in a Deep South High School." In *Desegregated Schools: An Appraisal of an American Experiment* edited by Ray C. Rist, pp. 89–113. New York: Academic Press.

Conley, Houston; Judith Bailey; Georgia Eugene; June Key; and Bernard Minnis. 1977. *Contingency Planning for a Unitary School System.* Nashville, Tenn.: McQuiddy Printing Company.

Coser, Lewis A. 1964. *Functions of Social Conflict.* New York: Free Press.

Cottle, Thomas J. 1976. *Busing.* Boston: Beacon Press.

Coulson, John E.; Sally D. Hanes; Dan G. Ozenne; Clarence Bradford; William J. Doherty; Gary A. Duck; and Judith A. Hemenway. 1977. *The Third Year of Emergency School Aid Act (ESAA) Implementation.* Santa Monica, Calif.: System Development Corporation.

Crain, Robert L. 1969. "Effects of Community Conflict on Community Attitudes." Unpublished paper. Chicago: The National Opinion Research Center.

———1977. "Racial Tension in Southern High Schools: Pushing the Survey Method Closer to Reality." *Anthropology and Education* 8, (May):142–151.

Crain, Robert L., and Rita E. Mahard. 1978a. "School Racial Composition and Black College Attendance and Achievement Test Performance." *Sociology of Education* 51 (April):81–101.

Crain, Robert L., and Rita E. Mahard. 1978b. "Desegregation and Black Achievement." *Law and Contemporary Problems* 42, no. 3 (summer):17–56.

Crain, Robert L., and Donald Rosenthal. 1967. "Community Status as a Dimension of Local Decision-Making." *American Sociological Review* 32 (December):970–984.

Crain, Robert L., and Carol Sachs Weisman. 1972. *Discrimination, Personality and Achievement: A Survey of Northern Blacks.* New York: Seminar Press.

Crain, Robert L., and Robert L. York. 1975. "Evaluating a Successful Program: Experimental Method and Academic Bias" *School Review* 84:233–254.

Crain, Robert L.; Morton Inger; Gerald A. McWorter; and James J. Vanecko. 1968. *The Politics of School Desegregation.* Chicago: Aldine.

Cusick, Philip. 1973. *Inside High School: The Student's World.* New York: Holt, Rinehart and Winston.

Davis, James A. 1973. "Busing." In *Southern Schools: An Evaluation of the Effects of the Emergency School Assistance Program and of School Desegregation*

Vol. 2, by National Opinion Research Center, pp. 83–118. Chicago: National Opinion Research Center.

DeFleur, M.L., and F.R. Westie. 1958. "Verbal Attitudes and Overt Acts: An Experiment on the Salience of Attitudes." *American Sociological Review* 23:667–673.

DeFriese, G.H., and W.S. Ford. 1969. "Verbal Attitudes, Overt Acts, and the Influence of Social Constraint in Interracial Behavior." *Social Problems* 16:493–505.

Delaware Committee on the School Decision. n.d. *Update: A Desegregation Resource Handbook.* Wilmington, Del.: New Castle County Public Building.

DeVries, David L., and Robert E. Slavin. 1976. *Teams-Games-Tournament: A Final Report on the Research.* Baltimore: Center for Social Organization of Schools, The Johns Hopkins University.

Douvan, Elizabeth, and Joseph Adelson. 1966. *The Adolescent Experience.* New York: Wiley.

Duncan, Otis Dudley. 1975. *Introduction to Structural Equations Models.* New York: Academic Press.

Ehrlich, Howard J. 1973. *The Social Psychology of Prejudice.* New York: Wiley.

Ewens, W.L., and H.G. Ehrlich. 1969. "Reference Other Support and Ethnic Attitudes as Predictors of Intergroup Behavior." Revised version of a paper presented to the joint meetings of the Midwest Sociological Society and the Ohio Valley Sociological Society, Indianapolis, Indiana, May.

Fendrich, J.M. 1967. "Perceived Reference Group Support: Racial Attitudes and Overt Behavior." *American Sociological Review* 32:960–970.

Festinger, Leon. 1957. *A Theory of Cognitive Dissonance.* New York: Harper and Row.

Finger, John. 1976. "Why Busing Plans Work." *School Review* 84 (May): 364–372.

Forehand, Garlie A. and Marjorie Ragosta. 1976. *A Handbook for Integrated Schooling.* Princeton: Educational Testing Service.

Forehand, Garlie A. and Majorie Ragosta; and Donald A. Rock. 1976. *Conditions and Processes of Effective School Desegregation.* Princeton: Educational Testing Service.

Foster, Gordon. 1973. "Desegregating Urban Schools: A Review of the Techniques." *Harvard Educational Review* 43:5–36.

Giles, Michael W. 1978. "White Enrolment Stability and School Desegregation: A Two-Level Analysis." *American Sociological Review* 43 (December):848–864.

Giles, Michael; Everett Cataldo; and Douglas Gatlin. 1976. "Determinants of Resegregation: Compliance/Rejection Behavior and Policy Alternatives." Report to National Science Foundation, RA–760179, June.

Gottfredson, Gary D. 1980. "Schooling and Delinquency Prevention: Some Practical Ideas for Educators, Parents, Program Developers and Researchers." Report no. 303, The Johns Hopkins University Center for Social Organization of Schools.

Gottfredson, Gary D., and Denise C. Daiger. 1979. *Disruption in Six Hundred Schools*. Report 289. Baltimore: The Johns Hopkins University, Center for Social Organization of Schools, November.

Grier, William H., and Price M. Cobbs. 1968. *Black Rage*. New York: Basic Books.

Hanks, Michael P., and Bruce K. Eckland. 1976. "Athletics and Social Participation in the Educational Attainment Process." *Sociology of Education* 49 (October):271–294.

Hawley, Willis D. 1978. "The New Mythology of School Desegregation." *Law and Contemporary Problems* 42 no.3 (fall):214–222.

Hawley, Willis D., and Betsy Levin. 1978. "School Desegregation: The First Twenty-Five Years." *Law and Contemporary Problems* 42 No.3,4 (summer and fall)

Heyns, Barbara. 1978. *Summer Learning and The Effects of Schooling* New York: Academic Press.

Hirschi, Travis. 1969. *Causes of Delinquency*. Berkeley: University of California Press.

Jencks, Christopher; Marshall Smith; Henry Acland; Mary Jo Bane; David Cohen; Herbert Gintis; Barbara Heyns; and Stephen Michelson. 1972. *Inequality*. New York: Basic Books.

Kardiner, Abraham, and Lionel Ovisey. 1951. *The Mark of Oppression: Explorations in the Personality of The American Negro*. New York: Norton.

Katz, I. 1964. "Review of Evidence Relating to Effects of Desegregation on the Intellectual Performance of Negroes." In *Policy Issues in Urban Education*, edited by Marjorie B. Smiley, and Harry L. Miller. pp.400–442. New York: Free Press.

Kluger, Richard 1975. *Simple Justice*. New York: A.A. Knopf.

Levinsohn, Jay; Louise Lewis; John A. Riccobono; and R. Paul Moore. 1977. *National Longitudinal Study of the High School Class of 1972, Data Users Manual*. Research Triangle Park, NC: The Research Triangle Institute.

Lincoln, James R., and George Zeitz. 1980. "Organizational Properties from Aggregate Data: Separating Individual and Structural Effects." *American Sociological Review* 45:391–408.

Marx, Gary T. 1968. *Protest and Prejudice: A Study of Belief in the Black Community*. New York: Harper and Row.

Mayer, Martin. 1963. *The Schools.* New York: Doubleday & Co., Inc.

McPartland, James M. 1978. "Desegregation and Equity in Higher Education and Employment." *Law and Contemporary Problems* 42 (summer):108–132.

McPartland, James M., and Edward L. McDill. 1977. "Research on Crime in Schools." In *Violence in Schools: Perspectives, Programs and Positions,* edited by James M. McPartland and Edward L. McDill, pp. 3–34. Lexington, Mass.: D.C. Heath.

Mills, Nicholaus. 1973. *The Great School Bus Controversy.* New York: Teachers College Press.

Mosteller, F.W., and D.P. Moynihan, eds.1972. *On Equality of Educational Opportunity.* New York: Random House.

Narot, Ruth E. 1973. "The Effects of Integration on Achievement" in *Southern Schools: An Evaluation of the Effects of the Emergency School Assistance Program (ESAP) and of School Desegregation.* Edited by the National Opinion Research Center, pp. 60–82. Chicago: National Opinion Research Center.

National Institute of Education. 1978. *Violent Schools—Safe Schools: The Safe School Study Report.* Washington, D.C.: U.S. Government Printing Office.

National Opinion Research Center. 1973. *Southern Schools: An Evaluation of the Effects of the Emergency School Assistance Program (ESAP) and of School Desegregation.* Vols. 1 and 2. Chicago: National Opinion Research Center.

———. 1981. *High School and Beyond.* Data Tape and Users Manual. Chicago: National Opinion Research Center.

New York Times. 1976. "Little Rock Central High School Is a Success Story Today." Sept. 8. p. 1.

Nunnally, Jim. C. 1967. *Psychometric Theory.* New York: McGraw Hill.

Offer, Daniel; Melvin Sabshin; and Judith L. Offer. 1969. *The Psychological World of the Teenager.* New York: Basic Books.

Orfield, Gary. 1978. *Must We Bus? Segregated Schools and National Policy.* Washington, D.C.: The Brookings Institute.

Payne, Charles M. 1979. "Who Runs This Chicago High School?" *Integrated Education* 17, nos. 1–2:9–14.

Pettigrew, Thomas F. 1973. "Attitudes on Race and Housing: A Social-Psychological View." In *Segregation in Residential Areas,* edited by Amos H. Hawley and Vincent P. Rock, pp. 21–84. Washington, D.C.: National Academy of Science.

Pettigrew, Thomas F.; Elizabeth L. Useem; Clarence Normand; and Marshall S. Smith. 1973. "Busing: A Review of 'the Evidence.'" *The Public Interest* 30 (winter):88–118.

Report on Education Research. 1979. "Blacks Score Lower Than Whites on SATs." *Report on Education Research,* 22, no. 48 (December 26):1–2.

Richards, Pamela. 1979. "Middle-Class Vandalism and Age-Status Conflict." *Social Problems* 26, no. 4 (April):482–497.

Rist, Ray C., ed. 1977. *Desegregated Schools: An Appraisal of an American Experiment*. New York: Academic Press.

Rosenthal, R. 1966. *Experimenter Effects in Behavioral Research*. New York: Appleton-Crofts.

Rossell, Christine H. 1978. "School Desegregation and Community Social Change." *Law and Contemporary Problems*. 42 (summer):133–183.

Rutter, Michael; Barbara Maughan; Peter Mortimore; and Janet Ouston. 1979. *Fifteen Thousand Hours: Secondary Schools and Their Effect on Children*. Cambridge, Mass.: Harvard University Press.

Schofield, Janet Ward. Forthcoming. *Behind Closed Doors: Race Relations in an American School*. New York: Praeger.

Schofield, Janet Ward, and H. Andrew Sagar. 1979. "The Social Context of Learning in an Interracial School." In *Desegregated Schools: An Appraisal of an American Experiment,* edited by Ray C. Rist, pp. 155–197. New York: Academic Press.

Schofield, Janet Ward, and H. Andrew Sagar. Forthcoming. "Integrating the Desegregated Schools: Perspectives, Practices and Possibilities." In *Impact of School Desegregation on Student Outcomes,* edited by David Bartz and Martin Maehr. New York: JAI Press.

Scherer, Jacqueline, and Edward J. Slawski. 1977. "Color, Class and Social Control in an Urban Desegregated School." In *Desegregated Schools: An Appraisal of an American Experiment,* edited by Ray C. Rist, pp. 117–153. New York: Academic Press.

Seeman, Melvin. 1964. "Alienation and Social Learning in a Reformatory." *American Journal of Sociology* 69:270–284.

Seeman, Melvin, and J.W. Evans. 1962. "Alienation and Social Learning in a Hospital Setting." *American Sociological Review,* 80 no 1:772–782.

Simmel, George. 1955. *Conflict and the Web of Group Affiliations*. New York: Free Press.

Slavin, Robert E. 1978. *Using Student-Team Learning.* Baltimore: Center for Social Organization of Schools, The Johns Hopkins University.

Slavin, Robert E., and Nancy A. Madden. 1979. "School Practices That Improve Race Relations." *American Educational Research Journal* 16:169–180.

Solomon, Frederic; Walter L. Walker; Garrett J. O'Connor; and Jacob R. Fishman. 1965. "Civil Rights Activity and Reduction in Crime among Negroes." *Archives of General Psychiatry* 12:227–236.

Suttles, Gerald D. 1968. *The Social Order of the Slum.* Chicago: University of Chicago Press.

U.S. Commission on Civil Rights. 1967. *Racial Isolation in the Public Schools.* Washington, D.C.: U.S. Government Printing Office.

Weisman, Frederic. 1969. *High School.* Boston: Zipporah Films.

RAND EDUCATIONAL POLICY STUDIES

PUBLISHED

Averch, Harvey A., Stephen J. Carroll, Theodore S. Donaldson, Herbert J. Kiesling, and John Pincus. *How Effective is Schooling? A Critical Review of Research.* Englewood Cliffs, New Jersey: Educational Technology Publications, 1974.

Carpenter-Huffman, P., G.R. Hall, G.C.Sumner. *Change in Education: Insights from Performance Contracting.* Cambridge, Mass.: Ballinger Publishing Company, 1974.

Crain, Robert L., Rita E. Mahard, and Ruth E. Narot. *Making Desegregation Work: How Schools Create Social Climates.* Cambridge, Mass.: Ballinger Publishing Company, 1982.

Elmore, Richard and Milbrey Wallin McLaughlin. *Reform and Retrenchment: The Politics of California School Finance Reform.* Cambridge, Mass.: Ballinger Publishing Company, 1982.

Gurwitz, Aaron S. *The Economics of Public School Finance.* Cambridge, Mass.: Ballinger Publishing Company, 1982.

McLaughlin, Milbrey Wallin, *Evaluation and Reform: The Elementary and Secondary Education Act of 1965, Title I.* Cambridge, Mass.: Ballinger Publishing Company, 1975.

Pincus, John (Ed.) *School Finance in Transition: The Courts and Educational Reform.* Cambridge, Mass.: Ballinger Publishing Company, 1974.

Timpane, Michael, (Ed.) *The Federal Interest in Financing Schooling.* Cambridge, Mass.: Ballinger Publishing Company, 1978.

278

OTHER RAND BOOKS IN EDUCATION

Bruno, James E., (Ed.) *Emerging Issues in Education: Policy Implications for the Schools.* Lexington, Mass.: D.C. Heath and Company, 1972.

Coleman, James S. and Nancy L. Karweit. *Information Systems and Performance Measures in Schools.* Englewood Cliffs, New Jersey: Educational Technology Publications, 1972.

Haggart, Sue A. (Ed.) *Program Budgeting for School District Planning.* Englewood Cliffs, New Jersey:Educational Technology Publications, 1972.

Levien, Roger E. *The Emerging Technology:Instructional Uses of The Computer in Higher Education.* New York:McGraw-Hill Book Company, 1972.

INDEX

Academic success, 21
Acceptance of school rules, 18, 20, t140,
    263
  and attitudes toward principal, 128, t129
  and bi-racial committee effectiveness,
    135–137, t136, t161
  and extra-curricular participation, t174,
    t194, 195, t196
  and human relations literature, t131,
    t160
  and knowledge of black experience,
    t140, t163
  and liking principal, t109
  and minority history course, t163
  see also outcomes
Achievement, 11, 21, t27
  and teacher racial attitudes, t219, t231
  and audio-visual specialist, t232
  and discussion of racial issues, t143,
    t158
  and duration of desegregation, by sex,
    t91
  and extra-curricular participation, t178,
    t194, t196
  and fine and performing arts teachers,
    t188, t204
  and gym teachers, t188, t205
  and knowledge of black experience,
    t163
  and minority history course, t163
  and minority history, t138

  and school racial composition, t52,
    54–55, 70–71, t71
  and socioeconomic status, 44
  and teacher perception of black achieve-
    ment, 120–121, t122
  and teacher racial attitudes and behav-
    ior, t104, t122, 123–124
  and tracking, 217–218, t219
  between school differences in, 24–26,
    38–50
  black:
    and duration of desegregation,
      70–71, t71
    and school desegregation, 68–70
    and white student socioeconomic
      status, by sex, t92
    and white student socioeconomic
      status, 71–72, t72
    male:
      and attitudes, 28
      by region of south, 90
  racial "gap", 25
  SAT units, 24
  white, and desegregation plan character-
    istics, 84
  see also outcomes
Adelson, J., 77, 236
Adolescence, and race relations, 19
Adolescence, 14, 236–238
Aggregation, 260, 266–268
Alienation, 19–20

Armor, D.J., 69, 76, 268
Aronson, E., 212–213, 229
Art teachers, see fine and performing arts
    teachers
Attenuation, 83
Audio-visual equipment, 221–223
Audio-visual specialist, t222, 221–226
    and achievement, t232
    and teacher-student contact, t223, t232
Aura of school, 16
Austin, Texas, 212, 229

Belonging, sense of:
    and attitudes toward principal, 128, t129
    and busing, t58–59, t59, 88, t89
    and effectiveness of biracial committee,
        135–137, t136, t161
    and knowledge of the black experience,
        t140, t163
    and liking principal, t109
    and minority history course, t163
    and school racial composition, t52, 53,
        t85, t86
    and teacher racial attitudes and behav-
        ior, 99–100, t99, 120, t121, 217
    and tracking, 216, t217
    see also outcomes
Benham, B.J., 20
Berman, P., 224–225
Bernstein, C., 240–243
Between school differences in outcomes,
    achievement, 42, 45
Between-school differences in outcomes,
    40, t41
Between-school variance and sampling er-
    ror, 268–271
Biracial committee, 134–137
    and outcomes, 159–162, t161
Black history, see minority history, 137
Bloom, B.S., 220
Bock, Darrell, 258
Boston, MA 61
Boulding's Law, 245
Brown vs Board of Education, 69
Bunche, R., 140
Busing, 56–61, 63–64, 84
    and outcomes, t88, t89

California High School, gym class,
    189–190
Campbell, E.Q., 72
Caplan, N., 77
Cataldo, E., 55
Causal analysis, 123–124, 200–203,
    250–253
Charleston, 134
Chicago, 62

Civil rights activity, 124
    and achievement, 149–152, t151–153
    and teacher racial attitudes and behav-
        ior, t125
    by students, 153–154
    see community conflict
Classroom discussion of race, see discus-
    sion of racial issues
Cobbs, P.M., 149
Cognitive dissonance, 111
Coleman, J.S., 24, 40, 44, 48, 49, 69,
    229, 239, 255
College attendance, and extra-curricular
    participation, 178–180, t202
College plans, t33, 34
    and knowledge of the black experience,
        141
    encouraged by staff, 193, t194, t196
        and extra-curricular participation, t173
Commission on Civil Rights, U.S., 69
Common school, 208
Community biracial committees, and
        teacher racial attitudes and behav-
        ior, t125
Community conflict over desegregation:
    and achievement, t167
    and racial tension, t152
    measurement of, 164, 165
Competition, 209
Computer-assisted instruction, 220
Conley, H., 184
Correlation coefficient, 27
Coser, L.A., 165
Cost-benefit ratio, and interpretation of ef-
    fect size 93
Cottle, T.J., 61–62
Coulson, J.E., et al., 1977, 257
Crain, R.L., 16, 36–37, 69, 70, 77, 166,
    255, 257
Cusick, P., 15, 20, 240, 222

Daiger, D.C., 227
Dallas, 57
Davis, James M., 58, 61, 78
De Fleur, M.L., 111
De Friese, G.H., 111
Delaware Committee on the School Deci-
    sion, 184
Delaware High School, recording extra
        curricular participation, 187
Delinquency, see nondelinquency
Detroit, 57
DeVries, D.L., 212
Differences, magnitude of, 91–94
Discussion of racial issues, 141–143,
    t142–143
    and achievement, t158

and racial attitudes, t158
and racial contact, t158
and self-esteem, t158
and student perception of teacher racial attitudes, t158
and student-teacher contact, t158
Disruption in school, 226–228
Douvan, E., 77, 236
Drama teachers, see fine and performing arts teachers
Dummy variable, 81
Duncan, O.D., 201
Duration of desegregation, 19, 73–75
and black achievement, 70–71, t71
and outcomes, 73–75, t85

Eckland, B.K., 191–192
Ecological fallacy, 78, 251
Educational Testing Service, 2, 191, 220, 232
Effects, Magnitude of, 91–94, 132–133
Ehrlich, H.J., 111
Elementary and Secondary Education Act of 1965, 12
Elementary school segregation, see duration of desegregation
Elementary school survey, 17
Emergency School Assistance Program, 257
Equality of Education Opportunity, 24
Evans, J.W., 37
Ewens, W.L., 111
Extra-curricular participation, 206, t207
and acceptance of school rules, t174, 175
and achievement, t178, 194–197
individual-level analysis, 206, t207
and amount of homework, t174, 175
and college attendance, 178–180
and happiness, t176
and like school, t174, 175
and parent involvement, 172, t173
and self-esteem, t176
and teacher encouragement to go to college, t173
by race and sex, 170, 171
and achievement, t183, t195, t197
in 1955 and 1977, 191–192
individual participation and school participation rate, t199
racial bias in, 181–184, t183
rates, 170–171

Factor analysis, of outcomes, 32–38, t33
Family, school as a, 4
Fendrich, J.M., 111
Festinger, L., 111

Fighting, 17
Fine and performing arts teachers:
and achievement, t188, 189, t204
and self-esteem, t188
Finger, J., 77
Football, 169
Ford, W.S., 111
Forehand. G.A., 2, 95, 134–135, 139, 145, 162, 184, 253
Foster, G., 77

Gallup Poll, 80
Gatlin, D., 55
Giesen, P., 20
Giles, M.W., 55, 76
Gottfredson, G.D., 227
Grades, 209, 213–214, 239
and eligibility for school activities, 135, 184
Grier, W.H., 149
Griffith, J., 78
Group work, training in, 185
Groups, 15
Gym teachers:
and achievement, t188, t205
and self-esteem, t188

Hanks, M.P., 191
Happiness, t33
and civil rights activity, t150
and community conflict over desegregation, t167
and extra-curricular participation, t176, t183, t195, t197
and opposite race socioeconomic status, 64–65
and school racial composition, t85, t86
Havinghurst, R.J., 19
Hawley, W.D., 76
Heyns, B., 255
Hirschi, T., 226–227
Homeroom, 187
Homework, amount of, 193
and extra-curricular participation, t174, t194, 195, t196
Human Relations Committee, 5, 134
see also biracial committee
Human relations literature, 159
and outcomes, 131–132, t131, t160
and teacher racial attitudes and behavior, t107
Human-of-the-Week Award, 8
In-service staff training, 133, 159
and like school, t133
and outcomes, t160
Instructional specialist, 226
Internal control, 34, 36, 37

Interviewer evaluation of school, see observer evaluation of school

Jefferson County, (Louisville), 184
Jencks, C., 12, 39, 43, 80, 218
Jenkins, Jean, 231
Jigsaw, 212, 229
Johns Hopkins University, 210–213, 229

Kardiner, A., 77
Katz, I., 111–112
Kluger, R., 76
Knowledge of the black experience, t33, 34, 137–141
  and belonging, sense of, t140
  and outcomes, 162, t163
  and student perception of teacher racial attitudes, t140

Learning centers, 56–57
Levin, B., 76
Like school, 20, t27, t140, 262–263
  and black socioeconomic status, t65
  and civil rights activity, t151
  and community conflict over desegregation, t167
  and duration of desegregation, t85
  and effectiveness of biracial committee, 135–137, t136, t161
  and extra-curricular participation, t174, t194, 195, t196
  and human relations literature, t131, t160
  and in-service training, t160
  and knowledge of black experience, t140, t163
  and minority history course, t163
  and school racial composition, t85, t86
  and teacher racial attitudes and behavior, 99–100, t99, 120, t121, t218, t230
  and tracking, t230
Lincoln, J.R., 266
Little Rock Central High School, 151
Los Angeles, 57–58, 220, 223, 232
Louisville, Ky, 184, 57

Madden, N.A., 210
Magnet schools, 186
Mahard, R.E., 70, 77
"Mainstream" schools, 144–147, 155–157
Maw, C., 257
Mayer, M., 187
McDill, E.L., 229
McLaughlin, M.W., 224–225
McPartland, J.M., 77, 229

Media, see audio-visual
Metropolitan desegregation, 57, 68
Middle-class bias of school, 155
Mills, N., 76
Minority history courses, 137–141
  and achievement, t138
  and outcomes, 162, t163
  and racial attitudes, t138
  and racial contact, t138
Moynahan, D.P., 70
Music teachers, see fine and performing arts teachers
Mutual adaption, 225

Narot, R.E., 78, 84
National Center for Education Statistics, 191
National Institute of Education, 26, 62, 227, 232, 239
National Opinion Research Center (NORC), 16, 77, 231, 233, 254
Nixon, R.M., 70
Nondelinquency, 83, 263
  and black socioeconomic status, t65
  and duration of desegregation, t85
  and school racial composition, t52, 54, t85, t86

Oakes, J., 20
Observer evaluation of school, 145, 155–156
  and like school, t145, t156
  and self-esteem, t145, t156
  and student perception of teacher racial attitudes, t156
  and teacher racial attitudes and behavior, t145
Offer, D., 174
Offer, J.L., 174
Orfield, G., 76
Organization of client groups, 168–169
Outcomes, student, t41
  and duration of desegregation, 73–75
  and school racial composition, 53–56
  and socioeconomic status, 26, t39, 40
  between-school differences, t23
  correlation between races, t27, 37
  factor analysis, 32–38, t33
  see between-school differences
Ovisey, L., 77

Parent involvement, and extra-curricular participation, t173
Parent visits to school, 193
  and extra-curricular participation, t194, t196
Payne, C.M., 246

Peer disapproval of racial contact, and school racial composition, 63–64, t64, t85, t86
Perception of teacher attitudes, 113
Pettigrew, T.F., 70, 76, 111
Plato, computer program, 220–221, 232
Principal attitudes and behavior, and teacher racial attitudes and behavior, t125
Principal, student reactions to and outcomes, 108–109, t109, 128, t129
Principal's racial attitudes, and teacher racial attitudes and behavior, t107, 108

Race relations, 21
and black socioeconomic status, 64–68, t68
and white socioeconomic status, 64
Racial attitudes, 21, 262
and student reactions toward principal, 128, t129, t109
and civil rights activity, t150
and community conflict over desegregation, t167
and discussion of racial issues, t143, t158
and extra-curricular participation, 176, t177, t183, t195, t197
and knowledge of black experience, t163
and minority history course, t138, t163
and teacher racial attitudes and behavior, 118–120, t119
and tracking, 217, t218
see also outcomes
Racial balance, 56
Racial climate, t33, 34
and school attitudes, 29
Racial competition, t53, 63
Racial contact, 17–19, 21, 29, 34, t27, 262
and black socioeconomic status, t65
and busing, 59–60, t59, t88, t89
and civil rights activity, t150
and community conflict over desegregation, t167
and discussion of racial issues, t158, t143
and duration of desegregation, t85
and extra-curricular participation, 176, t177, t195, t197
and knowledge of black experience, t163
and minority history course, t138, t163
and racial tension, 35, 38

and school racial composition, 35, t85, t86
and teacher racial attitudes and behavior, t101, 120, t121, t216, t230
and tracking, t216, t230
see also outcomes
Racial stereotyping, 18
and teacher racial attitudes and behavior, t98, 118–120, t119
Racial tension, 17–19, 21, 29, t27, 35, 38, 68, 263–264
and bi-racial committee effectiveness, 135–137, t136
and black socioeconomic status, t65
and busing, 60–61, t60, t88, t89
and civil rights activity, t152
and community conflict over desegregation, t167
and effectiveness of biracial committee, t161
and school racial composition, t52
teacher perception of, 17
see also outcomes
Radical critics of schools, 19
Ragosta, M., 134–135, 139, 162, 184, 253
Rand corporation, 224–225
Reference group theory, 111
Regression, 81
conversion to simulated cross-tabulation, 78–83
Research design, 16–17, 250–271
Richards, P., 239
Rosenthal, R., 102, 112
Rossell, C.H., 76
Rutter, M., 48, 49, 254

Sabshin, M., 174
Safe schools study, 26, 62
Sagar, H.A., 248
Sampling error, 268–271
Schofield, J.W., 245–246, 248, 253
School as a whole, 14–15; see also school as family
School desegregation, 17
and black achievement, 68–70
School effect on achievement, 42–48, f45
School racial composition:
and black achievement, 70–71, t71
and outcomes, 53–56, t85, t86
School violence, 26
School work interesting, 20, t33, 34
School work worth learning, 20, t33, 34
Schools don't make a difference, 24
Seeman, M., 37
Self-esteem, 21, t140, 261–262
and achievement, 37

and busing, t59, 59, t88, t89
and civil rights activity, t151
and community conflict over desegrega-
    tion, t167
and discussion of racial issues, t143,
    t158
and extra-curricular participation, t176,
    t183, t195, t197
and fine and performing arts teachers,
    t188, t204
and gym teachers, t188, t205
and knowledge of the black experience,
    t140, t163
and minority history course, t163
and school racial composition, t52, 54,
    t85, t86
see also outcomes
SES, see socioeconomic status
Simmel, G., 165
Size of effects, interpretation, 132–133
Slavin, R.E., 210, 212
Socialization, 12
Socioeconomic status, 40, 261
    and outcomes, 40
    white, and black achievement, 71–72,
        t72, t92
Solomon, F., 149
Sororities and Fraternities, 181
Southern schools, 231, 233
Spears, Harold, 15–16
Springfield City High School (pseud.), 2,
    95, 249
Staff racial composition and teacher racial
    attitudes and behavior, t107
Statistical significance, 94
Student biracial committee, see biracial
    committee
Student leaders' attitudes about desegrega-
    tion, 193
Student leadership, integration of,
    143–144
Student perception of teacher racial at-
    titudes, and discussion of racial
    issues, t158
Student racial attitudes, t133
Student Learning Team, 229
Student-teacher contact, 193
    and discussion of racial issues, t142,
        143, t158
Students attitudes toward self and school,
    21
Students for a Concerned Society, 9
Suttles, G.D., 77
System Development Corporation, 257

Teacher expectations of students:
    and achievement, 103–104
    and teacher racial attitudes, 103–104

Teacher perception of black student
    ability:
    and achievement, 120–121, t122
    and teacher racial attitudes and behav-
        ior, 120–121, t122
Teacher racial attitudes:
    measurement of, 96–97, 114–116
    between-school differences, 96–97, 115
    item correlations in scale, t115, t116
    student perception:
        and discussion of racial issues,
            t142–143
        and effectiveness of biracial commit-
            tee, 135–137, t136, t161
        and extra-curricular participation, 176,
            t177, t195, t197
        and human relations literature, t131
        and in-service training, t160
        and knowledge of the black experi-
            ence, t140
        and minority history course, t163
Teacher racial attitudes and behavior, 265
    and achievement, t104, t122, 123–124,
        t219, t231
    and belonging, sense of, 99–100, t99,
        120, t121
    and community civil rights activity, t125
    and expectations of students, 102–103
    and like school, 99–100, t99, 120,
        t121, t218, t230
    and principal attitudes and behavior,
        t125
    and racial contact, t101, 120, t121,
        t216, t230
    and racial stereotyping, t98
    and sense of belonging, 99–100, t99,
        t217
    and staff background, t125, t127
    causes of, 124–125, t127
Teacher racial behavior:
    and teacher racial attitudes, t117
    causes of, 105–107, t107
    item correlations, t114
    measurement, 112–113
Teacher-student attachment, and number
    of students seen by teacher, 227
Teacher-student contact, 20
    and audio-visual specialist, t223, t232
    and extra-curricular participation, t194,
        t196
Teachers, assaults on, 62
Team learning, 210–213
Teams-Games-Tournament, 211
Territoriality, 61–63
Test anxiety, t33, 34, 37
Tracking, 214–220, 266
    and achievement, 217–218, t219
    and belonging, sense of, 216, t217

and like school, t230
and racial attitudes, 217, t218
and racial contact, t216, t230
Tradeoffs, among student outcomes, 26
Trust, t33, 34
Turf, see territoriality

United States Office of Education, Office
    of Planning, Budgeting, and
    Evaluation, 257
University of Illinois, 233
Unstructured strategies for dealing with
    race relations, 146

Vandalism in suburban schools, 62
Violence, 62–63

Warren, Earl, 69
Washington, Mr. (pseud.), 2
Weisman, C.S., 36–37, 69, 77
Westie, F.R., 111
"White flight", 56
    and school racial composition, 55
"Whole child", 13
Wilmington, Delaware, 56–57
Wiseman, F., 238

York, R., 257

Zeitz, G., 266